PERFECT VICTIM

ELIZABETH SOUTHALL is the pen-name of Elizabeth Barber. She was born in Victoria in 1959, one of four children of Ivan Southall, a distinguished Australian writer of children's literature. Elizabeth herself is known for her work as a children's book specialist.

The disappearance and murder of Elizabeth and Michael's eldest daughter Rachel first made headlines around Australia in the first weeks of March 1999. Elizabeth kept a journal from that time on, including letters she'd written to Rachel. *Perfect Victim* stems from those writings.

Elizabeth lives in Heathmont, Victoria, an outer suburb of Melbourne, with her husband Michael who is a toymaker and designer, and their two other daughters, Ashleigh-Rose and Heather. Elizabeth has a Diploma of Arts in Professional Writing and Editing. She is currently studying for a Bachelor of Theology degree.

MEGAN NORRIS is a UK-born journalist experienced in the criminal justice system. Her career in journalism began in 1976 as a reporter in the UK covering courts, police rounds and general news. Later, specialising in court coverage, she wrote about the impact of crime on victims and their families. She has covered stories including the aftermath of the Port Arthur massacre and some of Australia's most high-profile serial killers and stalkers.

Her first contact with Elizabeth came when she was preparing a story about the Barber family for Australian Consolidated Press. Elizabeth and Megan became firm friends and a collaboration began. Megan's following of the Rachel Barber case and her research for *Perfect Victim* occupied her life for several years. She lives in Melbourne, Victoria, with her husband Stephen and their two sons Alex and Peter.

PERFECT

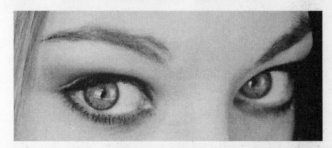

VICTIM

Elizabeth Southall and Megan Norris

Penguin Books

Penguin Books

Published by the Penguin Group
Penguin Books Australia Ltd
250 Camberwell Road
Camberwell, Victoria 3124, Australia
Penguin Books Ltd
80 Strand, London WC2R ORL, England
Penguin Putnam Inc.
375 Hudson Street, New York, New York 10014, USA
Penguin Books, a division of Pearson Canada
10 Alcorn Avenue, Toronto, Ontario, Canada, M4V 3B2
Penguin Books (N.Z.) Ltd
Cnr Rosedale and Airborne Roads, Albany, Auckland, New Zealand
Penguin Books (South Africa) (Pty) Ltd
24 Sturdee Avenue, Rosebank, Johannesburg 2196, South Africa
Penguin Books India (P) Ltd
11, Community Centre, Panchsheel Park, New Delhi, 110 017, India

First published in Viking by Penguin Books Australia, 2002
This edition published, 2003

1 3 5 7 9 10 8 6 4 2

Designed by Cathy Larsen, Penguin Design Studio
Typeset in Sabon by Post Pre Press Group, Brisbane, Queensland
Printed and bound in Australia by McPherson's Print Group, Maryborough, Victoria

National Library of Australia
Cataloguing-in-Publication data:

Southall, Elizabeth.
Perfect victim.

ISBN 0 14 300102 7.

1. Barber, Rachel. 2. Robertson, Caroline Reed. 3. Murder
– Australia. 4. Women murderers – Australia. I. Norris,
Megan. II. Title.

364.15230994

www.penguin.com.au

The extract from Margaret Mahy's *A Lion in the Meadow* on p.51 is reproduced with
kind permission from Margaret Mahy and Dent Children's Books.
Text copyright © Margaret Mahy, 1969, 1986

For Rachel
– E.S. and M.N.

CONTENTS

Some time in the first week of March 1999, the body of Rachel Elizabeth Barber was unceremoniously dumped in the wardrobe of a second-floor flat in Trinian Street, Prahran, an inner suburb of Melbourne. A black, old-fashioned telecommunications cable was still tight around her neck.

In another room were all sorts of scribblings: hate lists, catalogues, notes about Rachel, her family, her personality, her likes and dislikes – and one note in particular with the ominous words, 'All things come to pass'.

PART ONE

Vanished

A family is a unit, with a sense of belonging, even when separated by miles, even when separated by divorce, because everyone is aware of another's being and location, somewhere on earth. Our unit suddenly found a piece of the jigsaw missing.

ELIZABETH SOUTHALL

1

AN AUTUMN EVENING

Monday, 1 March

An uneasy thought occurred to me while I gave the two younger children their evening meal. It was only 7.15 but Mike and Rachel should have come, exhausted, through the door about 6.45 p.m.

I have a vivid imagination and this night I had Mike rammed between two other cars, or with a flat tyre, or yes, that's it, without petrol. We were always running on empty. They probably didn't have the cost of a phone call between them and, unlike many families, we didn't use mobile phones.

I looked at the clock again: 7.17. I picked at my food and thought back over the day. An easy day. An ordinary day beginning with an ordinary morning. Rachel had wanted me to drive her to Richmond because Mike was running late, and she hated travelling on trains. She was cross at my lack of understanding for even suggesting the possibility of a train. She hadn't wanted to miss breakfast with her new classmates at her friend Kylee's place. But it was my work-free day and Mike wasn't long ready and so the two of them sailed off. That's what it had seemed like. She called 'goodbye' and 'love you' from the door and leapt off the steps in her day-old Bloch dance pants and petite blue top. It was said of Rachel that she often appeared to neither walk nor run. The white sedan reversed up the driveway with Rachel smiling and waving goodbye.

After her fifteenth birthday in September 1998, and at the end of her third term in Year 9, Rachel pleaded to be allowed to leave school. She had the full support of Mike, but this was not an easy decision for me who had completed Year 12 and tertiary education. However, we were confident she would start a Diploma of Dance in late January, so when her English teacher claimed she'd danced down a row of desks, I said, 'Okay, Rachel, if you can find something constructive to do for the last term. But I'm not going to have you sitting idly at home.'

What followed was a two-week period of diligent experimentation for Rachel applying for part-time jobs: everything from café waitress to sales assistant. Unfortunately she was afraid of handling computer checkouts. Once, she had hidden for long periods of a two-hour try-out in the toilet of a café in Bridge Road, Richmond: scared stiff.

One afternoon when she went for a job as a kitchen hand she came out and sat in the car.

'I'm in shock,' she said. 'Do people really work like this?'

'Yes,' I answered. 'And what you have to remember is by leaving school you will be putting all your eggs in one basket. If you do this, Rachel, you must commit yourself one hundred per cent.'

'I am a dancer. I want to be an entertainer. You *know* that.'

'Okay, then,' I said. 'You know you'll have our full support.'

There was silence. 'The money was good though,' she said, her blonde-tipped ponytail bobbing with agreement.

'Oh, you don't get to keep it all. You have to pay about $70 to the government as tax.'

She laughed. 'Well, they're not getting any of my money.'

I was amazed she didn't fully understand about tax. 'Haven't you learnt about this at school?' But with her head filled with dancing there would be little space for a rendering of tax.

'Sorry, Rach, they will get your tax. They take it out before you receive your pay packet.'

She scoffed. 'Well, someone should do something about that.'

At the end of this long two weeks for Rachel, I received a

4

phone call from Dulcie, the artistic director at her dance school. She said Rachel had just been in her office.

'Dulcie,' Rachel had begun. 'You know my fourth term scholarship? Could you *please* extend this to a full-time scholarship? Mum said if I could find something constructive to do I could leave school.' Dulcie, who had apparently been so impressed with Rachel's handling of the request, had agreed, if this was okay with me.

Rachel struggled through school. Her academic grades were low, not because she was mischievous but because teachers could not get through to her. In Year 8 she had cried one night, telling me it wasn't that she deliberately didn't want to do the work, it was because she could not understand it. It was in dance she excelled, never receiving less than a high distinction for her Royal Academy of Dance or contemporary dance exams. Rachel Star – that was the name she gave herself. One day, she would have her own Rachel Star dance studio.

Now she was into the fifth week of a potentially wonderful two years and her dreams were being answered in an almost fairytale way. Everything was coming together. Life was good.

So what was keeping them tonight? Rachel hadn't called to say she would stay at Kylee's: she had already arranged with me to spend Tuesday night with Kylee. At lunch I had thought of calling the dance school, just to see how she was going, but I thought they would start to get annoyed with me if I rang them too often. I wonder now why I had sensed the need to make contact.

The phone rang. It was 7.40. At last, I thought, they've found a phone, and how silly I'd been to worry. After all, they were barely an hour late.

Mike's voice sounded concerned. He was ringing from his parents', Rose and Arthur's, in suburban Blackburn. Rachel had not got off the tram at Wattle Park. Had she called? Did I have any ideas? Maybe she had forgotten Mike was collecting her at Wattle Park? Not so. Mike said that this was the last thing they'd discussed. She'd be there for him at around 6.15 and had said, 'Love you, Dad,' as she always did.

He'd been there at ten past six and waited an hour. Kept hoping she'd step off. So where was she?

I could sense his panic stirring.

He'd go back to Camberwell and see if she'd got off the tram, mistakenly, where I had started to pick her up Tuesday to Thursday, the week before. After all, it was only her second pick-up from Wattle Park. If she wasn't there, what then? It was dark now and Rachel hated the dark. I'd call the police immediately. Call Mike back. Then I'd call Rachel's boyfriend Emmanuel and her dance school.

I rang the Box Hill police station around 7.40 and reported Rachel missing. They wondered how long she had been missing? An hour and a quarter. And how old was she? Fifteen. Yes, well, they didn't exactly laugh, but I had the feeling they thought I was over-reacting. But to give them credit we were told that if Mike could not trace her in Camberwell then we should come to the police station and fill in a missing person report.

I rang Emmanuel, and he immediately feared the worse. 'She meant it,' Manni said. 'I didn't think she'd go.'

Panic. She'd meant what?

During the day Rachel had taken Manni into a shoe shop and had pointed out a pair of chunky blue Spice Girl shoes she was going to buy the next day. How was she going to pay for them? She'd said to Manni that she had been told not to tell her parents or boyfriend, but she was going to a job where clothing would be provided and she would make a lot of money. Nothing immoral. No need to worry.

No need to worry? Manni was worried. Mike and I were worried.

She had definitely left the dance school. Waving goodbye and calling 'love you' across the road as Manni and his brother disappeared down an alley to get their car. She had said she'd ring him that night to tell him all about it and told her girlfriend Kylee that she would be there for breakfast on Tuesday as usual.

I called her school. I called Kylee. I called Manni back. She had simply vanished. Perhaps there was really no need to worry. Maybe I was over-reacting. But Rachel *knew* how I worried. She would know I'd over-react. She would know I'd contact the police. It was past 8.30. She'd have contacted somebody by now. And she hadn't.

Michael searched the leafy, middleclass streets of Camberwell but never imagined he'd find her there. The events of the evening were beginning to feel ominous. At 8.45 p.m. he officially reported her missing at Box Hill police station. Perhaps an odd choice, considering her dance school was in inner-city Richmond and we lived in suburban Heathmont about half an hour's drive from Box Hill, but it was at least near where she was to get off the tram.

Mike doesn't believe in over-reaction, and he was not over-reacting. Rachel had never disappeared before and it was so unlike her not to contact us if she'd been delayed. She hated the dark. She feared public transport. She would have phoned by now.

The police reaction was not to worry. What else could they say? She had most likely gone off with her friends and would turn up tomorrow.

My mother, Joy Southall, came to take care of our younger daughters, eleven-year-old Ashleigh-Rose and nine-year-old Heather, while we drove to Richmond to search for Rachel. Her dance school hadn't seen or heard from Rachel since she left around 5.45 that afternoon. They were closing when we arrived.

We searched the streets of Richmond calling her name. It's a dusty and busy inner-city suburb, famous for its footy club, and sitting in the shadows of the Melbourne Cricket Ground. But really our searching was pointless. We had no idea where she was. We knew, as others did who knew Rachel well, that the story she'd partly shared with Manni already reeked of foul play. I think we realised, even then, that Rachel had been baited with the equivalent of a bag of sweets a small child is warned about, and in her naivety been snared.

Another story.

The afternoon before . . .
Sunday, 28 February

Some time between five and six in the late afternoon, Rachel
was on the phone. She was laughing and gossiping, probably to
her boyfriend Manni, sharing with him the events of her day.
During the morning she'd had breakfast with her mum at
Doncaster Shoppingtown where she'd bought her new Bloch
dance pants. She had grizzled to her mum about wanting a new
top, and was upset that Mum had dismissed the need for extra-
strong deodorant.

Rachel's weekend had been full, too. Manni had been working
all weekend, so she busied herself on Saturday afternoon
handsewing him a giant purple velour heart created from some old
scraps she'd found in her dad's workshop. She would surprise
Manni with it on Monday, telling him to keep her 'heart' safe
somewhere, always.

On Sunday afternoon, at the Bayswater Family Pet Care Day,
Rachel finally persuaded her mum to allow her to have the kitten
she so desperately wanted, ever since Sable, their eighteen-year-
old cat, had been killed by two stray dogs outside her bedroom
window. The new kitten was to be named Humphrey.

But Rachel wasn't speaking to Manni that afternoon on the
phone. No one knew she wasn't speaking to Manni. She spoke for
some time. Telephone records indicate that during this one hour
period, two calls were received – a fifteen-minute call and a
twenty-nine minute call – received from someone with a silent
number. Goodness knows what that person was filling Rachel's
head with.

Later that night, Rachel, Ashleigh-Rose, Heather, Mum and Dad
sat together watching television. It was an episode of 'Vanity Fair'
on Channel Two. Rachel enjoyed the series because of the period
costumes and the tangled romance.

Rachel knelt on the floor in front of her mum, asking for a
back massage. But Mum was tired and said no. Rachel persisted.
Ever since she was little she had enjoyed massages. After a day

at primary school she would often come running up the long driveway, flinging her bag down at the front door. She would climb onto the kitchen table where a towel and pillow would already be waiting for her. A trail of clothes from the door. Her mum would massage her, with Rachel stripped down to her knickers.

This Sunday evening, her mother looked at the smoothness of her daughter's clear skin. 'Please,' Rachel's voice urged, and her mother just managed a rub.

Rachel went to bed happily this night, revealing to no one, as promised, the details of these private calls. Maybe she thought, yes it will be all right, I'll buy that new pair of shoes. The new pair of shoes she tried in vain, the week before, to show her mum, but the pair of shoes about which Mum had said, 'I'm tired. I haven't got time to look at a pair of shoes. And anyway, we can't afford them.'

2

THE SEARCH BEGINS

Day 1: Tuesday, 2 March

It is an incredible sensation to wake in the morning and realise that life may never be the same again. I wonder, now, why we even went to bed, but there was always the hope that Rachel would arrive at her dance school, apologetic and having made whatever money it was, with her new shoes in hand.

Now I face a dilemma. How honest should I be in telling this story? I say this in fear of upsetting people; in fear of upsetting police. But my account of events will not have its full impact unless I share the two struggles we first faced.

Our anger grew during Rachel's disappearance to a point of total frustration. Not only did we and our family and friends struggle with the grief of Rachel's disappearance but we also struggled with convincing the police that we felt Rachel was *really* in trouble. Into the second week, Lauren, an old school friend of Rachel's, rang: 'Elizabeth, you *know* she's not capable of running away. Don't stop looking for her.'

I look at Rachel's compelling green eyes, staring at me from her photograph, and sense her spirit saying, 'Come on, Mum, tell it all. I am with you.'

We took the girls to school on Tuesday morning, telling them not to worry. What else could we say?

At the Box Hill police station, the officer on duty at the desk did not know what we were talking about when, photographs in hand, we made our third contact with police. He explained that their shifts had recently changed but said he'd look for the report.

After failing to find it he went to a side room from where another police officer came out. Mike recognised him as the sergeant who had taken the report. The sergeant immediately went and lifted the report from a hook on the back wall. I couldn't help thinking that they had taken the report last night and hung it up on the hook, without further action. But, they said, police cars in the area would have been told to look out for a girl answering Rachel's description.

We left the photographs with the policeman. They were confident she would turn up of her own accord, that Rachel would be safe.

Rachel had not had breakfast at Kylee's, nor had she arrived at her dance school this morning. But then we really didn't think she would have because everything was feeling so horribly wrong.

We spent the rest of the morning discussing Rachel's disappearance with dance students and teachers. Nobody had noticed anything odd about Rachel's demeanour on Monday. She had been positive all day and her usual smiley self, although she'd had lunch on her own as her classmates were rehearsing for something connected to the Moomba festival or the Grand Prix.

Manni was alarmed that Rachel had not phoned as promised the night before. They had rung each other every night for the last ten months, much to the frustration of their parents. They saw each other every day and were so happy together and so deeply in love it did in all honesty concern me a little. I thought, if ever one of them left the other, there would be so many pieces to pick up.

Mike and I used to say that if she had to have a boyfriend at fifteen then she could not have made a better choice. My mother later said in her Victim Impact Statement, '. . . Rachel had visited me along with her parents and Emmanuel Carella a few days before she was so cruelly taken from us. He was her very first love, and Rachel adored him. As she was saying goodbye to me, she suddenly flung her arms around me and whispered in my ear, "Nan, don't you think Manni is wonderful? Wouldn't you love him in our family?" I can still feel the warmth of that hug and the delight in her, and as they drove away and I waved to her until they were out of sight, I thought, "Dear Rachel, may the magic last for a very long time."'

I went with Manni into the shoe shop in Swan Street to confirm what Rachel had said about buying some shoes, not for myself but because I knew the police would want confirmation. I went with notepad and pen in hand.

The shopkeeper remembered Rachel and thought she was a lovely girl. She was often in looking at shoes, and yes, she had asked the lady to put the shoes to one side. Rachel had been very excited. The shopkeeper repeated almost word for word what Manni had said. It was then that Manni recalled that Rachel had referred to an old female friend. 'It was nothing immoral because she was going with an old female friend.'

Old female friend? A friend from primary or secondary school? A friend from the Baptist or Anglican church youth groups? Or from a previous dance school? Or was she referring to an *older* female friend, a woman? It was an expression we could not associate with Rachel. Old girlfriend, yes, but 'female'? This sounded like the description of an older woman.

So then, our Rachel had never intended to catch the tram home on Monday night. She had planned to go somewhere with *someone* who was going to provide clothing and pay her a lot of money. Perhaps she'd thought we'd understand and praise her for her initiative. Or perhaps – and this thought wasn't very appealing to us – perhaps she didn't care that we would be worried. But I think not. Perhaps she'd been told by this *someone*, on meeting her later in the day, that her parents had been contacted during the day. Perhaps Rachel thought we knew where she was going and that it had been arranged for us to pick her up later.

A lot of money. To some, one would imagine thousands of dollars. To Rachel? She was planning to buy shoes, and it was also my fortieth birthday later that week. Mike remembered that he'd said to her not to forget it was Mum's birthday and she had said she remembered.

We seemed to live from pay packet to pay packet and with dance fees there never seemed enough for luxuries. Rachel was on a strict budget and I was always going on about part-time work. I told her she could have money for tram fares and coffee and take a packed lunch each day. Any extras she would need to find the money for. This didn't of course include clothing and everyday essentials. She had placed herself in an adult world and I believed we were doing the right thing by making her aware of where her own responsibilities were. I regret not paying her a weekly allowance. But the morning of the day she disappeared I had given her $10 – to buy two $5 tops.

Mike and I started a shop-to-shop walk with Rachel's photographs, starting with Bridge Road because this was the direction Manni had last seen Rachel walking in.

'Excuse me, could you please help us for a moment? Our fifteen-year-old daughter went missing last night. She was last seen at 5.45 near the corner of Swan and Church Streets, walking in the direction of Bridge Road.' We would show them Rachel's photo. A number of shopkeepers remembered seeing Rachel from time to time but not the previous day. They all sounded very much concerned for her welfare.

It began to sound like a stuck record after a while. Mike walked down one side of the street and I down the other.

There were some shop assistants in two girls' clothing shops who thought they may have seen her. One at Pretty Girls thought she had bought two $5 tops from their sales bin at the front entrance. She said Rachel had been by herself.

Mike met me on the street. 'I think I have something. Come and listen to this lady.'

This lady, a middle-aged shop manager, told us in detail about a report in Monday's *Age* concerning a man who had been released from jail. He had been in prison for coercing under-age girls into an illegal brothel he supposedly owned in

Fitzroy. The lady raised enough suspicion to suggest it may have been possible for Rachel, particularly with the tale Rachel had shared, to have been grabbed for this market.

We thanked her, left hurriedly and managed to purchase a copy of yesterday's *Age*. We returned to Rachel's dance school, expressing concerns about the article.

It was the middle of the afternoon and Rachel had made no contact with Manni, home or the dance school. I remember thinking, this *can't* be happening. Where was Rachel? Had she been grabbed like the lady thought? Was she scared? Somewhere in Melbourne our Rachel was in trouble.

3

_____

MISSING PERSON

We climbed the few steps into the Richmond police station, an old and dusty-looking fortress, with the disturbing newspaper article in hand. We turned into the area in front of the dark wooden counter, a room I soon discovered was called the watch-house. We sat and waited in the cramped space with just enough leg-room between a row of three or four chairs and the counter. There was a National Missing Persons poster plastered to the wall showing the faces of several missing people. I thought, our daughter is a missing person. Incredulous.

We explained our story again and our fears in connection to the article. Rachel's dance school had contacted the Richmond police earlier to express their own fear but the police officer was unaware of this contact. The police officer asked us what we would like him to do. We were beginning to think we should have reported Rachel missing at the Richmond police station instead and shared this with him. He explained he couldn't really do much as it needed to be investigated by the policeman it was first reported to, the sergeant at Box Hill. He also felt our fears relating to the newspaper article were unwarranted. Logically thinking, I believe his assumption was justified, but we were the parents of a newly missing person, with no leads.

The officer rang the Box Hill police to discover the sergeant's name and said we must contact him. I thought how useful it would have been if we had been made aware that the police officer we made the initial report to was also the same officer responsible for the continuing investigation. It isn't something one thinks of when, as distressed parents of a missing child, you go to the police. It seemed natural, now that we believed Rachel did not catch the tram to Wattle Park, that the investigation should be handled by the Richmond police.

We left the station feeling confused and at a loss to understand the apparent lack of co-operation on behalf of the police, and continued our shop-walking in Swan Street. Mike was told a disturbing story by a young woman who worked at the dress shop beneath the dance school. She recognised Rachel as one of the dance students who browsed in the store.

She told Mike a woman who had been in the shop on Monday had followed her onto the same carriage at Richmond railway station in the evening. She hadn't thought too much of this until the woman followed her off at her home station, Elsternwick, a bustling and cosmopolitan suburb within easy distance of the city and the bay. After walking behind her for a short while the woman spoke to her. She told her she was a very pretty girl and offered her a chance to make a lot of money by working at the Daily Planet. The girl refused but thought there may be a possible connection because of the story Rachel had told Manni – about clothing being provided and making a lot of money. She gave Mike a description of the woman: about twenty-eight, large and with shoulder-length blonde hair. She was wearing a pink top.

Mike shared this story with me and concerned dance teachers. 'Isn't the Daily Planet a newspaper?' I quizzed.

There was spontaneous laughter from the dance school teachers. 'No,' it was a legal brothel in Elsternwick.

Could Rachel have been approached by the same lady when she'd been having lunch by herself? Could Rachel have thought the Daily Planet was a newspaper too, or perhaps a magazine? Could Rachel have thought she was being offered a modelling job? After all, she had just modelled for the March edition of *Women's Fitness*

Australia, through the modelling agency where Rachel had completed a full-time course the previous year.

I was urged to ring the Daily Planet. The people I spoke to were appalled by the story, assuring me they did not operate this way. It wouldn't be worth their while. They thanked me for bringing it to their attention and suggested I ring the Victorian Prostitutes Collective and gave me their phone number.

'Oh, this is ridiculous,' I said. 'Rachel would have a fit if she knew we were even considering she was silly enough to get caught out with such a tall story.'

'Why not?' answered one of the teachers. 'You thought the Daily Planet was a newspaper.'

I rang the Prostitutes Collective, not even sure what I was going to ask. I was regretting that Mike had spoken to the lady in Bridge Road who had pointed out the original *Age* newspaper article. Coupled with the story of the Daily Planet, everything was beginning to sound just a bit too serious.

The lady I spoke to at the Prostitutes Collective could understand our concerns. She suggested that if Rachel had not been found by the end of the week then we should call back with a full description of her. They had 'staff' who went around the streets looking after the welfare of their sex workers. They'd be happy to keep an eye out for Rachel. I thanked her for her concern and said goodbye.

We spoke to tram travellers and pedestrians from about 5.30 p.m. in the vicinity of the dance school, showing them Rachel's photograph in the hope someone remembered something. We stayed hovering at the intersection of Church and Swan Streets, assuming that if Rachel had caught the tram it would have been from this corner.

No one saw anything. The 'nothing' people saw confirmed Rachel never caught the tram as expected. A young girl who happened to be a student at the dance school remembered how odd it seemed that Rachel was not on the tram. They had recently begun to sit together until Camberwell.

I went into the Café Montague beneath the dance school and the owner asked me to wait a moment. He said he knew Rachel and Manni as they often came in with a group of students to drink coffee or occasionally, when they were out of cash, jugs of ice-cold water. He was really concerned for Rachel because, like everybody else who knew her, this disappearance felt terribly wrong. He gave me the mobile number of a mate of his, Neil Paterson, who happened to be a detective in the Missing Persons Unit.

I went out onto the street holding this number in my hand. *Missing person, missing person.* Yes, 'missing person' because she was missing. I couldn't reach Neil Paterson so I left a message on his answering service.

Another shop-owner remembered seeing Rachel on occasion and offered to make a poster. She scanned Rachel's photograph onto her computer and made the first poster for us. We photocopied these at the dance school and then Mike and I, Manni's family and dance students started putting them up in Richmond and the city.

We continued to search the back streets of Richmond in a systematic order.

On the way home we called into the Camberwell tram depot because two tram inspectors we'd spoken to earlier had suggested we drop a poster off. Perhaps a driver had noticed her. We did this, but the person in charge was not so co-operative, saying that drivers were too busy to notice who gets on and off their trams. After gentle persuasion he did take a few posters and said he'd put them up in the canteen. We left, feeling like scolded children.

When we arrived home I rang my father Ivan Southall and my stepmother Susan, and told them Rachel was missing. They could come up with no answers either. But we discovered that while we had begun our first day's search, they had been hanging an exhibition of Susan's at the Centre for Contemporary Photography in Collingwood, close to the centre of Melbourne.

I had forgotten all about this. Rachel was at the heart of the whole exhibition. Susan, a contemporary artist, assembles photographic images within a collage to create her works, and Rachel was her muse. Susan paid her a modelling fee for each sitting. Rachel had, for years, been portrayed in Susan's artwork as Viking slave girls, sea captains' wives, dancing maidens,

heroines and sacrificial 'lambs', the Madonna and a host of angels from ancient, medieval and Renaissance literature.

This exhibition was on show throughout March. Susan was worried someone in the Richmond area may have recognised Rachel from the thousands of pamphlets distributed beforehand across Melbourne, possibly attracting unwanted attention. I didn't think this was likely but was prepared, as the week advanced, to accept all possibilities. So Dad and Susan hung a sign telling the public that the girl featured in the artwork had since disappeared and that if anyone had seen her they should inform the assistant at the desk.

Later that evening, at home, we rang the numbers given in several 'dancing girls required' ads in the local papers, on the off-chance that Rachel had naively rung them for part-time work. But applicants needed to be eighteen plus, as we had already assumed. And they had to provide proof of age, so it was highly unlikely she would have even been interviewed. Nevertheless, they did inquire for us, to see if there were any new girls with the name of Rachel. No Rachel.

We went through Rachel's address books and school diaries looking for names of old friends. When she was thirteen I sheepishly read some extracts of her diary. This was the age she discovered she was a teenager with developing boobs. It was the age when she and her girlfriends would sit in huddles giggling about boys. I didn't find anything I wouldn't have expected, apart from a few swear words, and I'd felt so bad that I never did it again. My own mother said she once read my elder sister's diary when my sister had been sixteen and vowed she'd never do it again.

Well, now I was doing it again. I still felt as though we were invading her privacy. We began to make a search of Rachel's room, finally going to bed about 4 a.m.

For the second night in a row Rachel had failed to contact Manni.

Since her birth we had known where she slept every one of those nights, for fifteen and a half years. This night our daughter was sleeping elsewhere.

4

Making Someone Notice

Day 2: Wednesday, 3 March

We didn't sleep on Tuesday night. It seemed disrespectful to sleep. It would be dishonouring our daughter to sleep. I was already feeling guilty for sleeping some of Monday night.

How could we sleep when Rachel might have been huddled somewhere so scared she perhaps feared for her life? Was she crying? Had she been raped? Had she been grabbed off Church Street and housed in an illegal brothel? Had some sleaze been watching her on the corner of Church and Swan Streets, while she cuddled Manni on the bench? Sometimes I would drive round the corner to see Rachel and Manni kissing their farewells and think, don't they realise someone could be watching? Had this sleaze dragged her off the streets, fondled his way through our daughter's clothing, stripped and raped her? Had he beaten and killed her, dumping her body somewhere in the bush? Was she dead?

I sat up straight. 'She's not dead. I don't feel it. I would know. We would know.'

Mike didn't reply. He wasn't asleep.

'Ring Ted. Michael! Ring Ted.' I grabbed the phone.

It was so early. I don't remember how early. But we rang Ted.

Ted and Betty are as near to family without actually being family. We met them when looking for land in 1982 and continued

20

to be close when we moved to Glen Alvie, a country hamlet between Korumburra and Wonthaggi close to the south-east coast of Victoria. That was when Rachel was six months old. Then, when Rachel was two, and both Mike and I were working at the Lance Creek Reservoir, our Rachel was cared for by Ted and Betty, as day carers. Betty would meet me and Rachel at the Reservoir gates at 10 a.m. and later in the day we would collect her from their dairy farm.

Rachel had a joyous year. She would walk into the dairy and stand on the dairy gate. She'd watch the milk tanker come, and bulls riding cows' backs, and calves born and poddy-fed. She'd throw scraps to the chooks, and search for extra eggs hidden in the garden. She milked the goat, played with kittens and puppies, and talked to the pet cockatoo. She was fed full-cream non-pasteurised milk, fresh vegetables, eggs, home-made cakes and the farm's own meat.

Mike also helped Ted with milking. A bartered employment. In exchange we received evening meals, vegetables, eggs and milk. I learnt how to make perfectly good-tasting butter in a food processor and be left with buttermilk to make delectable scones, which I served with homemade jams made from greengage plums picked from roadside trees, and cream skimmed from the milk and whisked.

Ted and Betty had once helped pay for Rachel's ballet fees. They saw Rachel like a grandchild and loved her dearly.

Seven years ago Ted collapsed in a coma at the dairy. He was rushed to hospital where he 'died' in casualty. His busy farming lifestyle prevented Ted from seeking medical attention when he felt unwell. He was an undiagnosed diabetic. Now he was dead. Betty was beside his bed but the doctors did not give up. They resuscitated Ted.

Ted's life changed from that day. Ted would say he was *told* things. He said he experienced a foretelling of people's lives. I haven't always been able to go along with this but now more than anything I wanted him to have *seen something*.

'Rachel's missing,' I said to him over the phone on that early morning.

Ted had sensed nothing. He said he'd do his best. He said we

21

should keep him in touch. Pray and keep strong, we were told.

It was then I realised that I had not prayed at all. This confounded me. How many times, in the past, had I prayed? I'd prayed when I was a child for the times I would forget to pray as an adult. I'd prayed for God to save me from persistent bullying in my first two years of secondary school because my youngest sister had Down's syndrome. I'd prayed when my parents divorced. I'd prayed for God to take my vivacious grandmother after a series of strokes left her with a death rattle, and bedridden, at seventy-four. I'd prayed for good results in exams. I'd prayed for God to bless our marriage. I'd prayed in bushfires. I'd prayed for my sister Robbie when her little boy Jonathon was stillborn at full term. I'd prayed during childbirth. I'd prayed for my children when they were happy and when they were cross, and when they were sad. Yet now my grief was so overpowering I had simply forgotten to pray. But I knew God would know my despair, and recall the prayers from my childhood when as an adult I forgot him. I prayed.

We found my mother out on the back veranda, under an overcast sky, and sat beside her sipping tea. We sat silent for some time. She thought it was an idea if she stayed until Rachel was found. We had taken this for granted. She thought it a good idea if Robbie came and collected our youngest daughter Heather, and took her back to Wonthaggi. We thought perhaps Ashleigh-Rose should stay home from school. Thoughts became plans. Decisions were made.

Family and friends were ringing. No one had any idea where Rachel might be.

I rang the Box Hill police station and spoke to the sergeant again. I explained to him what had happened the previous day. The shop walk, the disturbing story from the dress-shop girl, the story in the *Age*. He knew about this because of the contact from the Richmond police. He said somebody from the Box Hill police would visit the dance school later in the morning.

Our first contact with Neil Paterson of the Missing Persons Unit was at around this time. Neil was very helpful. He phoned to say that at this early stage the unit could not do anything. But

he did sound concerned for Rachel and said he would contact the police station to see that everything that could be done would be done. He said it wasn't possible for the Richmond police to transfer the investigation because this was the responsibility of the officer to whom it was reported. I persisted. 'Could I perhaps go to the Box Hill police to take it off them? Then I could make a fresh report with the Richmond police.' The answer was that it didn't work like that.

It rained on Wednesday morning. We said goodbye to Ashleigh-Rose and Heather. Said we'd do our best to find their sister. I rang work, for a second time, and explained that Rachel had not come home. Said I must look for her. They wished us the very best and would be thinking of us. Told us to keep positive.

Yes, our daughter was living, somewhere. She was not dead. We would find her. We *must* find her. How could our day-dreaming butterfly cease to exist?

We searched through the back streets of Richmond again. Down small streets, hidden behind Bridge Road shops and bluestone churches. Streets only wide enough for single lanes of traffic. Tiny single-storey terraced houses with rusting tin roofs, flaking paint and collapsed front veranda posts. Battered red and navy vinyl chairs sitting by themselves on front porches.

'Rachel, Rachel, RACHEL!' Two parents calling, for their first-born, walking down each side of the lanes. An odd sensation. So much of Rachel's disappearance was surreal. We were beginning to live a life that should not have belonged to us.

Looking over fences. Walking through into unit carparks.

For the first time Mike began to open dump bins.

'Don't do that!' I snapped. The thought was too final.

'Elizabeth, I must.' Pause. 'If she's been grabbed . . . someone may have dumped her bag.'

Some time later we gave up looking and returned to the dance school, hoping the Box Hill police were doing their bit. Vicki, the dance teacher, was distressed. The police had not been to visit. Vicki had called the Richmond police twice this Wednesday morning, to inform them the Box Hill police had not arrived. We were all trying desperately to make someone notice.

Vicki suggested I ring Neil Paterson again.

Once again Neil sounded sympathetic. He repeated what the Box Hill police had said – generally speaking ninety-seven per cent of missing people turn up within forty-eight hours. And if not, at least by the end of five days.

I thought, so that's it. The police will get serious after five days. She should have been the daughter of a Prime Minister or been related to someone wealthy and famous. It didn't matter she was our daughter. She didn't warrant enough attention. Rachel's life was cheap. To them she was just some fifteen-year-old kid who had decided to clear off for a few days. Well, that's how it seemed anyway.

Neil had been concerned about the *old female friend* story and suggested we start writing down the names of Rachel's friends. Not just present friends but old school friends. So the first of many lists began.

I found it difficult to remember all her friends' surnames so it was suggested I ring Canterbury Girls Secondary College. I rang and explained Rachel had been missing since Monday night and although Rachel had not been a student for the last six months could they perhaps provide me with a list of her friends' surnames. I was told they could not give out this information and suggested I ring the local police to make the request.

I put the phone down, understanding their situation, and phoned the Box Hill police. And again I needed to tell the story of Rachel's disappearance to yet another officer. The policewoman told me she didn't know where the school or I had got the idea that the police could request a list of names from the school, because they couldn't do it.

It really did feel as if, apart from family and friends, we were receiving little support. Did they expect us all to go home and wait? Wait to see if she would return? Wait to see themselves proven right that her life had never been in danger?

Wait. What sort of waiting game is this when one waits until it *is* too late? Wait until her body is found? Wait to hear them say, we were wrong, she wasn't a fifteen-year-old statistic who chose to go of her own free will.

It was now midday on Wednesday. We had made our first

contact with the police an hour and a quarter after Rachel's disappearance, but the only police help we'd apparently received were a few well-meaning comments.

We discussed ringing the newspapers and television news without the help of the police, but something stopped us. We feared, *really feared,* for her life. If someone was holding her against her will and saw the press, could they panic? Kill her?

While we were still at the dance school we received a phone call from Richmond police asking us to come to the station to make a statement. I felt a new surge of adrenalin! We did not know what activated this fresh interest, but, thank God, at last someone was listening. Immediately I began to feel better. Now the police were taking us seriously, we would surely find her.

Vicki, her dance teacher, had lent us her mobile phone, so we grabbed it and left a message at the dance school for Vicki to follow: if an independent person gave a character reference of Rachel the police would no doubt realise it wasn't just over-reacting parents who feared for her safety.

At the police station we met a new face behind the counter and found ourselves retelling the story, *again.* This officer disappeared for a moment, returning to say the detective senior sergeant would speak to us shortly. We sat waiting while people filed into this toilet-sized watchhouse. It didn't feel like a welcoming place.

There were statutory declarations signed. Complaints against parking tickets, a lost handbag and some complicated story about a lost licence. A middle-aged man came in verbally abusing the police officer, who remained remarkably calm.

Mike asked how long we would need to wait. It felt as if we were doing too much of nothing. The police officer tried to explain about police procedures while we were waiting and then I remembered that we'd left Vicki's mobile in the car. Mike decided to go and collect it.

While Mike was out the detective senior sergeant came through. I told him that Mike had just gone to collect the mobile phone from the car. The detective senior sergeant thought this an excellent idea because of the high theft rate from cars. I suggested we wait for Mike, but he said Mike could just follow us up. I was led through the first of many glass security doors that

we'd encounter over the next two weeks and walked up two flights of wooden stairs. We went through to an office where I again asked if we could wait for Mike.

The detective suggested I start with my statement and explained that this type of report is not usually investigated by CIB. I gathered something had been going on in the background – I sensed he wasn't particularly pleased. However, he appeared to be very thorough and I was glad that we had someone taking us seriously.

But I was embarrassed by Mike's absence, mentioning on a number of occasions how concerned I was. The detective senior sergeant told me not to worry. Mike had probably just been held up. I gave my statement as objectively as I could, so we didn't look like hysterical parents. I gave him details of our own investigations. Names of shops and shopkeepers, and the description of the woman approaching young women. But I kept thinking, *where's Mike?* I felt as if Mike had deliberately taken a long time so it would all be over on his return. I was concerned with how this must have appeared to the detective.

When the statement was finished the detective senior sergeant excused himself. Shortly after, another detective came through and offered me a drink. And finally, Mike came through with another detective.

'Where have you *been*?' I uttered, agitated.

'I've been downstairs.'

'All this time,' I answered in disbelief.

When Mike returned with the mobile phone Vicki was already waiting. Before he'd had a chance to speak, the constable behind the desk questioned him aggressively concerning the presence of Vicki, claiming she had already phoned twice that morning. Mike said Vicki was there to verify Rachel's character and show that she was no runaway, something no one in authority seemed to want to believe.

The constable replied that if and when the police wished to talk to Vicki they would make that decision and not Mike. He followed this statement with yet another description about the correct procedures when dealing with the police and how things were done, and in what order.

Mike said that every time he tried to say something he was told to hold on because he, the constable, was talking. Eventually Mike became so tired of this that he raised his voice and said, 'No, *you* hold on. If you don't mind, I would like to get a word in.' Mike explained again why Vicki was there, and said, 'I don't really care about the right or wrong way of doing things. I have a daughter missing and finding her is the most important thing to me and I don't appreciate being attacked for it.'

The constable immediately backed off and suggested that Mike sit down and calm down. 'I *am* calm and I should be with my wife giving a statement,' he said. But the constable insisted, so Mike sat. Some time during this trauma Vicki withdrew and returned to the dance school. Eventually Mike was shown upstairs to discover I had already given the statement.

We were then introduced to a woman detective and another male detective who were to investigate Rachel's disappearance. We handed them a copy of our poster and, I think, some photographs. Could we find some more photographs and bring them in the next day? Could we make up a list of Rachel's friends, not just recent friends, but names from old school photos, kindergarten friends . . . ?

After looking at our first poster the detective senior sergeant was concerned we had included our phone number on it, because of the risk of prank callers. We agreed we would white-out our phone number, but a lot of posters had already been distributed so we decided not to worry about it. The possibility of contact with prank callers in contrast to the possibility of one call that might help us find Rachel seemed acceptable. In reality we didn't receive one prank phone call. But the detective senior sergeant's advice was well-intentioned. His advice for us not to stay out all night was too – searching for her and wearing ourselves out, when we had no idea where she was. If we went home and slept we would be refreshed for the next day. But we were parents faced with a lost daughter and this seemed an impossibility.

He also asked us to check under the house with a torch at night. We thought this preposterous. Didn't he realise our daughter was afraid of the dark? He qualified his request by

saying that quite often young adults who go missing still feel the need to be close. It was just possible she could be hiding there. If she was not, well, he reiterated, get some rest because 'a person who doesn't want to be found won't be found'.

We left the station feeling disturbed. Had he really listened? Maybe I had been too objective. Perhaps I should have been crying. Perhaps ranting and raving. But Mike and I had agreed that we would hold off the tears, hold off the collapsing, because if we did either of those things we would not be in a position to help our dearly loved daughter.

I returned to the dance school and shared our experiences. Vicki was distressed by her treatment at the station because as a concerned member of the public she had willingly visited the police to provide information. But police opinion appeared to be that Rachel was a runaway. Why weren't the police asking *why* Rachel would *want* to run away?

We discovered in the next few days that they would. They would question Manni in front of his dance teacher because, at sixteen, he was under-age. Is she pregnant? Even here they were apparently making false assumptions that Rachel would feel unable to come to us. Were they assuming we would be parents unwilling to give their daughter support? Mike's first wife, when I was only seven, was a pregnant teenage bride. She miscarried on their wedding night and three years later their marriage ended. So yes, we *would* have been there for Rachel. And yes, Rachel would have known we would have been there for her.

The police read her school workbooks where she wrote of a sore back. Perhaps she was running away because dance was becoming too strenuous? The previous year Rachel suffered from shin splints caused by trying to out-do her best. She visited the physiotherapist twice weekly, for five weeks, and although unable to dance she still attended class every day so she could learn the new dances in her head.

Meanwhile, Mike once again searched the back streets of Richmond, checking every dump bin. He also decided to have a chat with the photographer who had taken the pictures of Rachel for the magazine *Women's Fitness Australia*. Considering she was

the most recent contact Rachel had had with a photographer we wondered if there was a connection. Not because she was guilty of wrong doing, but maybe she had given Rachel another contact.

When Mike returned to the dance school he was full of these ideas so I rang the modelling school for, I suppose, a character reference for this photographer. As far as they were concerned she was completely up-front and trustworthy. They were worried Rachel could have become involved with some dodgy photographer – they warn their students not to go anywhere unless it is verified through them. Could Rachel please contact them on her return so they could make this safety issue clear to her.

On Wednesday afternoon we visited Cathy, the mother of Ellen, one of Rachel's closest friends. Although Rachel and Ellen had not visited each other for a number of months, they were like soul mates and no doubt still in telephone contact. Perhaps Ellen knew something.

Rachel was in the fortunate position of having a number of friends who thought they were Rachel's best friends. The truth is, she did have a number of best friends from her different interests in life. Best friend at church. Best friend from primary school. Best friend from secondary school. Best friend at dance school and so on. The Baptist minister described Rachel as a butterfly, flittering from one group of friends to another, in her different interests, but always making people feel special.

Ellen had not heard from Rachel. Ellen was very concerned. It was not like Rachel to let people worry. She said she would ring up the radio station her age group listened to and get word out. Ellen became upset and Cathy went to collect her from school.

Cathy also contacted one of her friends, John, who was a pharmacist who owned printing equipment. He offered free access to this equipment with an unlimited quantity of paper to produce as many posters as we would need. David, a friend of ours and graphic artist, had already offered to design another poster for us and gave his time to go and produce these posters,

which he did after a full day's work and long into the small hours of the night.

A phone call came through asking us to contact the woman detective at Richmond police. Someone had rung in response to one of the posters. A girl answering Rachel's description was seen with two other girls getting on at East Richmond railway station. It was now about 5 p.m., and the police said they would contact Camberwell station because surveillance videos for this region were stored at Camberwell. We assumed we would be contacted when they were going so we could accompany them.

The dance school was also informed by Richmond police that they would interview teachers and students on Thursday morning regarding Rachel's disappearance.

At last.

5

DESCENT OF LOSS

Wednesday Evening, 3 March

We returned home at about 5.30 p.m., for a short while, to see our younger girls and give them some loving. They must surely be feeling insecure as well.

The house seemed to be full of caring family and friends, who listened to the events of the day. Robbie, my sister, had arrived from Wonthaggi. She would take Heather back. Nine-year-old Heather was happy to have an unscheduled holiday from school.

David, our graphic artist friend, arrived not long after us, and he was happy to pick up a number of photographs of Rachel to design the new poster. We could collect it tomorrow morning from his work.

I remembered David had called into the house last Saturday, when Rachel had been by herself for a while, and I asked him how she had seemed.

He told us she was fine. She had shown him the heart-shaped cushion she was making for Manni, and had spoken of how much she loved Manni. She had also wanted to make a cake but discovered there were no eggs and asked David if he would go and buy her some. He wanted to know why she hadn't just walked to the corner store. She replied that she was too scared to go to the local shops because sometimes men followed her.

Someone suggested I ring Telstra and find out the details of incoming and outgoing phone calls for the weekend. I thought this an excellent idea but I could only obtain the outgoing calls because to access incoming calls would be breaking the privacy act. The Telstra lady was extremely helpful though and gave us a list of all the phone calls made from our house over the weekend. The only mystery phone-calling that weekend had been from Heather and Ashleigh-Rose, who had rung some new friends whose numbers we were not yet familiar with.

When I informed the detective senior sergeant that I had rung Telstra and obtained a list of outgoing calls he told me I had saved them the job because they were just about to do that. I asked him if he could get a list of incoming calls because I felt the so-called female friend may have tried to contact her over the past weekend. He told me this wasn't possible. I thought – not *technically* possible.

I was given the impression that the following morning a press statement was going to be released, possibly with 'Crime Stoppers'.

It was as if there had already been a death in the family. It wasn't that I believed Rachel was dead. It was the chasm of the not knowing which felt – like death. Rachel was now approaching her third night out. She had spent three nights away from home before, but then we knew where she was. Either at Manni's, or a girlfriend's, on holiday, or with a grandparent. It was the helplessness of it all. A family is a unit with a sense of belonging, even when separated by distance, even when separated by divorce, because everyone is aware of another's being and location, somewhere on earth. Our unit suddenly found a piece of the jigsaw missing. Even second and third cousins and great-great-aunts and uncles in England, the Shetland Isles and America were feeling anxious about Rachel. Manni's family in Italy was feeling anxious about Manni's girl, the girl they'd seen dancing on birthday and Christmas videos.

What must it feel like for the parents of children sent to fight or nurse in wars?

My father said, 'The not knowing. This is what wartime is like. Imagine five years of it, every person, in every household.'

Mike stood up. 'It's dark under the house. I'll grab a torch,' he said and left the room.

'What's he on about?' asked Michele, my cousin.

'He's looking for Rachel . . . under the house.'

Everybody stopped talking. I realised my mistake.

'She's under the house!' yelled Heather and ran, but I grabbed her.

My mother stood up, ashen-faced.

'No, Heather. I'm sorry. I didn't mean it like that.' I wrapped my arms around her, giving her a comforting cuddle. 'The detective senior sergeant asked us to look under the house, just in case she had run away and was hiding there.'

My mother was appalled.

My Aunt Babe said, 'Now, Joy, he's just doing his job. He had to ask Michael.'

We heard the door to the area under the house open. We heard Mike say, 'Rachel, Rachel, are you here?' We heard him walking right underneath. 'Rachel . . . Rachel . . . Didn't think you'd be here.'

Emmanuel Carella's mum, Rosa, met us at about 7.00 o'clock in Richmond. She came with Tony, Manni's dad, who had brought more photocopied posters. We told them we were having a new poster designed which would hopefully be available tomorrow. During the day the Carella brothers had thought Rachel's disappearance may have had something to do with the Grand Prix, as did my father. They thought it possible Rachel may have been hoodwinked into believing some clever story about part-time dancing for the Grand Prix, because the older dance students were rehearsing for something connected to the Grand Prix. Could Rachel have naively gone to some tabletop dance club and be held up somewhere for the week? Could she have realised her mistake and now just be biding time? My father hoped she might appear at the end of the week.

The Carella brothers and cousins and their friends decided they would frequent clubs and tabletop dancing venues, just in case. Tony said he would walk around the city gardens with Robert, the eldest Carella brother.

Rosa, Mike and I walked the streets behind East Richmond railway station. I couldn't imagine why Rachel would be here but we all felt the need to do something. We stuck posters up and called . . . Rachel, Rachel, RACHEL.

If it was at all possible she was behind one of these walls, even if she couldn't answer us, she would at least know we were continuing to search for her.

We were walking back across the bridge over East Richmond railway line when a car pulled up. A door opened. It was the detectives. They asked us if we'd had any luck. No. Had they?

They had been to Camberwell station and viewed the videos for the hour of 5.30 to 6.30 p.m. on Monday, and said they couldn't see Rachel. I thought it odd that they hadn't asked us because I felt, as Rachel's parents, we would have had a better chance of identifying her on a video surveillance than the detectives.

We talked to them for a little while before they were called away to do another job. They were genuinely concerned for Rachel.

By the time we returned to the dance school, classes had finished. It was then I realised I hadn't eaten all day. I can't remember exactly what we did for food but I have an idea Vicki ordered pizza. We ate, only because we needed to keep up our strength. We knew we would not be going home.

Instead we did the hospital walk. We had phoned the hospitals on Tuesday only to be met with this damned privacy act. If Rachel had been admitted under 'Rachel Barber' she had the right for her parents not to know, if she didn't wish them to. So we soon learned we had to ask if a girl, answering Rachel's description, had been admitted, named or unnamed. But there had been no injured or deceased girls answering her description admitted to any of the hospitals over this period.

We drove back to Richmond, drove slowly around the streets, over and over again. The words *a person who doesn't want to be found won't be found* stirred and challenged our thoughts. As Rachel's parents we had considered this an insult. But what were the alternatives? Would we rather our daughter be missing of her own free will or would we prefer the alternative? To be proven right and find a decomposing body or a badly

beaten and raped shadow of the Rachel we'd last seen?

'You do realise that when we find her she won't be in any condition to dance,' I said. 'She may have to take a year off. I think she'll need special counselling.'

'Don't underestimate Rachel,' Mike answered. 'She'll be back dancing within the month. Dancing will heal her.'

The detective senior sergeant had warned us not to stay out all night. Trying to find her would be like looking for a needle in a haystack. Another cliché, but a true one. He told us we could drive down one road only to turn into another just as she might walk into the road we'd just left. Futile, it seemed. It was. We were now approaching the third night without any further leads. In all honesty we could not expect the police to take us seriously in the search if we did not consider what they thought, too – that Rachel may have run away. The search for Rachel should be a two-way partnership, family and police working together. So we decided to search for her as if she really *was* a runaway, so we would have credibility with the police, not because for any one moment we thought she was.

Exhausted, at about 2.00 a.m., we drove into the city.

6

No Foul Play

Day 3: Early hours of Thursday, 4 March

I would not recommend making a tour of Melbourne at two in the morning. It is a different city then.

We drove around but soon realised we needed to be on foot. We parked the car somewhere near the corner of Lonsdale and Russell Streets, grabbed a handful of posters, an exercise book and pen, and made our way towards Swanston Walk and Flinders Street. The heart of Melbourne. This was scary stuff. There were clusters of people. Smoking, drinking, sleeping. No one appeared aggressive but there was a belligerent undercurrent. The city felt as if a haze had slipped over it like a pillow case.

We spoke to a few people and handed them posters. They wished us luck. We spoke to a flower-seller outside the Town Hall. Still selling flowers. Selling flowers, I thought, at this hour?

There were teenagers asleep, huddled against the columns of St Paul's Cathedral. Teenagers standing in groups, shifting from one foot to the other foot, drawing on cigarettes, downing Coke. Staring. Staring at us. Two crazy parents with posters in hand. We walked up to some of these young people, just children really, and asked them if they had seen any new girl answering Rachel's description. They shook their heads but one boy said, 'She's lucky.' We paused and looked at him. He drew on his cigarette and added, 'She's lucky to have parents like you . . . who care. You'll find her.'

I felt like we were stepping over bodies beneath the clocks of Flinders Street station. Not all these people were homeless, but a lot of them looked as if they should have been tucked up in bed with a teddy bear, the dregs of a hot chocolate dried out in a mug beside them.

Our posters were already taped to notice boards. Someone mentioned a public notice board somewhere in Swanston Walk. There were posters there as well. It seemed as though every available spot to place posters already had posters. The Carellas had done well.

I distinctly remember one poster where Rachel's eyes had been burnt out with a cigarette. I felt as if a dagger had sliced through my heart. Mike took down the eyeless poster and replaced it with another. He took my hand and led me away. It felt like an omen.

An alcoholic, destitute man kept following us. Three or four times he spoke to Mike. He followed us for several blocks. I found this unnerving, but Mike was courteous to him. It was as if Mike had collected a stray while going for a walk.

We quickened our step as we made our zigzagging way through the streets. We spoke to several security guards outside Timezone fun parlours and similar places, finally being convinced by one guard that this was not the right place for us to be.

'We're not going to find her, Mike,' I said, nervously squeezing his hand, and agreeing with the guard. 'It's not going to do anyone any good if we both end up dead.'

Mike nodded.

When the car was in sight we ran the last few metres and locked ourselves in quickly. I felt ashamed.

Mike said, 'Did you notice the police presence?'

'What police presence?'

We had been in the city for close on two hours, maybe longer, and had seen one patrol car.

'Shall we drive to Rose Street?' I can't remember whether it was Mike or me who said it, but we couldn't go home. So we 'cased out' our first brothel, the one that was the focus of that story in Monday's *Age*. By day eight we had noted the goings-in and the goings-out of five brothels and one escort agency. And why? Imagined fear coupled with exhaustion. This was the phenomenon the detective senior sergeant was probably trying to save us from.

We drove slowly down Rose Street, not even sure what a brothel looked like, and into the back streets of Fitzroy. Mike was driving now because I couldn't trust my concentration. We were stopped at one of the back street corners when a group of colourful, and young, dreadlocked adults surrounded the car. Oranges and reds, purple stripes and blue stripes marked their fashion statement.

Mike wound the window down. I couldn't believe it. We could have been mugged!

To my surprise we found that they were worried about us driving around the streets so slowly. They thought we were lost. Mike told them our story and they asked for some posters, offering to put them up. I was ashamed, again, at my preconception. They were warm and caring, and I had grossly misjudged them.

About 4.30 a.m. we found ourselves outside a pink, illuminated 'house of ill repute' in Richmond.

'She wouldn't be here,' I said. 'It looks too legal.'

'Right district though,' said Mike.

'No,' I said. 'She's not here.'

Mike drove over the bridge and on until we stopped the car near a small park. We watched a man walking two Great Danes on leashes while we sipped lukewarm coffee which tasted of vacuum flask. We walked around the park, looking under shrubs and in children's play equipment. Mike checked more dump bins.

'Enough,' he said. 'Let's go home.'

We did not sleep. We did not talk. We mulled over our unfolding tragedy, independently, for the two hours rest we allowed ourselves.

There was a gentle knock on the bedroom door. 'Are you awake?' came a whisper.

'Yes,' answered Mike.

My mother opened the door with tea and toast. 'Don't get up,' she said. 'I heard you come in.'

She sat down beside us. 'Robbie rang last night and Heather's fine. She'll go to the nursery with her today.'

We sipped our tea in silence. No words, just pain.

'Your parents rang, Mike,' said Mum. 'They've asked the Major at Inala if the Salvation Army can help.'

'Good idea,' answered Mike. Mike's parents lived at Inala, a retirement village not far away.

'We walked through the city last night.'

'*Elizabeth*,' said Mum, with her concerned mother's voice from my childhood.

'It's so sad,' added Mike. 'The city at night. It was terrible. There was this drunk . . .'

'Is Ashleigh-Rose okay?' I asked, breaking yet another silence.

'She settled late after letting me read to her in bed,' answered Mum.

The phone rang. It was Ted, our old friend. Mum left the room to refill our cups. She took the plate of cold toast with her.

'I don't know,' Ted told Mike, 'but I don't sense she's come to any harm. I feel she will turn up at the end of the week.' Mike passed this news to me. I felt relieved.

'Ted wants to know if you know of an old woman who lived in Mont Albert,' Mike asked me. 'Someone who has died.'

'Not that I can think of.'

'Someone who is perhaps blind,' added Mike. 'Ted says he's had a message that the blind see. And this blind person is watching over Rachel.'

'Old Grandma,' I said. 'She was blind. But lived in Surrey Hills. Same postcode as Mont Albert, though.' Grandma died when Rachel was about five. Rachel was her namesake, Rachel Elizabeth, although Grandma hated both names and always called herself Bessie. She told me when she found out I had named Rachel after her that she couldn't think why. But I think she thought the idea of having a grandchild named after her was appealing.

'That's it, then,' said Mike. 'The blind see.' He paused. 'There's another call coming through. Ted, can you hold on?

. . . Okay then . . . Bye, we'll see you later in the day . . . Hello
. . . Oh, Mum . . . no, we haven't found her yet.'

I relaxed and leant back onto the bed. Some moments later
Mike said goodbye to his mother, but dropped the phone. I
reached across him, and put it back. Mike stayed where he was,
his body over the bed, his arm dropped loosely to the floor, with
his fingers flailing.

'Mike . . . Mike!'

He was sobbing, uncontrollably.

I had never seen him cry.

'Oh, Mike,' I said and wrapped my arms tightly around him,
feeling his pain, empathising with his fatherhood's loss.

'She's dead!' he wailed.

'She's not!' I cried out.

He flung my arms away and rocked recklessly on the bed,
flinging his body around in anguish. 'She's dead.' He sobbed and
sobbed, and then suddenly his body fell back, and dropped like
a rag doll, limp. Still. His eyes glazed.

I thought he was dead. 'Mum!' I shrieked.

Mum came in as Mike raised himself again. 'I'm sorry,' he
sobbed, shaking. His whole body racked with torture. Trembling. Almost inaudibly he said, 'I love my children, I love my
children, I love my wife, I love my wife.'

I had never seen him look so terrifying. It was like he was
possessed.

Ashleigh-Rose came in. Looked at her father, tried to hold
him. He fell back again, limp as a doll, unable to move. She
stroked his head.

I ran from the room. Mum ran after me. We left him with
Ashleigh-Rose stroking his head, crying in her arms.

I rang our doctor in Mont Albert. Told them what had happened. But because we lived in Heathmont they were unable to
make a house visit. They gave me the phone number of a locum
service.

Ashleigh-Rose came out and sat on the couch. 'He's quiet now.'

The phone rang again and Mum returned to Mike with a
glass of water and two paracetamol. It was my father Ivan and
stepmother Susan ringing.

Before I could tell them what had happened they asked if Ashleigh-Rose would like to stay with them in Healesville until Rachel was found. Ashleigh-Rose replied with a firm 'yes' and started to cry. She had never seen her father cry either – now she had witnessed him sobbing. She was a very scared eleven-year-old.

The locum arrived within the hour and stayed talking, privately, with Mike for another hour. He prescribed medication and rest, but he knew the rest would be highly unlikely.

Mike did rest until noon. We knew the Richmond police were interviewing teachers and students at the dance school so we decided it was best not to interfere.

My father and Susan came to collect Ashleigh-Rose, who had hurriedly packed her bags. We rang one of my aunts to come and sit with my mother so she would not be by herself while she was busy answering phone calls.

Mike was now convinced that Rachel was dead. No amount of persuasion could alter his mind. Rachel was a girl who was afraid of the dark, and tentative in new surroundings. She was a girl who needed the security of family and friends. When we moved to Heathmont she hated having a downstairs rumpus room as a bedroom – she begged to come upstairs. 'I want to be with you guys.' So her father emptied his study and she moved upstairs.

I had described her to police as a creature of habit. 'Rachel was fifteen going on eighteen going on twelve.' My girlfriend Chris said, 'She couldn't help being naive, just look at her mother!' She was not mature for her age. But we could not deny that from the time Rachel had left school she had blossomed. Young womanhood agreed with her. Mike and I were looking forward to her future.

Thursday and Friday now tend to blur together, but to the best of my memory we left home early Thursday afternoon.

On the way we called into our friend David's employment where he was just completing the new poster. We had decided not to include Rachel's name on it, I suppose, for her privacy on her return.

But by now it had been three days and we knew Rachel

wasn't coming home. We knew she loved her family and boyfriend too much to let them worry. There was always the chance she had been raped or kidnapped for a brothel. Some well-meaning friend had informed us about a date-rape drug. We were told she could have been given this in a drink, drugged, even shipped out of the country. I thought this was a fairytale, but by the end of our search we had heard more of a trade where occasionally girls *were* kidnapped and taken overseas. Mike said that if one of the alternatives was being kidnapped for child prostitution, with no chance of rescue, he would rather she was dead.

We decided to call briefly into the dance school before connecting with the police, who in the meantime, thank God, had been to take statements. Monday she was reported missing, Wednesday afternoon we get past the front counter, and finally, Thursday morning some action.

Vicki the dance teacher said, 'Elizabeth, can I speak privately with you?' Her tone made me feel insecure, and I followed her into the office of Dulcie the artistic director.

'It's about Emmanuel. They interviewed him in considerable detail, and I was present because he was under-age.'

I sipped my tea and thought, what on earth is she going to say?

'They asked him really private questions. I felt so sorry for him. Like, is she pregnant?'

So that was it. They thought she was running away because she was pregnant. I laughed, and said, 'They're not even sexually active.'

'That's what I thought,' she replied, and said something like, 'I thought they were as pure as snow.'

Well, maybe not that pure, I thought.

'Elizabeth, apparently within the last month . . . something did happen, but he swears she's not pregnant. It was protected.'

So, I thought, it had to happen sooner or later. How long had they been a couple? Ten months, and so deeply in love I had been quite concerned by their obvious devotion to each other. He truly was her Romeo.

Silly thoughts come to mind at times like these. Like, Rachel would die if she knew Manni had been through the third degree. Like, poor boy, fancy finally consummating your love only to have some idiot kidnap your girlfriend.

I remembered a time when Rachel was twelve and had gone on a Baptist church youth camp to a place called Gum Creek. She came home 'in love'. She hurried me into her room and closed the door, and with a great grin on her face said, 'I've had my first tongue kiss.' Giggle, giggle.

I looked at her, flummoxed by this delighted child. This really did require some kind of answer. I leant back against the window-pane and said, 'Did you get lots of shivers running up and down your spine?'

'Yes,' she answered, sounding absolutely amazed. 'How did you guess?'

She called this young man Macca and fortunately he lived far far away, over the distant hills. Our phone bill went up dramatically, for at least a month.

Her very first love was her kindergarten friend Ryan, her childhood chum. Together they made mud pies and were fun beach pals at Cape Paterson. There was Anthony who, according to his mother, was besotted with her. Sadly for Anthony, Rachel was not besotted with him, but regarded him as a good friend. There was well-mannered Hugh, her St Hilary's friend, until Ben crept onto the scene for a few weeks, or was it days? Young teenagers often fall in and out of 'puppy' love and these five boys were special memories in Rachel's life.

'Elizabeth,' said Vicki, interrupting my thoughts. 'Elizabeth, I thought I had better say something in case the police come out with it. They told him it was confidential but . . .'

The door opened. 'There you are,' said Mike. 'I've been looking for you.'

I told Mike in the car about Manni's interview. 'How does that make you feel?'

'How should it make me feel?' Mike is clever at answering questions with more questions. I call it beating around the bush.

'Your little girl . . .' I said. 'Our little girl.' I wasn't sure how I felt.

'Well, to be quite honest, all things considered, it doesn't bother me. If somebody has dragged her off and . . . raped her, then it's a comfort to know she's experienced some sexual tenderness with someone who obviously loves her deeply.'

Dear Mike. He immediately made me feel comfortable.

We arrived at the police station, to see yet another new face behind the counter. However, this police officer seemed to treat us with some empathy and knew who we were. He apologised; there would be a short delay. We sat and waited. The missing persons poster glared at us from the wall.

While we were waiting, another concerned officer came through. He meant well, but he told us a story of another young girl who had been reported missing for six months when she was recognised by a truck driver who picked her up in country Victoria.

'Rachel's not a runaway!' I shouted, and stood up. Mike attempted to still me. 'She's got innocently involved in something that's got out of hand! When they find her four days dead they'll say, "Oh, the parents were right after all."'

I can't remember the police officer's reply but I can remember Mike speaking on my behalf.

I asked if I could go to the toilet. On the Wednesday the detective senior sergeant had allowed me to use the station toilet. This police officer told me to go around to the security door and he'd let me in.

The doors opened and as I was about to go through, unaccompanied, a policewoman asked me where I was going. I told her I wanted to go to the toilet. She replied I could not use the station toilet and if I went outside I would find a toilet around the back of the building. But when I stood outside the front door of the police station I was so angry I walked one and a half blocks to the McDonald's toilet instead. On my return, Mike, who had heard the earlier comments of the policewoman said, 'You went to the McDonald's toilet, didn't you?'

I nodded.

'I would have done the same,' he said.

We sat in front of the detective senior sergeant sitting at his desk, the woman detective standing beside his chair. Formidable.

44

We felt like criminals. Why? It felt as if it was our fault that they were being put to all this trouble. My impression of this man was that he would have been excellent at interrogating villains. But we were not villains. He should have been head of Fraud Squad, head of Drug Squad, head of Arson.

We handed the detective senior sergeant more photographs of Rachel and showed him the new poster. David had also given us a zip disk of the photographs for the police.

The detective thanked us for the photographs but mentioned that if we displayed the posters outside Richmond we would need to inform the police stations. Other stations would not know who the girl on the poster was otherwise. He also warned us to be careful where we displayed these posters as it was an offence to put them just anywhere. It was possible to incur a $70 fine for each poster. It was important to obtain permission from shops and offices if we wanted to place them on the inside of windows.

Lost dogs have more rights than lost children, I thought.

The detective senior sergeant then shared what he considered to be a positive sighting of Rachel. Another independent detective, not from Richmond, was on his way to a court hearing when he noticed an unusual occurrence in Bridge Road outside some shops. He'd seen a girl counting out coins with a blond-haired man, and was so concerned that he'd reported this to Richmond police. The detective senior sergeant had shown this detective photographs of Rachel and he was ninety to ninety-five per cent sure the girl was Rachel. So the detective senior sergeant told us that he believed Rachel *was* a runaway and repeated his advice: people who do not want to be found are very difficult to find. We obviously didn't know our daughter as well as we thought we did – *they* had discovered something about our daughter that *we* didn't know. He did not say what this was but I jumped to conclusions. 'The loss of her virginity?' I said. 'What fifteen-year-old *would* tell her parents?'

'You surely can't be serious,' said Mike. 'That girl could not *possibly* have been Rachel!'

Can you be so sure? was the sentiment expressed by the detective senior sergeant.

I considered this for a moment, not believing a word of it. If Rachel was a runaway why would she be sitting in Bridge Road, Richmond, where she would no doubt be recognised? It seemed preposterous that the police could have even considered this.

I had the idea from the woman detective's body language that she didn't necessarily agree with the detective senior sergeant either.

We had been given the impression that a press release or announcement through 'Crime Stoppers' was likely today. But now we were told that it would not be possible. There was no evidence, other than our gut feeling, of foul play. And the detective senior sergeant added that he didn't necessarily think it was a good idea to involve the press at present.

We had mixed feelings about a press release because we feared for Rachel's safety. We still believed she was being held against her will. So we said we didn't think it was a particularly good idea either.

But if we were so unsure about the idea of a press release why were we so clear about our need to distribute posters? There is a contradiction here, and I have thought about this in detail. I believe the posters were important as active participation for Rachel's family and friends. The posters were necessary as mind therapy. The alternative would be to sit back, wait on the police, and go mad. By distributing posters people were kept moving, and spread the news by word of mouth. And just maybe we'd be rewarded with a living, breathing Rachel.

We continued to put up posters all Thursday afternoon, concentrating our efforts on the Punt Road end of Bridge Road. We asked staff at every shop on both sides of the road if they had seen a girl with a blond-haired man counting out money.

Nobody could remember seeing a girl counting out money with a man. We asked people in offices, in the corner milk bar, workmen renovating a shop, people in the Epworth hospital and its pharmacy.

We told our story to a muscular and tanned man washing his car and boat, outside his house at the back of Bridge Road. He told us there were a number of legal brothels in the Richmond area and gave us the address of one – we tried to find it later that night but were unsuccessful. Feeling washed-out, we returned to the dance school.

We had arranged to meet Ted and Betty at 7.30 p.m. at the corner of Church and Gipps Street where Manni and Domenic, one of Manni's brothers, and Rachel's new dance classmates Tamara and Kylee, had said they'd last seen Rachel smiling and waving goodbye.

In fact, seven of us, all of us except Tamara, stood on the corner.

'Now, is this where you said goodbye to Rachel?' I asked.

'No,' said Dom. 'Further up.'

We walked along Church Street tentatively, as if we were looking for buried treasure. Rachel *was* our treasure. We needed a treasure map. X marks the spot.

Rachel's friends grouped together and said 'Here,' almost simultaneously, indicating a spot opposite the lane where they had parked their car on Monday.

I stood on the driveway, breathing in the space of her last known contact. 'Oh God,' I said. 'Where is she?'

'It was like she vanished,' said Dom.

'She was here, and then she wasn't,' said Manni.

'She just disappeared,' said Kylee.

'And we were only gone a matter of minutes,' added Dom.

Manni said, 'She didn't have time to walk out of view, in either direction.'

'So she was taken quickly,' said Mike.

I said. 'No. Remember there's been no evidence of foul play.'

Ted was at a loss, too. I wondered if 'psychics' could sometimes be too close to the situation themselves. Ted wanted Rachel to be living as well.

'I wonder if the police have done a doorknock.'

'Doubt it,' said Mike. 'But neither have we put posters in household letter boxes.'

An hour later we met again, having delivered posters to every letter box, to every flat in the street. Rosa, and Manni's brother Frank, met up with us.

For some reason Ted directed us to a flower shop in Carlton that had recently been robbed. He couldn't explain why he felt this shop had special significance. He said he kept seeing flowers, lots of them. He felt we should put a poster in this flower shop and others in Lygon Street.

This was a most peculiar evening, which I discovered Manni later reported to the police. Ted came up with the name of a street, Berkeley Street, and insisted Rachel was there. 'But which suburb is this street in?' someone was demanding. I went back to the car and felt we were on a wild goose chase, but because we didn't have any other leads I was happy to go along. Stranger things have happened.

Ted, under obvious emotional strain, came up with map co-ordinates and a page number, straight out of his head. Berkeley Street, G4, map 43. We looked the co-ordinates up in the street directory and found Berkeley Street. The atmosphere was intense. I leapt from the car and started to cry. 'You mean we'll find her? Tonight! Mike!'

I remember this night with excitement. Of course I don't intend to sound insensitive but this night *was* like an emotional roller-coaster. If we had not been searching for our daughter I could have described the night as a car rally or, indeed, like a treasure hunt.

But we didn't find her. The street consisted of warehouses. The street was empty except for nine people walking up and down calling Rachel . . . Rachel . . . RACHEL.

I know that Ted has been greatly affected by this night. No one wants to be faced with the prospect of a loved one dying. The following week he said he was told to stay out of it. What had happened could not be changed.

It was very late at night when we received a mobile call from David who had finished printing two thousand posters. We arranged to meet him in Richmond, where we were to drop Ted and Betty back at their car.

Thursday night was the opening of my stepmother Susan's exhibition at the Centre for Contemporary Photography. The Centre had offered to postpone the exhibition, but Susan had declined in the belief that its continuation may help towards Rachel's discovery. The Centre placed a sign: 'If you have seen the girl in these pictures recently, inform gallery staff immediately.'

Richmond police had visited the Centre during the day. I remember thinking that maybe the police thought Rachel's disappearance was a publicity stunt for the exhibition. If they did they never mentioned it.

During the opening, guests commented on the beauty of Susan's muse. Our Rachel. One of Susan's art teachers said, 'I sense a ghostly presence in this room. I'm too Irish to discount these things.'

7

THE RUNAWAY NOTE

Day 4: Friday, 5 March

It was mid-morning before we left home. We thought it important to have some thinking space. What had we missed? Police had asked for lists of Rachel's friends and apparently contacted several of them. Why would any of Rachel's friends want to harm her? We felt dreadful for having to include them on a list.

Richmond police contacted us on Friday morning to say they were coming to search Rachel's bedroom. We thought of being present for this, but as my mother was in the house we decided not to waste any more time and get on with our own inquiries. We were all, family and police, working together.

I laugh now at the memory we have of replacing Rachel's mattress and bed base back on its legs before the police came through. I was conscious of her room looking bare, but Rachel was in the process of redecorating it, changing it from a young girl's into a young woman's room. In late December she had been excited to find polished wooden floorboards beneath her carpet and begged to be allowed to pull it up. 'You know I've always wanted a wooden floor. Please, Mum.' One of her greatest unfulfilled wishes – practising her dance exercises on her own wooden floor.

I agreed, and absolutely everything, and I mean everything, was

50

dragged into the hallway. Her bed base dismantled. Her desk given to Ashleigh-Rose. Picture books and unread novels handed down. Her special autographed picture book, *A Lion in the Meadow* by Margaret Mahy, remained. *In rushed a big, roaring, yellow, whiskery lion. 'Hide Me!' it said. 'A dragon is after me!' The lion hid in the broom cupboard.* Rachel was the big, roaring, yellow, whiskery lion. 'Boo!' she would squeal, and rush out giggling. If I missed one sentence, even one word, she knew she'd been cheated.

Her favourite junior and teen novels by Margaret Clark remained on her bookshelf. I pulled *Diary of a Street Kid* off in case the police got the wrong idea. And I hid the unfinished manuscript I'd encouraged her to write.

'It'll have swear words in it, Mum . . . I'll write it like a Margaret Clark.'

'Go for it,' I'd said, thinking, anything to make her brain do a daily workout.

She stripped the room bare. Packed childhood belongings into boxes and stored them in the cupboard under the stairs. Manni ripped up the carpet, under her instructions. She gave Wally, her baby-blue soft toy whale, to Manni. Special Teddy, Nutmeg, and Yellow Teddy remained on her bookcase, with a sequined clown, make-up, dance shoes and Manni mementos. Wooden-sculptured flying machines stayed suspended from the ceiling.

Rachel had lifted her op shop mirror, a metre in diameter, off the wall and onto the floor beside her mattress, so that she could study her feet while dancing. The *Revoke*, a print of naughty fairies and koala bears; the glass-framed Giselle which Rachel had painted out with bright pink lipstick during her 'I hate ballet' stage; the photograph Nanny Joy took of us all at a dance concert in September 1998; and the 'Rachel loves Manni' collage – these remained on her walls.

She asked me if I'd take her to Ikea, whose furniture offered the young adult look she was after. During Rachel's disappearance my mother lay staring at Rachel's night sky, the luminous stars decorating her ceiling, wondering where our Rachel Star was.

On the Thursday night at the dance school we found an old pair of pants in the lost property box, the same design as Rachel's new pants. Vicki suggested we take these to the police so they could see what she was last seen wearing. We thought we'd go to the Malvern shop, a few doors from my work, Books In Print, where I had bought the little blue top she was wearing.

On our way to the dress shop we put up more posters. Mike had it in mind to place a poster at the dance school Rachel had attended for six years but I was apprehensive about this. Rachel would cringe if we hung a poster there. There had been a time when Rachel had admired and felt close to her teacher at that school, but Rachel had left with unhappy memories.

Rachel received counselling after she left that dance school and when she joined her new school, its artistic director Dulcie was probably the one whose advice helped her the most to move forward. She told Rachel that regardless of how she felt about her teacher now, she was an excellent teacher. If it hadn't been for her, Rachel probably would not have been so technically good – so graceful a dancer. Rachel had a lot to thank her for.

It was necessary, said Dulcie, for Rachel to resume classical training, even though the dance school's emphasis was predominantly training for stage musicals. Classical classes were the basis for all professional dancing. In the fourteen months that Rachel attended her new dance school, she regained her self confidence and was beginning to acknowledge her love of classical dance as well.

On the way to Malvern, Mike noticed a young girl standing at a bus stop. She stepped aboard a bus and the bus drove away.

'Did you see that girl?' said Mike urgently.

The girl was wearing black dance pants, a blue top and carried what appeared to be the same dance bag Rachel had. She wore her hair like Rachel's and was about the same height.

'Follow the bus,' said Mike.

Silly, really. We followed this bus from the corner of Malvern Road and Orrong Road through to Caulfield North, the inner suburban areas. Every time we got near the bus we would get caught by a traffic light or the bus would take off. Eventually Mike ran after the bus, banging on the side to catch the driver's attention. I saw Mike talking to the driver and was surprised

Mike was permitted to go and check. It was not Rachel. I could see the disappointment on his face.

I was unlucky at the dress shop in Malvern but they did say their factory outlet in Bridge Road, Richmond, of all places, might have the top I was after. I went back to Books In Print to speak to my work colleagues, only to discover Mike was there, frantically trying to locate me. He'd had a call from the police, at our house, to say they had found a possible runaway note in Rachel's bedroom. Could we meet them at the station in about half an hour?

I was stunned. Total disbelief, relief, denial . . . what now?

My mother had not liked the attitude of the detectives, but I think at first they were annoyed by our absence. Mike's parents were just leaving when they arrived and the police asked where we were. 'Where you'd expect them to be,' answered my mother-in-law, Rose. 'Out searching for Rachel.'

Apparently they spent a long time in Rachel's room, coming out once to ask about a bottle of tablets they'd discovered. My mother explained they were hers – she was sleeping in Rachel's room.

We drove to the police station with apprehension.

'Michael, I don't believe this.'

'I'm finding it difficult to grapple with too,' answered Mike. 'But maybe it's what we should hope for. Even if we don't want to believe it. It gives us hope she's still alive.'

The detective senior sergeant was not there on our arrival.

We waited.

Eventually the glass security door opened and we were asked to follow him upstairs.

The detectives had found what they considered were two notes written by Rachel, indicating that she had planned to run away.

The first said, 'Station, Go to Manni, $50-$80, 3 special things.'

The second said, 'Running Away.'

'Where did you find these notes?' I asked.

On the back of stapled sheets relating to her modelling course back in November, we were told.

'They're four months old,' I said. Not believing this furphy for a moment.

This did not convince the detectives.

Mike explained that while Rachel had attended the two-week modelling course she had arranged for Manni to collect her because of her uneasiness about public transport. They would travel to Richmond together on a tram which departed from Flinders Street. Staff at the modelling school could confirm this as Manni often waited for Rachel to finish. They thought he was lovely. And Mike explained that before Christmas Rachel had wanted to buy Manni three special things and had asked Mike to take her to the Reject Shop to see what 'special things' her money could buy.

I told the police I had explained to Rachel we would only be able to spend approximately $50 to $80 on her for Christmas because of the cost of the full-time dancing fees. This she had understood.

We were asked about the words 'running away'.

I didn't have an answer for this just then. But there would have to be a reasonable explanation.

Can you really blame the police for the position they were taking? At the time I could. I was angry. I felt helpless. But on reflection, and looking at the available hard evidence and the statistics for this age group of missing persons, I know the odds were really stacked against Rachel.

The police were looking for a close. They had searched Rachel's room in the belief that she was a runaway. That's how it appeared to us. Again the detective mentioned the police sighting reported the day before.

'But we asked every shop down the Punt Road end of Bridge Road,' I said. 'No one recognised Rachel and no one remembered seeing a girl counting out coins to a blond-haired man.'

The detective said it had happened between 8 and 8.15 a.m.

'Ah, yes,' said Mike. 'But I spoke to workmen who'd been in the street since 7 a.m. and Liz spoke to the milk bar owner.'

A gesture of hands was the detective's reply. There was enough evidence to suggest Rachel had disappeared of her own free will. She had said she was going with an *old female friend*.

There were no sightings of foul play. There was the detective's identification. It was obvious – they had discovered things that even *we* did not know about our own daughter. Clearly she had a secretive nature.

I could not believe what I was hearing.

His advice to us was to go home to our 'obviously' two smaller children and seek special counselling. He put the stress on the 'obviously'.

Seek special counselling, I thought. So that's it. I started to cry. Not because for one moment I believed Rachel was a run-away, but because I knew she was in trouble and could see the police investigation coming to an end.

Calming down, I said, 'I've brought you these dance pants. They're the same type Rachel was wearing. I thought you might need them.'

The detective shook his head.

Michael stood up and shook hands with the detectives. He especially thanked the woman detective because he felt that regardless of her opinion, she had always been caring.

We left the station with Mike surprisingly good-tempered. He told the detectives we would still continue with our search and put up more posters.

The detective senior sergeant smiled. He said he would be off duty over the weekend but if we needed a detective there would still be some on duty.

Where to now? Where to now? Everything had come to a stand-still. Maybe there *would* be detectives available over the weekend, but we felt as if we, family and friends, were on our own. Mike's father had offered us $3000 to pay for a private detective but we still thought this shouldn't be necessary. We would take up the offer only when no further help was forthcoming from police. A friend suggested we ask the police what they planned to do in the next twenty-four, forty-eight and seventy-two hour periods. We never did. The police would think I was being too much trouble. Maybe we could hire a skywriter and have RACHEL drawn into the sky. At least she'd know we were still searching for her, that we wouldn't give up until we found her.

On leaving the police station we decided to visit Dulcie from the dance school, who lived near by.

'Dulcie,' I said. 'Please think back to last Monday. Was there *anything*?'

'She was positive all day . . . The body language of Rachel that day was not that of a teenager contemplating running away. I should know. I work with kids all the time.'

'What . . . then?' asked Mike.

'I feel she's been taken,' answered Dulcie.

'Then why don't the police . . .'

'Because it's only our gut feeling,' said Mike, interrupting me. 'There's no *evidence* of foul play.'

'He's right, Elizabeth,' said Dulcie. 'The police don't know Rachel.'

True, I thought. To them she's just another fifteen-year-old girl.

I asked Dulcie what she thought about Mike's need to hang a poster at Rachel's previous dance school. She felt it an excellent idea because she knew their studios were leased to other dance groups.

Then Mike told Dulcie about a problem I had had with a male friend of ours. Mike was becoming concerned that this man might have been involved in Rachel's disappearance, although I thought it highly unlikely.

Dulcie was amazed we hadn't reported him already. To an outsider it seemed a very reasonable possibility.

'I'll think about it,' I said.

'Elizabeth! You'll only *think* about it?' Dulcie cried.

We went home late in the afternoon.

School friends of Rachel's were calling in to collect posters. Other friends had begun to drop in casseroles, coffee and cake.

My cousin Ian had phoned. A work colleague's husband was an inspector in the police force. He suggested I write in an exercise book the events of Rachel's disappearance and he would hand it on.

James, my 44-year-old cousin, came to help where he could. He grabbed a large cardboard box of odd socks to match, discovering only one pair. It was the sock box from Rachel's play-group days: odd socks were brilliant for hand puppets.

News was spreading fast. Letters of support were arriving. The phone rang constantly. My mother was tiring from the responsibility of answering the phone. My Aunt Babe, ravaged by emphysema, gave my mother respite, and answered the phone with authority.

Ashleigh-Rose was calmer, having spent the day at Montrose Library with my stepmother Susan. She had shelved and covered books. Susan recalled Ashleigh-Rose saying, 'I had to get out of the house. Mum and Dad are crying all the time, and Nanny Joy cries, too. Then I cry because I can't stand to see Mum and Dad crying.' Ashleigh-Rose told her about going in to see her father and being frightened by his hard grasp. 'Daddy said, "I don't want to lose you, too. I've already lost Rachel. I've let Rachel down . . ."'

Robbie had reported that Heather was having a lovely time. Robbie's friend Dianne took Heather fishing and Heather caught her first fish. When Heather heard that Rachel had not been found she'd said, 'Good, that means I can stay with Auntie Robbie and go fishing again.' But then added, 'You know I don't mean that.'

My brother Drew rang to say he would be down on Sunday to take over the phone. He'd always been a very distant brother. But tragedy is a catalyst. It was the catalyst that brought sister and brother closer. It was the catalyst that brought a separated family together. My mother, father and stepmother put differences aside. I felt completely at ease in the company of all three: I'd been working on that for twenty-five years. We all had one focus: to bring Rachel home. At the end of this first week it was beginning to feel as though it was becoming 'bring Rachel home, dead or alive'.

We were so exhausted but sleep was still not a possibility. The 'ifs, why dids, what fors' consumed us. We were Rachel's parents. We were responsible for Rachel. We had let her down. We were guilty. Tragedy had swept fifteen years of loving, fifteen years of energy, fifteen years of Rachel into a cavity, unseen, unfound.

Mike said he knew she was dead. He was looking for a body.

The doctor, who considered Mike to be suffering from shock, had said, 'Mike has begun the grieving process already because he believes Rachel is dead.' But still I couldn't believe that Mike felt this. Why would he continue to search for her in areas where she could still be alive? We were making little sense as our tortured minds battled fatigue and denial. I either didn't *feel* she was dead or didn't want to admit it. No one who knew Rachel would want to harm her. The other possibility that she had been grabbed, drugged, and raped was, in my despair, becoming more likely.

On Friday night we decided to extend our search to the Grand Prix. We had planned just to walk around but found the place surrounded by what seemed like three-metre-high wire fencing. So we went to St Kilda and drove around the red-light district, very slowly. We didn't even bother looking at the street map.

8

QUANTUM LEAP

Day 5: Saturday, 6 March

Our friend David had been producing more posters overnight. He rolled up on our doorstep early this Saturday morning. We plastered posters on the inside of our car windows. We gave him a list of people who wanted to distribute more. He would be delivery man.

We mulled over the words 'running away', 'running away'. We knew Rachel would never run away, yet the detective senior sergeant had shown us these words written in Rachel's handwriting.

'Running away . . . Running away . . . Runaways,' said Mike. 'Perhaps she meant runaways. Sounds like . . .'

'Shoes,' I said. 'That's it. They're gym shoes. You know her preoccupation with shoes.'

And suddenly, after trying so hard, I remembered something Rachel had been telling me about her day at the modelling school. She had handed me the sheets to read. I had turned over the notes and read on the back, 'running away'.

'What's this?' I'd asked.

She'd laughed. 'It's a pair of shoes.'

But this would not be enough for the police. We had to find the shoes.

Alex, a friend, called in with two mates. They had decided to doorknock Church Street. Before they left we discussed the problem male friend. I told Mike about the photographs he had given me a few months before which I had thrown in the bin, because they seemed really off. Scary almost. Photographs of places, empty chairs, where we had consumed legitimate cups of coffee on the way home from business meetings.

This man had progressively made me feel more and more uncomfortable. It wasn't all his fault. Mike tells me I have an infectious and sometimes flirtatious smile. I enjoyed his company and assumed we could be friends, like girlfriends.

Rachel knew he made me feel uncomfortable. She didn't like him. She had seen him turn up at the dance school, looking for me in the pizza shop, where I would sometimes eat and read a book, while I waited for night classes to finish.

He would turn up at my workplace. He would sit in his car waiting for me to leave work. Sometimes I would get to the car and discover his business card on the windscreen. Once I found a card sitting on the steering wheel when I had forgotten to lock the car.

Two weeks before Rachel's disappearance I was home alone and so nervous that I closed all the curtains and would not answer the phone. Sure enough, he arrived. Mike's car was not in the drive. He rang the front doorbell as he dialled his mobile. Our phone rang. I went into Heather's bedroom. He walked around to my bedroom window, trying to look in, and dialled once more. Our phone rang again. He went back to the front door and pushed the bell again. I sat where I was, hiding. Eventually he left. I rang Mike.

Later in the day the phone rang. I decided to pick it up and not talk. If it was Mike or my mother, or someone from work, they'd speak. No one spoke, for a long time. Then, 'Elizabeth . . . Elizabeth.' It was him. I hung up, waited a minute and picked the phone up. He had not replaced the receiver. I pulled the plug from the wall. This was a game I didn't like.

It was such a hot day this Monday. After school Ashleigh-Rose, Heather and I had had a swim. I had been showering, and came out dressed to discover him in the kitchen. Heather had let him in. He said, 'Your phone appears to have a problem.'

Enough is enough, and this was enough. Ashleigh-Rose and Heather stood looking at him.

'My phone is not out of order. I just didn't want to speak to you. In fact I am fed up with you following me around and I think I should ask you to leave the house. Right now.' Silence. His body language was awkward. I do believe he was genuinely surprised. He said goodbye and left the house.

This was two weeks to the day that Rachel went missing. I had not heard from him since.

'Elizabeth, you must report him,' Alex said.

'It's only a game to him,' I said. 'He wouldn't hurt Rachel. You know that, Mike.'

Mike didn't answer me.

'Mike.'

Alex stood up with his friends. 'Look, we'll go to Church Street now, and then report our findings to the police. Elizabeth, think very carefully about this man. I think you're acting very naively.'

We sat on the couch. Mike's silent mood disturbed me. 'We must tell the police,' he said.

'Mike, you know he wouldn't hurt Rachel. It's not in his nature.'

'But going after other men's wives is?' he answered. 'You shamed him in front of the other children. You haven't heard from him in two weeks. And what does he give you every birthday, Christmas, or even Mother's Day . . . a small present?'

'So?' I said.

'So what if he told Rachel his business needed a model or dancer for the night? What if he said they would provide the clothing? If he told her it was okay with us, she'd probably believe him. What if he thought you would phone him to say Rachel is missing? Then he could miraculously find her and bring her home on your fortieth birthday, tomorrow.'

'Michael.'

'Listen,' said Mike. 'We don't know that by not ringing and asking him for help we haven't backed him into a corner. Now he can't come to your rescue. He can't be your knight in shining armour . . .'

'Oh, Michael,' I interrupted, thinking how melodramatic he was sounding.

'How do you know he just won't decide to give her back to you, dead. A present for your fortieth.'

I started to sob. 'You can't be serious. He wouldn't do that. Rachel's not dead.'

Mike shrugged his shoulders.

'Don't you give up on her. Don't you!'

My mother interrupted. 'Elizabeth, it does sound feasible.'

'It's a game to him. Just an annoying game.'

'Dulcie didn't think so,' said Mike. 'We're telling the police. I think he would too, in similar circumstances.'

This just couldn't be possible, but Mike was creating such a strong image of what *could* have been. Even so, the story didn't seem to agree with Rachel's account to Manni. This man was not an *old female friend*. Rachel would recognise him. How could he possibly get away with holding her for a week?

Mike reminded me that this man's family owned a holiday house. Perhaps the house was empty. And what about the memory-loss drugs we had learnt of?

By midday I was convinced we needed to inform the police. Rachel's survival could depend on us discovering her today.

My cousin Michele arrived and offered to drive us into Richmond. Before we left, Alex returned. He and his friends had doorknocked Church Street and had not received a warm welcome at Richmond police when they reported their results. The police were annoyed that we were still carrying out our own investigations.

Michele drove us to the Richmond police station. We asked Mum to continue ringing shoe shops and Mike suggested she try some shops in Moonee Ponds, where Manni lived.

We received a phone call from Mum at about 2 p.m. A shoe shop in Moonee Ponds sold a range of cross-trainers called Runaways. They cost from $50 to $100 and there had been a display of them for some months in their window.

We walked into the Richmond police station feeling that we

had exonerated Rachel of the runaway note theory. It reaffirmed our sense of urgency.

But we were told by a policewoman that no detectives were available. I explained that the detective senior sergeant had said there *would* be detectives. She said they left at 2 p.m. and 'like everyone else were entitled to time off. You have already had a lot of police hours this week and you're not the only parents of missing persons.'

A lot of police hours. You've got to be kidding.

I tried to explain that we had new information. She didn't appear to want to deal with us. We were a nuisance. We were parents of a 'runaway' who wanted the police to find their naughty child. This was not their job any more. *Go home . . . seek special counselling*. This was the feeling, the perception.

The knot of anger and despair gripped my chest. A single atom multiplied in a second. I ran from the police station and, standing on the steps, wrenched my handbag from my shoulder, aiming it at a stationary police car window. Then I stopped suddenly and ran into the street.

I screamed, 'They're going to let our little girl die! They're going to let our little girl die!'

I was cheap entertainment for the Saturday afternoon coffee minglers, sitting outside cafés at tables for two. Street fumes mixed with inhaled smoke. Cigarette ash flicked into the dusty, grimy gutters. Chairs appearing to teeter on the edge.

Michele followed me. Wrapped her arms around me. 'Elizabeth,' she pleaded, 'come back. She said she'll listen.'

I looked to the upstairs window of the detective's office. Were you up there looking down at me?

Mike and the policewoman met me on the step. She asked me what this new information was, insisting that I could tell her on the street.

'There's this man,' I began and stopped. How *could* I tell her on the street? I tried to explain about one of our best friends betraying us. It sounded so ridiculous. I felt invaded, as if *I* had committed a crime. Could she think we were trying to come up with just any reason to keep the police investigation open?

We left, dissatisfied. Michele drove us to Dulcie's.

Dulcie rang Neil Paterson of the Missing Persons Unit to tell him we were not happy with the response from Richmond.

'Look, even if Rachel hated her parents, she'd still come to dance,' I heard her say.

Whether our fear was justified or not we now believed one hundred per cent that my fortieth birthday was crucial to Rachel's survival. We *had* to find her tonight.

Dulcie was told we could contact the Ethical Standards Department, or the Ombudsman, or the inspector at the Victoria Police Centre, Duty Office Region One. We rang the number for the inspector. Labour Day long weekend. No one there. I left a detailed message. It was impossible to give up. We just couldn't say, 'Oh what the heck, let's go home. See if Mike's wrong or right.' What if we did receive a large package, sent by courier? What would the policewoman say then?

We all decided to go back to the police station. Maybe the policewoman would be off duty.

The policewoman was still there. We repeated our request for a detective. No, no detective available. So, crime didn't happen on long weekends. My suppressed anger tried to speak to her in a controlled but loudening voice. I told her we'd left a message on the inspector's phone. We were taking matters higher. I told her I had nearly thrown my handbag through the police car window in frustration. I was emotional. Extremely noisy. I was becoming one of her worst nightmares.

The policewoman cautioned me: she could put me on a charge if I continued in this manner.

'Go ahead then!' I yelled, baiting her. 'It'd be a very good idea.' How good would it look to jail the mother of a missing girl. The press would love it. 'YOU FUCKHEAD!' I screeched. I can still remember the shock of hearing my own voice.

I was delirious. Crying and swirling in circles. Michele tried to hold me tightly. I have little recollection of Mike and Dulcie during this, only enough to know they witnessed the sad scene.

When I calmed down, the policewoman said she would take a handwritten statement at the front desk but if the phone rang she would need to answer it because she was the only one there.

And then she would offer her opinion. I agreed.

For the first time, I now realise how fortunate I was not to have been charged. If I had been a police officer I wonder how I would have responded.

I spoke very slowly and deliberately. I needed to be careful with the story because now, under the circumstances, this male friend of mine, with his silly game, had incriminated himself. I remember saying we weren't having an affair, because I thought it could have appeared so. Mike had never been threatened by our friendship. This man and I were best friends, that's all, until his hide-and-seek game started. A bit of harmless fun for him, I'm sure. He had told me once that he was steadfastly stubborn and always got what he wanted.

The policewoman looked several times at the clock.

Finally, after a long half-hour at the watchhouse counter, I finished the statement.

'I'll run a check on him.' And she disappeared.

'They won't find anything,' I said.

'His name is clear,' said the policewoman when she returned. 'So what do you want me to do?'

We were stumped. I thought the police should come up with the ideas.

'Maybe you could contact his local police station. An officer could make general inquiries at his house, like . . . Rachel Barber went missing this week and we're just asking people who knew her whether they've seen her.'

We were told this was not possible.

She said, 'I feel you are making a quantum leap. You are not just talking about a missing person here, you are talking about an abduction and murder.'

9

GROWING FEAR

It was Saturday evening. We dropped Dulcie home and Michele drove us to St Hilary's. This was Rachel's church, where I had seen ourselves as Rachel's guests. She had been a member of the Balwyn Baptist Church, but when she started at Canterbury Girls Secondary College, her friends introduced her to the St Hilary's youth group, Wipe Out. I thought the church needed to know about Rachel's disappearance. Since we moved to Heathmont, a forty minute drive away, she had only attended spasmodically. She had made me promise I would still drive her to Wipe Out and the Sunday evening youth service, where she was also a member of the choir. Work-tired, I had broken my promise.

The minister was out for the evening, but I left a message with their babysitter, so her youth group friends could pray for her. The church immediately became supportive, as did Balwyn Baptist. Rachel went down on many prayer lists, in many churches. Not only Christians responded. We have Jewish and Buddhist friends, too. There was quite a prayer network on the go.

An hour later we drove slowly past the house of the man we had reported, in Michele's car. Mike and I slid down the back seat. His car was not in the driveway.

At home I rang a mutual friend and asked if she had seen this man during the week. If she had not seen him I would have been concerned. She had seen him twice and his behaviour was the same as always.

My nephew Shaun and his girlfriend Renée arrived. We had not slept since the few hours on Monday night, and though we had found strength in our diet of adrenalin and coffee we had become incompetent drivers. Shaun was to be our wheels.

Around seven o'clock Shaun decided to go with Mike and place the man's house under surveillance. If his car was not there they would drive to his family's holiday house.

Michele, David, Renée and I drove to a supermarket and bought the largest torches we could find. Perhaps we should *not* ignore what police felt – that Rachel was a runaway. We certainly couldn't sit at home, and with no new leads we were running out of options. Maybe if the police could see we weren't closing down on their options they would not close down on ours, and keep searching.

But if Rachel had run away, where would she go?

We decided to walk around Mont Albert, where we had lived for five years, renting my stepmother's house. We walked through the grounds of the local primary school. I felt ridiculous searching under shrubs, walking behind shelter sheds, and sussing out the play equipment, calling Rachel, Rachel, RACHEL. I checked in the shadowy brick corners of the old school building. Would I find a sleeping child like the children we saw by St Paul's? I knew she would not be there.

We split up. David and Renée, Michele and I.

'Tape the posters to all the light poles,' I said. 'We'll put posters in the letter boxes of our old friends.'

I hesitated outside a two-storey house, pausing at the letter box. 'Gail Reid lives here,' I said.

Michele said, 'Go and knock on the door.'

I put one foot inside the front fence, stepped back and pushed the poster through the letter box.

'Elizabeth?' said Michele.

'I can't.'

It was a large sombre-looking house in the night light.

We walked hurriedly around the corner. 'Do you think anyone saw us?'

'No,' she said, looking back.

A few moments later she said, 'Look at that gargoyle. Makes you want to shudder.'

'Part of Gail's house,' I said. 'It's not a happy house.'

I remember, one afternoon, a few years before, Gail sitting at our dining-room table. We were enjoying a cup of tea and a chat. She had been to see a clairvoyant whom she hadn't seen in a long while. I recall Gail saying she was feeling a little cheated. The clairvoyant was talking more about her Barber friends. We were a family Gail should not lose touch with, she said. We would remain lifetime friends.

A phone call came through from Mike. They had driven past the man's house several times. His car was in the driveway. Everything seemed okay. They had sat for an hour at the entrance to the no-through road. They decided not to check his family's holiday house, so they drove to Wattle Park.

Mike considered it possible that Rachel might have arrived at the Wattle Park tram stop *after* he left on Monday night. Perhaps she had gone to buy those two tops she had been interested in, forgotten the time, and on arriving late and finding no Mike, waited at the tram shelter, only to have been coaxed or dragged across into the park.

A week had gone by. Mike went into the park looking for a body.

Mike and Shaun split up and covered the whole grounds, checking the old trams, checking beneath tree canopies and around the creek. They half expected to find some kids shooting up or evidence of recently used bongs, but he knew she wouldn't be there. We knew she hated drugs, intensely. 'Mum,' she said to me, on at least one occasion while on the phone, 'are we doing anything this Saturday? I've been invited to a party.' All the while shaking her head. She later said she'd recently discovered the girl smoked dope and didn't want to go to the party.

Mike walked along the boundary of the golf course and

around to the back, discovering walkways and footbridges he didn't know existed. It was eerie in the dark.

There was a party up at the café near the tennis courts. People were out and about, glasses in hand, laughing. What would these people think of the torchlights searching the grounds? Nobody noticed, or if they did – what was it to them?

The creek was densely overgrown, dirty-looking. Mike searched the undergrowth and along the edges – looking for Rachel lying beneath a film of murk, green algae braiding her hair. What did this father imagine now? What of his living grief? It wasn't an imagined fear: it was a real fear that he would come across the distorted body of his first-born.

I can still see the pride in his face when he first saw her. He was thirty-seven. He had called her Rachel from the moment we knew of her conception. We had not found out through ultrasound that we were having a girl. He instinctively knew. He desperately wanted a daughter. We had always agreed our first girl would be named after my grandmother. I remember saying early on in the pregnancy, 'Don't keep calling the baby Rachel! What if it's a boy? You'll be disappointed.'

'I won't be disappointed,' was his reply. 'The baby is Rachel.'

And as my stomach bloated with new life Mike would rest his hand there, feeling his daughter's movement. The unborn Rachel and I would relax together, daily, on the couch. Headphones brimming with classical music held to my naked stomach. Chopin, Grieg, Mozart, Liszt. Her favourite, Mendelssohn's *Midsummer Night's Dream*. We knew this by her body movement. Is it any wonder she was born to dance?

'Don't dance to the music,' I said to my six-year-old Rachel, 'dance as if you are a part of the music.' She will forever be a part of the music.

Later that Saturday night we watched a building in Church Street, Richmond. 'Keep an eye on the grey stone building. It's a halfway house with about forty rooms,' Mike was told by a man in a local restaurant. The man had a friend who lodged there. Didn't like what he saw. Kept to himself. There was a steady flow of male-only traffic that did seem suspicious. Was this a drug drop-off and collection point? Were there prostitutes inside? Could this have been why Rachel had disappeared so quickly?

Shaun went across to ask one of the waiting taxi drivers what they were doing. The driver told him through a mouthful of food that they dropped off clients.

In an adjacent block of flats Michele's attention was drawn to the top floor where a group of men, naked down to their pubic hairlines, were dancing and drinking beer. We stood on a low concrete fence on the opposite side of the road, watching these men, who were drunk and obviously enjoying themselves, in the seclusion of their own unit. We felt like Peeping Tomasinas – invading their privacy.

Then the place took on a more sinister feel. No women were visible, and Michele did not like the way the men were apparently taking turns going into a side room.

'Imagine,' she said. 'Rachel could be there.'

'Holding her hostage.'

'Taking turns.'

Mike could see our concern and gestured he would investigate. He walked around the back of the older-style block of flats. There were curtain-free windows but when he climbed the wooden steps to look inside all he could see was blackness. It was amazing he was not reported to the police for prowling.

Obviously Rachel could not be in all these places at once, but our emotions were extreme. We were, as the policewoman said, making quantum leaps. We felt abandoned, and in our despair, our anger and our fear, it was what we believed.

But I am imparting this to help local police understand why parents faced with missing children are not consoled by the known facts, or the statistics. It wasn't irrational fear that made me swear abuse at the policewoman who did not know our daughter. It was absolute despair. Was Rachel crying, slumped in a slimy dark corner of a Melbourne street, wondering why we hadn't saved her? Was she about to face death, or had she already faced the *hurt* of death? It was this that sent us searching into the hidden stories behind Melbourne's streets.

It's strange that family members also felt the need to justify excessive behaviour. We were adamant we were right and the local police were adamant we were wrong: *go home to your two smaller children and seek special counselling.* How much we wished we *were* wrong.

We regrouped at McDonald's in Richmond, just before closing time. We were laughing. It's an odd experience to laugh when faced with exhaustion and looming defeat. Nature's way of saving your sanity, perhaps. I've always thought so. 'Even in war,' my dad once told me, 'laughter can keep you on track.' Not only were we laughing, but noshing into hot chips and coffee.

Shaun or Renée suggested we visit the refuge houses for young people. I argued that she wouldn't be there, but we needed to cover all options. But where do you find refuge houses? We borrowed the McDonald's *Yellow Pages.* Nothing under 'Refuge Centres'. We looked under 'Emergencies' and found a reference to 'Organisations – Family Welfare.' Four columns. It all looked so confusing.

We were tired, couldn't think straight, and wanted an answer now. Two or three main refuge centres, listed in the *Yellow Pages* under 'REFUGE CENTRES', holding information for the others. We wanted to visit them. Now. In the middle of the night.

'There's a public phone across the road. I'll ring Lifeline.'

Renée came with me. We felt exposed. A dishevelled-looking man crab-walked unsteadily towards us. An offensive body odour hung on him. Trousers soiled? Dried vomit? He turned around and crab-walked away.

The phone number was engaged. Continuously. I thought if I was on the brink of suicide I'd kill myself out of frustration simply because I couldn't get through.

I rang Telstra. 'Suburb please.'

Poor woman got a life story. She became *my* lifeline. We whinged sympathetically together about the engaged phone number. My inability to find a refuge centre. Her inability to satisfy others who needed Lifeline.

'It's always engaged this time of night.'

She wished me luck in our quest, but couldn't help us without a name. She suggested that perhaps refuge centres were not listed as refuge centres because then they would not provide refuge.

Michele and David left first. Shaun, Renée, Mike and I drove around the streets of Richmond again, finally making our way home at about 2.00 a.m. We stopped off at the Ringwood police to tell them about posters we had taped to telephone boxes in the district. Mike told the police what we were told regarding fines and posters. Their response: 'Who's going to fine you when your daughter's gone missing? Just do it.'

10

THE POSTER CAMPAIGN
CONTINUES

Day 6: Sunday, 7 March

My fortieth birthday. The avoided day. I can't remember even considering my birthday on the Sunday morning, other than being thankful that a large parcel had not been delivered by courier.

Mike phoned Richmond police about 10.30 a.m. to see if the woman detective had been informed about our Saturday report of the man. The woman detective asked Mike if we were still concerned about him because records showed he didn't have any prior convictions. Mike told her we had checked him out ourselves and felt with hindsight he was not involved.

We organised a railway station walk. Shaun, Renée and Manni would cover the Frankston and Pakenham lines from Malvern. David would cover Glen Waverley and possibly the Alamein line. Mike and I would cover the Belgrave line from Ringwood and from Richmond to Malvern, and the Carellas would break up and cover Zone 1 of the western suburbs. Our plan was to place a poster in most of the Zone 1 and Zone 2 railway stations, on both platforms.

Sunday was a boiling hot day and it took two days to achieve our goal. But we had to make the public aware of Rachel's disappearance.

'Yes, this is Rachel Barber,' I wrote on the posters for East

Camberwell station because it was the station most of Rachel's old secondary school friends used. But within two days most of these posters had been pulled down by diligent cleaners.

David decided to walk around the Glen Waverley shopping centre as well. We had received a phone call saying that security personnel at a department store reported seeing a girl answering Rachel's description at a checkout counter. David said he would drive around the suburb.

It was the last day of the Grand Prix, so if the Carellas and my father were right, Rachel may have shown up this day, this night. She didn't. Could the police have also been waiting for the end of the Grand Prix?

We met up at Carlo's single-storey terrace house in Richmond, in the late afternoon. Carlo was a close friend of Mike's brother's family, and had on occasion taken the girls to the zoo with Tamzin, our niece.

Police thought it a possibility that Rachel may have absconded with her cousin. 'York Street, Prahran. Who lives there?' we were asked. 'Telephone records indicate a phone call to this number in the last three months.'

'Tamzin did. Rachel's thirty-year-old cousin. But not any more.'

'And who lives at Windsor?'

'Tamzin.'

Tamzin drove round the Prahran streets at night, looking for her little cousin and distributing posters.

Carlo said he would organise a website and also help with the posters. Tate, a friend of Carlo's who led youth discos and knew gang leaders of street kids, said he would see if they had heard any whispers. I was not aware that a lot of street kids hung around in gangs, providing a network of comparative safety for themselves.

Then Carlo ordered in pizza.

We were sitting there in the comfort of Carlo's living room. I remember thinking that I wished we'd known he'd lived so close to the dance school. It could have been a safehouse for Rachel. But then we didn't know she'd needed one.

Carlo's friends were preparing a fruit salad, tossing chunky pieces of fruit into a giant-sized glass bowl. The atmosphere was relaxing.

'I suppose,' said Carlo to Manni, 'we should be asking, is Rachel pregnant?'

This comment was said in jest but I could sense a sudden change in Manni's demeanour. He was sitting alongside Mike, on a cosy two-seater couch.

Manni's pizza hovered in front of his opened mouth. 'No,' he said uncomfortably. 'She couldn't be.'

'Why not?' asked Carlo, completely unaware of Manni's earlier interview with the police.

'Impossible. We haven't done it.' He studied his piece of pizza.

This was not an ideal conversation to have in the presence of your fifteen-year-old girlfriend's parents, particularly when sitting on a cosy couch with her dad.

Mike leaned across him. I thought, be careful, Mike.

'Are you sure, Manni?' he asked in a knowing but friendly manner.

'Definitely,' replied Manni.

'Manni,' I said, in the same tone as Mike. I placed my hand on Mike's arm, cautioning him.

'Are you absolutely sure, Manni?' Mike asked again.

'Never,' said Manni, his face turning beetroot red.

Everyone paused, their attention suddenly on Manni. 'Jeez, Manni,' said Carlo, reading between the lines. 'My big mouth. Sorry, mate.'

'Manni, are you *absolutely* sure?' persisted Mike. 'Because information we have has it otherwise.'

Manni smiled nervously. 'Really,' he said.

We both nodded.

'It's okay, Manni,' I said, trying to ease his embarrassment. 'Normally I wouldn't have been so impressed but . . .'

'Only just,' he blurted out. 'It was protected, and . . . lovely.'

Every man in the room, even Mike, suddenly found themselves in Manni's place. Everyone was waiting for Mike's reaction. They didn't expect what they got.

I started to laugh.

Manni was looking confused.

'Elizabeth,' said Carlo, 'it's not a laughing matter.'

I knew that, but sometimes laughter is very close to tears. Mike looked at me.

'It's okay, Manni,' I said. 'Really, look, we're okay with it . . . now,' and I thought, was I really? Or was I just trying to relax this incredibly embarrassed young man?

Mike put a reassuring arm around Manni's shoulder. 'Not fair, is it?' he said, sympathetic. Mike knew how it felt.

'N-no,' Manni stammered. 'But please don't tell Mum and Dad. They don't know.'

Everyone laughed then, with nervous relief. Manni must have been terrified about our reaction, but now he seemed more worried about what his mum and dad would say.

He really is a sweet kid, I thought.

Manni's parents were unaware that Manni had been interviewed by the police at the dance school with his teacher. And they felt, considering he was under-age, that they should have been present, or at least contacted. And Manni had been nervous of the detective senior sergeant: he seemed to think Manni knew where Rachel was.

We left Carlo's at about 10.30 because we were absolutely beat. We felt guilty about going home, but we needed rest.

There were a few presents for me on our return. One of them was a collage from Ashleigh-Rose with a 'I miss you heaps from your *middle* daughter with love' message on the back.

Shaun, Renée and Manni decided to continue with the posters. They went into the city and obtained permission to put posters up at the Moomba ticket offices and at all the rides. The annual Moomba festival, which covered the Labour Day holiday weekend, brought many thousands of people – tourists and families – into the city of Melbourne to enjoy the entertainment. The Moomba office advised security men to make sure none of our posters were pulled down. Shaun said one ride manager told him ten thousand people a day rode on his ride and would see the posters.

The Carella brothers continued working through the night as well. Frank said he was taken aback by the number of street kids he met. One said, 'I hope you find her. She's too beautiful to be on the streets.'

Any kid is too beautiful to be on the streets. I wondered how many of these street kids were listed as missing persons.

Into the second week there was so much knowledge about Rachel's disappearance that if someone had recognised her they *would* have reported it. It seemed that every second person the Carellas spoke to knew of her story.

My brother Drew arrived this Sunday afternoon and sent Mum home for a rest, but she was back the next day. Drew added more phone messages to Mum's list. Our former neighbour Gail had rung in the morning, distressed by Rachel's disappearance, and offered to help. And at 9.15 p.m., although I was not aware of it until much later, Gail's eldest daughter, Caroline Reid, had also rung and left her silent number.

11

ESCORT AGENCIES

Day 7: Monday, 8 March

The beginning of the second week. Our obvious defeat was dis-illusioning. I had to act positive. I could not help Rachel with a defeatist attitude. I still couldn't sense Rachel's spirit so I chose to believe she was alive, being held captive.

It was decided that Renée, who was a catwalk model, should pretty herself up and walk around the streets of Richmond, try-ing to entice the woman who had followed the dress-shop girl off the train. Obviously this woman didn't work for the Daily Planet, but she was working for someone. Thankfully, though, Renée in the end didn't need to offer herself as bait.

On the Sunday or the Monday, against my better judgement, Mike visited Rachel's old dance school in Prahran and left a poster. (We all decided that when Rachel was found safe we would distribute 'I HAVE BEEN FOUND' posters to celebrate and thank people for their support.)

Then Elaine, a secondary school friend of mine and Rachel's godmother, rang to say she had some thoughts about the *old female friend*. 'Elizabeth,' she said, 'this friend could not be a school, church or dance friend, because Rachel would have said – old school, church or dance friend.'

She was right. Why hadn't we thought of this? So, who were

we looking for then? A friend of the family? A friend of a friend? Perhaps someone more distant?

Mike and I were at Carlo's when a phone call came through from Drew. The mother of two of Rachel's past dance school friends had rung. The older girl, Alison, had arrived home from work to hear her younger sister, who had been in the same class as Rachel for six years, say, 'You'll never guess who's gone missing! Rachel Barber. She was last seen in Richmond at 5.45 p.m. last Monday.'

From a very early age Alison was known to have an almost photographic memory and she could remember seeing Rachel on the same night, Monday 1 March. Rachel, she said, had climbed quite happily onto the number 6 Glen Iris tram, at the intersection of Chapel and High Streets at about 6.40 p.m., with another girl. Drew said that Alison had reported this sighting to the police.

I rang Alison's mother immediately. Mike and I would go and speak to her. We had not seen each other for about two years, but it felt as if little time had passed. The younger sister had been one of Rachel's closest friends at the old dance school and quite often I drove both sisters home.

'How sure were you that it was Rachel?' I asked Alison.

'I saw her last week at the Princess Theatre, and anyway I couldn't mistake Rachel for anyone else. I couldn't get over what she looked like.'

I felt a bit embarrassed because I thought she was going on about how scantily dressed Rachel may have been. 'Didn't she have a windcheater on? I've told her time and time again to wear something over her dance top when she leaves the school. The students don't realise how "undressed" they sometimes look.'

'She was fine. She had a little top on. I meant, she looked beautiful.'

I realised she would have thought nothing of Rachel's little top because she was dressed in very similar clothing.

'Who was she with?' asked Mike. 'Can you give a description?'

'For starters, I couldn't work out why Rachel would be with her. Although they were very chatty, and obviously knew one another. And I don't like saying this about people but the girl was heavy set and not attractive at all. Very plain. She obviously wasn't a dance student.'

'Where did they get off?'

'At the corner of Williams Road and High Street. They stood outside Honda for a while.'

'I'll just ring Carlo,' I said. He would meet us there shortly.

'I met Rachel at the "hire a crowd" night at the Princess Theatre,' said Alison. A number of dance schools had been approached because a crowd was needed for a show by an American choreographer. 'I don't know whether I should say this or not, but I think Rachel got tipsy that night,' she said.

'Tipsy?' I said. I found it very surprising and felt further embarrassed. I had never seen Rachel tipsy, although I suppose there is always a first time.

'Well, she was all over her boyfriend.'

'No, she wasn't tipsy,' I scoffed, remembering that Rachel had come home about 9.30 that night, with an empty bottle of soft drink. She'd kept the bottle because of the star logo. She'd gone to Planet Hollywood for a little while with some friends, before being brought home by Domenic and Manni. 'It was Rachel being Rachel,' I said, and reminded her how over-the-top Rachel could sometimes be. 'Yes, Rachel was very giggly this night, but no more giggly than usual. She was being happy. Exuberant with love.' I found out later, much later, that she *was* tipsy that night. One of her friends had put some vodka in her soft drink, and with her knowledge. Oh dear.

Alison told us the number 602 bus travelling down Williams Road ended up at Brighton. Perhaps they had caught this.

We finished our tea and thanked her for contacting the police. Perhaps the police should now be looking for two missing girls? Surely with all the posters around the other girl must have seen at least one. Why hadn't this other girl come forward?

We arrived at the corner of Williams Road and High Street and were met en masse by Rosa, Robert, Manni, Kylee, Shaun, Carlo, Tate and Richard.

Carlo and Tate had arrived first to scout around. Tate considered there was a suspicious-looking business in the middle of the shops because the inside was screened off and there were cameras pointing out, not in. We went around the back, where Mike started opening dump bins again. I hated him doing this but he reminded me that he was looking for Rachel's dance bag.

He disappeared into the darkness, down a narrow walkway behind the shops. I started to follow, sliding my hands across the wooden fence as I groped along. My open sandals standing on rubbish I could not identify. Used syringes? Don't think about it, I thought.

Memories of Saturday night returned.

I could just make out Mike's shadow when I saw him stop suddenly. Was there another figure in the shadows? I stood very still. What were we dealing with here?

Mike and Tate came towards me, laughing. Tate had already been investigating the back and was returning when he walked into Mike. They had both received a fright.

'There's definitely something going on here,' said Tate. 'The back entrance to the shop has a very high fence. I couldn't even jump to see over the top.'

'Snoop,' I said, jesting.

'Elizabeth, it's the only high fence. What are they hiding? She could be in there,' said Tate. 'Have you thought that the person Rachel was with on the tram could be the person recruiting from Richmond?'

'It's a possibility,' said Mike.

'Too right it is,' answered Tate, excitedly.

'No, the girl Rachel was with is too young, and Alison felt Rachel knew her.'

Tate and Mike weren't listening. They had found a rubbish bin and were taking it down the walkway to stand on and peer over the fence.

This was a silly game, very nearly dangerous.

I don't know how many rolls of thick tape we used putting up more posters. We put them on the traffic lights so they could be seen in every direction. We walked down Williams Road and High Street in all four directions. We walked down neighbouring streets. Normanby Street. Newry Street. Trinian Street.

Mike was told by two local business owners that the business we were interested in was fairly new. 'Telemarketing agency,' they said with a smile.

'Corporate business?'

'Telemarketers, you know, escort.'

'You mean, women?' I said.

They smiled again.

'See, I told you,' said Tate.

We gathered around the corner to discuss what our next move should be. Contact police? And say what? No, we would keep watch. Richard excused himself and said he'd keep an eye on the website that Carlo had set up.

Manni and Kylee disappeared into High Street. We couldn't believe it. Kylee climbed onto Manni's shoulders and, as he ran past the business, she jumped up so she could see inside. They wanted to look like two kids larking around.

'Hardly an undercover surveillance,' said Rosa.

Robert started keying in car numbers on his mobile phone. It became evident that there was a steady flow of female traffic. As the night progressed women were being escorted elsewhere, and later returned. We must have staked out this corner for three hours or more.

Rosa and I decided to drive to a local petrol station and look through the *Yellow Pages* for the names of escort agencies. The young attendant asked us what we were doing. I told him I felt my daughter was being held captive in an escort agency and I needed to find out the phone numbers and addresses of agencies in the area.

'Well, you won't find any addresses in there,' he answered. 'You need to be looking in the girlie magazines.'

He picked up a couple from the shelf and flipped through. 'See, there're lots of them.'

I looked at the price. 'Could I perhaps borrow them?' I asked. 'I'll bring them back. They're not really the type of magazine I'd normally buy.'

He was a bit hesitant. 'You can trust us,' said Rosa.

'Yeah, all right,' he said. 'But just see if you can return them before seven. That's when I finish. I don't want to get into trouble with my boss.'

We bought a couple of chocolate bars and said thank you.

I drove around the block. I wasn't intending to park directly in front of the agency but I noticed a laneway opposite so I reversed in as far as I dared, and turned the headlights off. Forgetting our white car must have looked like a beacon. Through my rear-vision mirror I could see someone riding circles on a bicycle, down the end of the lane, in the street lights. A light switched on in the red-brick house on the other side of the fence.

Rosa and I slid back the front seats, and lay flat so we wouldn't be noticed, and started to flick through the girlie magazines with a torch. Boobs and pubic hairs winked back. We couldn't help but laugh. It was like a scene from a sitcom. We sat there for at least half an hour, not having achieved anything with the girlie magazines, so we started to write down descriptions of the girls sitting in the upstairs windows over the road.

Rosa freaked out. 'Someone's opening the door.'

A woman spoke to Manni and Kylee.

Kylee was still on Manni's shoulders. I could almost see the strain on his back muscles while the woman spoke to them. He grasped Kylee around the knees.

They told us later that she said, 'Would you mind not peeping in our windows, please?'

Kylee had answered, 'Oh, we're just waiting for a tram.'

'At two o'clock in the morning?' The woman was not pleased.

The kids retreated, unable to control their laughter.

A short while later a woman in the upstairs window, smoking a cigarette, seemed alarmed and was pointing in the direction of where I thought Carlo and Tate were standing. The woman opened the front door and appeared to be searching. She had a mobile phone in her hand.

'Elizabeth,' said Rosa apprehensively. 'This lane's a dead end. I think we should get out.'

We started to wind up our seats. Carlo and Tate walked past, quickly.

My seat got stuck. A black car, one we'd noticed before,

drove slowly past the laneway and continued down High Street. Mike suddenly came into view, looking for us, and quickened his step.

'Get out of here, quick!' he said, opening the door and jumping in.

I couldn't believe it.

'They've spotted you!'

'No kidding,' said Rosa.

'Where's Shaun?' I yelled.

'He's running to his car. We'll pick Robert up on the corner. I don't know about the others. Quick. Move it!'

Scared plus. I had visions of those great big burly men, dressed in black and looking like pub bouncers, in their big black cars, bouncing us out of history.

I drove the car out into High Street as another black car came from the opposite direction and made a quick U-turn, while the woman in the street pointed out Shaun's car.

'He's going the wrong way!' I yelled.

The black car followed and chased him, picking up speed.

I'm sure Robert jumped into our car while it was still moving. Thank God the green light was with us.

The Carellas' car was left behind, to be picked up the following day.

In my rear-vision mirror I just caught sight of Carlo's red sporty car making a quick turn into Williams Road followed by yet another great black charger, or was it the same one?

'Stop,' yelled Rosa. 'The kids!'

My God, there they were, totally stranded. They had made a run for it. I did a U-turn to collect Manni and Kylee and they clambered into the back seat.

A police van drove past, turned around, and came back in our direction.

'Look as if you're strapped in.' I didn't dare look to the right. The police van came alongside. Kylee was hidden under Manni's legs in the back. Four people in the back seat, front seats halfway down. I'll lose my licence, I thought. The police drove on and stepped up their speed. They were after someone else. I couldn't believe my luck.

I turned into a side street, thinking I'd be able to turn right, stay hidden for a bit and come out into High Street further down.

'It's a dead end,' shrieked Rosa.

No place to turn in this narrow street with cars parked on either side, so I reversed towards High Street and took the next road. I didn't want to stay on High Street. Nobody was following us now but that didn't alter the way I felt.

'It's another dead end,' cackled Rosa.

Everybody was laughing in the back seat. I was too scared to laugh. This was movie stuff. How did I know they wouldn't suddenly appear in my rear-vision mirror and block us in?

There wasn't enough room for people to sit properly. Rosa and I wound the seats back up and fastened our seat belts. How could they laugh when we didn't know if Shaun had made it clear, or if Carlo and Tate had got back? I couldn't for the life of me work out why the police had not stopped us.

'We'll have to go and look for the others,' I said.

'How?' said Mike. 'Where?'

Somehow I ended up back in Williams Road. As I drove past the petrol station Rosa said, 'The girlie magazines.'

'I can't, Rosa,' I said. 'I'm too scared someone will catch us. I'll ring him from your house.'

We drove back towards Richmond to take Kylee home to her unit, but when we got there she was too scared to stay. Couldn't blame her. We drove on to Moonee Ponds with me still freaking I'd lose my licence. I was convinced we were a marked car.

'Elizabeth,' said Kylee, rather sheepishly, 'do you mind if I tell you something the detective asked me. He told me not to tell you because he didn't want to worry you.'

'Whatever is it?'

'He asked me what Rachel's bra size was because the detective who'd seen the girl counting money in Richmond said she was chesty.'

'*Chesty*,' I said.

'Yeah,' said Kylee. 'Well, I just laughed and said Rachel's like me.'

Rachel's bra size was 10A. Why couldn't he have just *asked*? This has got to be a male thing, I thought. But then there was a

85

woman detective. The detective's identification of Rachel could have been quite easily disproved the same Thursday morning. For any man, detective or not, to have noticed a girl was chesty while driving along in a car, the girl would most certainly have needed a bra cup larger than a 10A, push-up or not.

I found out later that Shaun had been chased first by the black car and then by a police car. He had turned into a street, where they did a figure eight in the middle of the road, cutting him off. The police got out of their cars with a megaphone and demanded that Shaun come out and place his hands on top of his car with his feet apart. Shaun obliged.

The escort agency had reported us to the police. The police wanted to know what we thought we were up to. Shaun showed them the poster of Rachel. Apparently they knew of Rachel's disappearance. It was to their station that Rachel's dance friend had made her report.

They relaxed towards Shaun when he explained that he was Rachel's cousin and that we had reason to believe Rachel was inside the escort agency. The police told him they knew the agency ran a legal business. We need have no concern that Rachel could be there.

Shaun said they were very understanding. Before they left he asked them for directions home because, as he told them, he lived in the country and had absolutely no idea where he was.

1. Elizabeth with her three daughters: from left to right – Rachel, Heather and Ashleigh-Rose in November 1991.

2. Rachel, aged nine, at ballet class in Prahran.

3. A Christmas ballet performance, 1992.

4. At Grandad Ivan's, dancing in the garden, 1995. Heather is in the background.

5. Rachel, aged eleven, wearing her wings.

6. With her grandfather, distinguished writer Ivan Southall, looking through her Manni memento album.

7. Photographic portrait of Rachel by Susan Southall, 1995. This was one of several photographs that captured the attention of Caroline Reid.

8. In late December 1998, Rachel receives the Elisabeth Membrey Award for Most Improved Student at her dance school.

9&10. Rachel modelling clothes for a professional dance production in 1999.

11. Rachel in February 1999, a photograph taken by Manni two weeks before her death.

12. Rachel and boyfriend Emmanuel Carella (Manni) at a Christmas party, 1998.

A GUT FEELING

Day 8: Tuesday, 9 March

Ashleigh-Rose was frightened by many dreams the Monday night. She dreamt over and over again of Rachel coming home, everyone being happy. I found these dreams puzzling. Why should they frighten her? But deep down, even for this eleven-year-old, she sensed that her dream of Rachel coming home would probably never be.

Heather's unscheduled 'fishing' holiday with her Aunty Robbie was beginning to lose its 'good excuse to be away from school' feel. At first Heather preferred to think of a simple explanation for Rachel's disappearance: she'd gone off with her friends, and isn't she going to be in trouble! Heather could see no reason to fear the worst.

This Tuesday Robbie had organised a special day at the beach. Her seven-year-old son Sam and Heather were looking forward to it. Robbie's girlfriend and her small daughter joined them. The children were having fun playing and making sandcastles. Robbie leant across to her friend and said, 'This is probably the last time Heather will go to the beach thinking she still has an older sister.'

For Robbie there was no hope. 'Knowing your family and knowing Rachel, there is no way Rachel wouldn't come back if she could,' she said.

Soon after this, Heather's attitude began to change as the gravity of Rachel's disappearance began to creep up on her. Perhaps Rachel was lost. Why hadn't she been found? If parents look for their children they should be found. Why hadn't *her* parents found *her* sister? Robbie almost went demented trying to keep the looming seriousness of Rachel's disappearance from Heather.

On Tuesday morning we received a phone call from Richmond police asking us to come in. They were ready to do a media release.

I was feeling very nervous of the Richmond police now, more so because of my Saturday afternoon antics. I asked six-foot-two Drew to accompany us. He would be a protective barrier for both parties.

My brother refused to come at first because he said we wouldn't listen to him.

'We will,' I said.

'You *won't*,' he growled. 'You don't listen to me when I tell you to come home at night. When I tell you to rest. You're not going to help Rachel if you both end up dead.'

'Please,' I urged. 'We'll behave ourselves, won't we, Mike?' Silly thing for a forty-year-old woman to be saying to her fifty-one-year-old brother, in front of her fifty-two-year-old husband, but I did not trust us. I did not trust *myself*. I knew I would become irrational. And I knew Drew could stop me.

Finally Drew agreed because Mike agreed, and he drove us to the police station.

We were waiting at the Richmond watchhouse for the detective senior sergeant, when a phone call came through on the mobile from a David dePyle of the Missing Persons Unit, wanting to speak to us before we spoke to the Richmond police. The phone call broke up. I tried to ring out but couldn't.

'I'll ring him after,' I said to Mike.

'The message was – *before*,' he answered.

'Ask to borrow their phone,' said Drew.

'Oh, I don't know.' I was in a real quandary. I stood up.

'What are you doing?' Drew put his hand out to me. 'Don't you leave this station!' he said in an authoritative voice.

'The detective senior sergeant's not here. I'll ring from a phone box,' I said, and ran out before Drew could protest. Mike followed.

David dePyle, the analyst from Missing Persons, told us he had seen a poster at his railway station on the way to work. When he arrived at the office he had spoken to Neil Paterson for some time. He thought the story of Rachel's disappearance would be a classic for the television program 'Australia's Most Wanted'.

'But what about the Richmond police?' I asked. 'They're going to do a media release today. Can we do both?'

Apparently we could. David told us to tell Richmond police that 'Australia's Most Wanted' were interested.

When we returned to the station Drew was in a foul mood. We had left him to deal with the detective senior sergeant, who appeared to be agitated by our absence. Drew said he would not go to the detective's office with us because it was obvious that we would not take his advice. With yet more persuasion he came.

The detective senior sergeant sat behind his desk. Mike and I sat in front. I cannot remember where the other two detectives were, but I felt safe with Drew there. He was offered a chair but said he preferred standing. Bravo, Drew.

We were told again that they were going to do a media release.

I said words to the effect, 'I realise we have both disagreed about the reasons for Rachel's disappearance but couldn't we just keep to the facts? Rachel said goodbye to her dance friends at 5.45 p.m. on Monday the 1st, and only last night a witness remembered seeing her an hour later getting off a tram at the corner of High Street and Williams Road . . . You *do* know about that?'

The detective senior sergeant inclined his head. He knew. I also had a feeling that he knew what we'd been up to as well.

He let me ramble. 'Do you think there could be two missing girls? Is it possible that another police station is also investigating a missing girl?'

No other police station was investigating another missing girl. The detective senior sergeant remarked that Rachel was the first missing person he had investigated. He had wanted the

Missing Persons Unit to do the investigation but pointed out again that there was no evidence of foul play.

'Please don't say that she's a runaway.'

He considered the possibility she still was.

'We've disproven the notes. Runaway is a pair of cross-trainers.'

He showed me the note. It quite clearly stated 'running away'.

'Yes, but Rachel isn't good at spelling. It's a pair of *shoes*.'

I could see there was no convincing him.

I remembered I had brought a copy of the March issue of *Women's Fitness Australia*. I opened the page to a photo of Rachel. 'Is this what you call chesty?' I demanded. 'Why didn't you ask me?' I was becoming heated. Drew reminded us we had to understand the position the police were in. The detective senior sergeant was pleased with his presence, too.

I told him that 'Australia's Most Wanted' were interested in Rachel's case. He told us they must be short for a story. He rang Victoria Police Media Liaison and repeated what he had just said to us.

In the late afternoon we were contacted again by David dePyle. The Missing Persons Unit was interested in hearing about Rachel's disappearance.

The police complex in St Kilda Road is formidable. A pipe organ would not be out of place there. But when David dePyle appeared, he led us over to an easy chair, away from reception. Already I was feeling better. This man respected our privacy. He wasn't intimidating. He said the Missing Persons Unit was not concerned with *why* a person goes missing. Their priority was to find the person. He repeated the all-too-familiar missing person statistics, but this time we found them reassuring.

It didn't occur to me that the Missing Persons Unit would have also considered Rachel a runaway.

We gave David dePyle the website address Carlo had set up and before saying goodbye he asked us if we would just limit ourselves to being poster people. The police knew of all our 'private' investigations, particularly the one on Monday night.

For the first time since Rachel's disappearance we felt at ease, and agreed.

We went home for dinner. Can you believe it? A house full of people wanting to know everything. Mike was beginning to feel closed in, but even though he found himself in an immense tragedy, his attitude towards people had changed for the better. He was overwhelmed by support from family and friends, and total strangers.

He was surviving.

13

FRONT-PAGE NEWS

Day 9: Wednesday, 10 March

Nine days after Rachel had waved happily from the door her disappearance made front-page news.

As day breaks I walk across to the petrol station to buy the papers. I am numb. The newspaper and media attention emphasises our loss. Will I ever see her again? You read the headlines 'Family Fear on Missing Teen', you read the story and make your judgement. Bad feeling about that girl. She's dead. And you realise that the thing that always happens to someone else is happening to Rachel, to Mike and Elizabeth, to Ashleigh-Rose and Heather. Not strangers. Me. Us. Our family. The paper tells your own story. The paper makes it final . . . and life goes on.

More phone calls. More sorrys. More help offered. More food left. Radio calling. Television calling. Attention plus.

Drew drives to Healesville to pick up more recent photographs and a Christmas video.

Victoria Police Media Liaison arranges for all the television stations and press to visit our house together so that we need only tell our story once. 'Australia's Most Wanted' will be coming after the news media. All other inquiries can be directed to Detective Senior Sergeant Steve Waddell at the Missing Persons

Unit. There is a sense of protection. I vaguely remember the presence of a kindly policewoman.

Furniture is rearranged. Lights are glaring. Television cameras. Fluffy microphones. Sound technicians. Reporters. Our living room is transformed. It is a long morning. A blur. There is a video fiasco. Competition between channels or programs from the same channel, with Drew caught in the middle. Apologies given. Apologies accepted. I remember thinking, *why is this happening to our family?* Will they help us find our beautiful daughter?

The media people were caring. They wanted their story but they were compassionate. Though for us it was mentally exhausting. And after we had told our story, again, to 'Australia's Most Wanted' we were so glad for the liaison part of Police Media Liaison because it meant with only two interview sessions we had covered most of the media. It was mid-afternoon before all the media left. 'Australia's Most Wanted' had the video from the dance school, which made them happy. The woman interviewer was taken aback when she saw Rachel's solo. 'Is that Rachel? She really *can* dance. She's so graceful.'

Before the team left they filmed us at the local railway station taping up posters, and they wanted us to travel with them to St Kilda to film us in the street. It was decided that we would do this at about 8 p.m. as we had been notified that the Missing Persons detectives were coming to the house at six. Thank God they were acting quickly.

We were signing a document for 'Australia's Most Wanted' when I noticed the date: 10 March. 'It's our twentieth wedding anniversary today,' I said.

'So it is,' said Mike.

'Today?' said the woman from 'Australia's Most Wanted'. 'I thought you said you've just had your birthday.'

'That's right. My fortieth on the 7th and our twentieth wedding anniversary on the 10th. Mike wouldn't marry me until I was twenty because he was nearly thirteen years older. So we married three days after my birthday.'

'There's no way Rachel would have run away,' said Mike.

'I believe you,' said the woman.

Drew was still answering the phone for us. Mum's sandwich and coffee-making hands were in retirement. Mike and I sat staring into space, wondering what we could do next. Mike stood up and started to gather posters.

'What do you think you're doing?' asked Drew.

'We just can't sit here,' said Mike.

'Yes. Yes, you can,' said Drew. 'I know the police said you could be the poster people but . . .'

'I don't need the police to tell me anything,' answered Mike, slightly ruffled.

'Yeah, I know, mate,' said Drew. 'But not now, hey. Just think how many more people have heard about Rachel today through the press coverage. No, you two go to bed.'

'Drew . . .'

'No, I don't want to hear any more. You're so tired you didn't even remember your wedding anniversary. Go to bed.'

Big brother had said his piece. We went to bed.

Ten days since Rachel disappeared, and maybe we had only slept ten hours each. Now we were in bed, awake, fatigued, unable to sleep in the daylight. I rolled on my side and cried. 'Tell me this isn't happening.'

'I can't tell you that,' said Mike, and held me close.

'Tell me you think she's alive.'

'I can't tell you that,' said Mike, and held me closer.

There was a softness in the room. A haze. This was a dream. Have you ever had the feeling that you are on the outside looking in? I was outside looking in. We were living in the wrong people's lives. The two people in our bed couldn't possibly be us. But they looked like us. Their names were our names, but how could their sorrow be ours?

Mike moved closer. He was aroused. Oh no, I thought. He nuzzled his head into the corner of my neck. I lay there and the words, 'oh think of England', immediately went through my head. I could not believe I'd thought it. It wasn't that I didn't need this comfort. It was guilt. A form of indecency I had never experienced.

What would Rachel think?

Michael's hand came round and squeezed my nipple.

I was so weary. Mike was weary. Too tired for sleep.

Oh, Rachel, I thought, as her father gently entered me.

'This will relax you,' whispered Mike.

He rocked with me gently.

We curled up together in a foetal position. Paused, and cried together.

'Our baby's gone,' I cried.

'I can't tell you that,' said Mike, and held me closer still.

There was a quiet tapping at the door. 'Would you two like a cup of tea?' asked Drew.

'Thank you,' said Mike.

We pulled ourselves together and a few moments later Drew opened the door and left two cups of tea on my bedside table.

My bedside table drawer was partly open, and when I picked up Mike's tea I noticed my contraceptive packet.

'Oh no,' I said. 'Since Rachel's disappearance I've completely forgotten to take these.'

Mike laughed.

'It's not funny, Michael, I'm in the middle of my cycle.'

'What will be will be,' he answered.

I started to cry again, and he cuddled me.

We didn't share this intimacy again for another four months.

At six o'clock that evening we shook hands with the police officers greeting us at our front door. Introductions and good evenings. Detective Senior Sergeant Steve Waddell and Detective Senior Constable Neil Paterson. Two officers sitting, facing two parents sitting.

Lengthy discussions. A story without an ending, repeated. Again the mention of a list of friends.

'We've already made two lists.'

'Make another.'

The phone rang.

Drew interrupted us. 'Your friend Chris, do you want to speak to her, Elizabeth? She rang earlier.'

'I must,' I said, and excused myself.

I hadn't heard from Chris for almost a year but I considered her, along with Elaine, to be my best friend. Time had simply parted us.

'I've just heard.' Chris started to cry. 'Oh, Elizabeth, I can't believe it.'

'She hasn't run away.'

'I know she hasn't.'

'Chris.'

'Elizabeth.'

Silence.

'I left a message earlier,' she said, 'but you were resting in bed.'

'Oh, I'm sorry, I haven't caught up with messages yet. We've had the media here.'

'I want to help you look for her. I've taken time off work.'

'I need you with us.'

'Yes, yes,' she said, 'anything.'

My cousin Michele drove us to the bayside suburb of St Kilda. People wound down their windows at traffic lights and pointed to the posters on her car. 'Hope you find her. My oath.' Thumbs-up signs. Many good wishes. 'Hope you find the bastard.' And, 'Needs his balls ripping off.'

We met the team from 'Australia's Most Wanted'. They had spent the latter part of the day filming in Richmond and Prahran. I was particularly taken with the cameraman. I know one could say, 'Elizabeth, they wanted your story.' But the team of three were also especially caring, gently helping us to perform for their camera. It was an awkward situation, like starring in a role which is just a little too real for comfort.

Microphones were clipped to our clothes. Instructions given. Three times we walked down the same street. 'Make sure you stay on the same side . . . No, you were holding the posters in the other hand before.' Their car moved at walking pace alongside us until the scene was shot.

The cameraman wrote a week later, 'Of all the horrible crimes I have had to cover in my time I have never been so affected as by what has happened to your family. I have two little girls – I feel I never want to let them out of my sight . . .'

Family and friends were continuing to distribute posters, long into the night. A volunteer from a food van for street kids in Brighton contacted us. The van would put Rachel's poster up. Rachel's Grade 4 teacher from Mont Albert Primary School rang to distribute posters, and parents from the school rang, too. They organised a casserole round-up, and by the end of the week they wheeled into our house a freezer full of food.

14

THE LIST

Day 10: Thursday, 11 March

Mike and my friend Chris went to Prahran to speak to people whose businesses were closed on the Monday night, and ask permission to hang posters on windows and leave small handfuls at counters. While Chris was busy speaking to businesses on the south side of the road Mike decided to go and apologise to the escort agency. I didn't go with them. I was scared of being recognised from the Monday night. I stayed at the dance school.

There were two doors to the escort agency, one leading straight upstairs. Mike walked up to the shopfront door with his posters in hand and pushed the buzzer. There was a long silence before a voice came through the intercom. 'Who's there?'

Mike had the feeling he was being observed, and was prepared to deal with whatever reception he received because he had gone to apologise. A hostile one was a possibility.

'It's Mike Barber.'

Not long after that the door opened and an attractive woman came into the street.

'I'd like to apologise,' Mike said. 'I was part of the chaos you suffered the other night. I also wondered if you could put a poster in your window.'

'All you had to do was knock on the door and ask,' she said kindly.

The woman spoke to Mike for some time. They had been annoyed by our behaviour Monday night because it was obvious we were targeting their business. But now the woman understood, and told Mike she probably would have done the same had their teenage daughter been missing.

There had been a lot of fuss on Tuesday because detectives had questioned the agency throughout the day. But they were one of the top two legal escort agencies and had been in business for eighteen years.

The woman invited Mike in for a cup of coffee and he met her husband, who had been the driver of the black car. They had already started to carry out some investigations of their own. It was highly unlikely that anyone would have taken Rachel into the business because the escort industry preferred experienced women. Unless it was an illegal business: they knew some of these and had checked them out. Their girls would continue to ask about.

They sat around the table together, sharing coffee, being chatty. How normal they are, Mike thought. They had children themselves. They'd been shocked by the whole affair, too; it was a parent's worst nightmare.

And the stories of young women being drugged for an over-seas market were not just movie material. And yes, there really were date-rape drugs.

Meanwhile, at the dance school, I received a phone call from David dePyle. He wanted to show me a photofit image of the girl who'd been seen with Rachel. When I saw it I broke down.

The girl in the picture didn't mean anything to me. I felt so angry. Who *was* she?

Instinct was telling me I would never see Rachel again.

'The eyes, and the chin,' I said. 'I recognise those.'

Then Mike returned from Prahran.

'You've been a long time.'

'I was apologising to the escort agency.'

David dePyle smiled. I'm sure I blushed. We really had got ourselves involved in some silly activities.

'Do you recognise her?' I asked Mike.

He came up with one name because of the hair. But I dis-agreed. Again the eyes and chin. Mike knew them but couldn't think of a name.

We went home for lunch to say farewell and thank you to Drew, who was returning, exhausted, to Harmers Haven. He said he needed a break from *us* because *we* wouldn't rest. But we couldn't just sit at home. We'd drive ourselves crazy. So we were driving everyone else crazy instead.

Ashleigh-Rose had started cutting roses. Dad and Susan had a rose garden the size of a tennis court out at Healesville, a beautiful bushy area east of Melbourne, past the suburban sprawl. Their roses were in full bloom. Normally they would probably have stopped her, but she filled all of Susan's vases with the roses. When the vases were filled she went around the garden collecting the fallen heads and placing them in shallow dishes. The house smelt like a florist's.

Missing Persons contacted us at the dance school in the late afternoon. Had we thought about the list?

We had, but could not come up with any new names.

My friend Chris felt positive that we could. She opened our exercise book of 'ideas' and divided a page up into groups: school, church, dance, Princess Theatre.

No new names.

'*Anyone* else, Elizabeth. Come on, Mike.'

'There were a couple of mystery names we found on loose pieces of paper in Rachel's room,' said Mike.

She wrote down the mystery names.

'Neighbours,' she said.

'Oh, I don't know, Chris.'

She looked at me in a 'come off it' Chris manner.

'I don't know.'

'Neighbours, from Mont Albert?'

'No, why would they?'

'Names!' she demanded.

'The Reids, but they lived two houses away,' I said.

'Don't be so literal.'

'Okay then, Caroline Reid and her middle sister. The youngest is a friend of Ashleigh-Rose's so she wouldn't be old enough.'

Chris wrote them down in our ideas exercise book, and then faxed the list to Missing Persons.

It was almost five and I needed to get to the dress shop in Bridge Road before it closed. Might they have a blue top like Rachel's? We hurried to the store and parked outside. They had sold out. While the sales assistant was on the phone to their factory, I saw a traffic warden writing us a ticket. I rushed out.

'Please!' I begged, 'I've only been here five minutes. Our daughter's gone missing and the police asked me if I could find clothing similar to what she was last seen in . . .'

'That's not my problem. It's yours,' he said, and slapped the ticket on the windscreen.

'One hundred dollars,' I said. 'Since when is a parking ticket a *hundred* dollars?'

'Clearway,' he said. 'If you don't move it by five it'll be towed away,' and he left.

I stood in the street, crying.

'Don't you worry about him,' said Chris. 'We'll sort it later. Good news, we can go to their factory tomorrow and they'll let us look on their racks.' I'm sure that if she'd had a handkerchief she would have been dabbing my tears and wiping my nose. It was good to have her around.

It was night and we were in St Kilda with Chris, in the red-light district again. We spoke to a young prostitute in Grey Street. She didn't look older than fifteen. I showed her Rachel's photograph. She shook her head. 'She wouldn't be fool enough to get mixed up in anything like this.'

'I know . . .' I began, but cut myself short. I didn't want this girl to feel I thought ill of her. 'If you do see her though?' She nodded her head and smiled.

Chris said, 'Let's try the backpackers' hostel. Good place for a poster.' Again I felt like I was stepping over bodies. This place seemed so alien. I had never backpacked anywhere.

We walked into a Salvation Army refuge centre where wasted-looking beings sat waiting for help. A strong smell of recent vomit permeated the building. Internet cafés, vegetarian eating houses, trendy restaurants. Everyone willing to display posters.

Chris was high spirited, and she renewed our fervour. She ran up to a police van stopped at traffic lights and handed the officer a poster through his half-open window.

'Can you put this up at your station?' she asked.

'Sure,' he said. The lights changed and they moved on.

I still can't believe it, but we walked into a sex shop to ask if we could display Rachel's poster in the front window. A middle-aged man, with his beachball-sized beer belly sitting on the counter, looked up from his *Age* crossword. 'Sure,' he said as well.

I'd never been in a sex shop before. I was amazed at the variety of sex toys; vibrators and dildos and unimaginables. What did people use *those* for? If Rachel would cringe at having a poster displayed in her old dance school, she'd pass out if she knew we were here.

We drove through Elsternwick on the way home, mainly because we got lost leaving St Kilda. There was already a poster up at the station. We were getting reckless with posters now and were sticking them everywhere.

We sat watching a large building for a while from our car. Young party-going men arrived. Maybe a bucks' night? Everybody appeared to be screened at the door by bouncers. Most men went in together. A car stopped near us and a retirement-aged man and another, looking like his son, locked the car and walked across to the brothel. What night was it? Thursday night. Perhaps the women were at bingo, perhaps they were home with pots and pans and baby's nappies. I'm sounding sexist. Perhaps the women were out with their toy boys or down at the local strip club. Perhaps they didn't care, or didn't know, where their men were going.

Chris suggested we drive through Brighton in case Rachel had indeed caught the number 602 bus from the corner of Williams Road and High Street. We drove aimlessly through the suburban streets, just looking, and thinking we were wasting our time. Somehow we ended up on Kooyong Road and went home.

There was a note from Mum when we got back. Carlo had rung to say that someone had contacted him through the website to report a girl answering Rachel's description being seen in St Kilda a week before her disappearance. I remembered the girl Mike had chased on the bus down Orrong Road, and how like Rachel she appeared. I wondered how many other girls answering Rachel's description must be out there.

15

'DO WE KNOW A CAROLINE ROBERTSON?'

Day 11: Friday, 12 March

Missing Persons called again on Friday morning to see how we were getting on with the sample of Rachel's clothes for the new media release.

There were so many clothing racks at the factory outlet that I thought we would be there for hours, but they had their system worked out.

'This is all we have left in the range.'

It's surprising how, when faced with a rack of similar colours and designs, how confusing it could be. We offered to pay but they refused. Rachel would have been in a seventh heaven here.

On our way to the police with our clothing samples we drove up to a set of lights that were changing to red and were confronted by the faces of two determined windscreen-washers.

'I'm sorry, I haven't any small change,' I said, as their squeegees hovered over our front and back windows.

'No change at all?' They sounded surprised.

'No,' said Chris. 'Really. We're on our way to police headquarters with . . .' and on she went with our life story. The lights changed to green, back to red, to green and back to red again. Fortunately there were no other cars behind us.

'Jeez, man,' one of them said. 'Have you got any spare

posters and we'll hand them out to the cars whose windows we wash.'

'Thank you . . . so much,' said Mike, sounding slightly overcome, and shaking their hands through the window. Even small offers of help meant a great deal.

A short while later we received another call on the mobile from Missing Persons.

'Do we know a Caroline Robertson?' Mike asked me.

'No,' I said. 'Why?'

Mike asked. Apparently telephone records indicated that a Caroline Robertson had rung our house before Rachel went missing.

'The only Caroline we know,' said Mike, 'is a Caroline Reid.'

The police wanted to know where we were and what we were doing.

Mike said we had samples of Rachel's clothes and were on our way to meet them.

I remembered that I had thought it wasn't technically possible to get a list of incoming calls. But it must have been. Why had I got the impression that it wasn't possible when I asked last week? Perhaps it wasn't within the other detective's jurisdiction or something.

At the St Kilda Road complex the three of us waited a short while with our visitor passes pinned to our fronts, before David dePyle came through. I had thought the Richmond police station was like a stronghold, but this police complex was an acropolis by comparison. A haven of security. You needed a pass to get through every department door. I was amazed the toilets were not security-locked.

We were so many floors up in the lift when David said he would just leave us here for a minute.

I panicked. 'What? Here? Locked in this lift?'

Everybody laughed. 'No,' said David. 'At the cafeteria.' I had been so preoccupied with the security arrangements that I had not heard him say he was going to take us to the cafeteria while he delivered the clothes.

'Detective Senior Sergeant Steve Waddell will be with us shortly. He is organising the media release. They will be dressing a mannequin and setting a caravan up at the corner of Williams Road and High Street.'

He left us with coffee and a magnificent view across South Yarra and Richmond. The building looked into the green grounds of Melbourne Grammar School, our landmark for our first directions to the complex. We were so high that the windows appeared to ripple in the wind. I walked to the edge and thought, looking down at the concrete path, how desperate people must be to hurl themselves from rooftops.

I went back to Chris and Mike. 'It's a beautiful green city,' I said, 'and yet somewhere beneath those rooftops, somewhere in those tree-lined streets Rachel is . . .'

'Elizabeth, don't,' said Chris putting her arm around me.

'No, no, it's all right,' I answered, looking at the expanse of sky. 'You know, if the Missing Persons detectives don't come up with anything, maybe our skywriting idea isn't such a bad one after all. Can you imagine Rachel's name spanning the breadth of Melbourne's skyline?'

Mike and Chris were smiling and their faces had the 'oh, Elizabeth's dreaming big again' look.

Shortly, David dePyle returned and brought us some sandwiches and more cups of tea and coffee.

'Tell me about Caroline,' he asked, and opened his notebook.

'Caroline Robertson?' said Mike. 'You mean Caroline Reid.'

David dePyle nodded in a laid-back manner. 'We're just making some inquiries.'

Why didn't we jump up and demand to know more? What inquiries, and why? What possible connection could Caroline Reid have with Rachel? But we didn't ask. We sat casually and chatted, in a relaxed atmosphere, while he jotted down notes.

'We haven't seen her since December 1997,' I said, 'when we moved from Mont Albert.'

'We were friends with her mother,' said Mike.

'And Ashleigh-Rose, our middle daughter, was friends with her youngest sister. Rachel was more a friend of the middle sister.'

'Why Caroline?' asked Mike. 'She was always very much in the background. The eldest daughter . . . the older sister.'

'Would you know why she rang your house on the 28th of February late in the afternoon?'

'I didn't know she had until today.'

'She rang twice.'

'I thought Rachel was on the phone to Emmanuel. She didn't say.'

'Caroline kept to herself,' said Mike. 'She struck me as an unhappy girl.'

'What about their father?'

'David. I didn't really know him,' I answered. 'I only met him a couple of times, if that. We hadn't been in Mont Albert long before David left Gail and applied for a divorce. We were a shoulder for Gail to cry on. Became good friends . . . I don't see what any of this has to do with Rachel.'

'I saw Caroline recently,' said Mike, becoming animated. 'I remember now! Ashleigh-Rose had been invited to her younger sister's birthday at the Dunloe Avenue swimming pool. They'd gone ten pin bowling. It's in the same centre.'

'Would you like some more tea?' asked Chris, taking our cups and, not waiting for our answer, she went to get some.

'When I went to collect Ashleigh-Rose I was speaking to Gail, and Caroline was speaking to Rachel through the car window. Rachel didn't get out. I didn't hear what they were talking about . . . She's got something to do with all this, hasn't she?'

'What else can you tell me about her?'

'Gail told me she won a scholarship to Camberwell Girls Grammar,' I said. 'They were really disappointed because she had done so well, and then she became really unsettled. Always staying away from school. Didn't seem to have any direction or friends.'

'Caroline liked to think she dominated the household when her father left,' said Mike. 'If Gail came over to our place for a cup of tea Caroline would phone to check up on her.'

'Caroline has epilepsy,' I said. 'She was really down. Gail was concerned because when she left school in Year 9 she would stay in her room for long periods. Gail used to say she stayed there for almost a year.'

'But she went back to school,' said Mike. 'She did her last year of school at Box Hill Secondary Senior Campus. Her computer broke down when she was doing her final assessments, so we let her use ours. She stayed in the house all day while we were at work.'

'She babysat a couple of times.'

'So would you say Rachel and Caroline were friends?'

'More like acquaintances,' said Mike. 'She was distant. Very much in the background,' he repeated. 'She was always polite to us, but we were told she was difficult at home.'

I became anxious about the time. 'It's getting late. Where's Steve? What about the media release?'

David dePyle excused himself and used his mobile. 'There's been a delay,' he said when he'd finished.

We talked about other things for a while. What was it like to be a detective? The view. The weather. Books. He enjoyed reading crime novels. He recommended I read an American crime novel based on a mother whose daughter had gone missing.

His mobile rang and he moved away from the table.

When he returned he asked Mike if he knew if the Reids owned any other property.

'Ah-ha,' answered Mike, 'I know her father has a place in the country somewhere.' He paused. 'And I suppose that could be quite a good place to hide someone.'

'That's right. A hobby farm in Kilmore,' I said. 'Gail was always upset that he bought this after they broke up because it was something they were always going to do together. Ashleigh-Rose was invited there, by Caroline and her youngest sister, on several occasions, but this never eventuated.'

Mike expressed concern about the possibility that Rachel was being held captive by Caroline.

'But why?' I asked. 'It doesn't make sense.'

Mike said, later in the day, that he felt relieved with the developments because he had always believed that if a man had grabbed Rachel she would be dead. The possibility of Caroline's involvement offered Rachel a chance of survival. But why would Caroline want to hold her hostage? There was no way Rachel would have worried us by just disappearing the way she had.

David dePyle said they were following several leads in this direction, but warned us not to get our hopes up because in their business they could spend days following up leads only to have them come to nothing.

We were there a long time. I had the feeling we were being gently detained. Perhaps they didn't want us out on the streets. David asked us what we would be doing when we left him and we said we had planned to go back to the Prahran corner where Rachel was last seen.

'And be the poster people?' he reaffirmed.

'Yes,' said Mike. 'The poster people.'

Chris was concerned it was getting late, too. She needed to go to the bank. There was a bank within walking distance, so Mike went with her.

They had been gone some time when I jokingly said perhaps they had gone to Prahran. David dePyle stood up quickly. 'Yes, they have been gone some time,' and went over to a phone to make a call.

He came back and asked me if I'd be okay for a minute if he left.

When Mike and Chris returned they said there had been a long queue.

Steve Waddell contacted David to tell him the media release was done.

David asked us if we would go home rather than go to Prahran. We told him we would, but we had to go via Richmond to collect Manni who wanted to stay the night with us, and then take Chris home to her family.

I didn't question David dePyle's request. I didn't ask why he didn't want us to go to Prahran. I thought that the police were actually getting somewhere with their investigations and I didn't want to get in their way. We needed to leave them to it now. Our curiosity did not even allow us to drive down High Street to have a nosey at what the police were up to.

At about 9.30 that evening we received a phone call from Missing Persons. A detective asked us if we could come down to the police complex immediately and identify some items.

I felt really hopeful. We all did. Maybe Mike was right. Perhaps Caroline was holding Rachel captive at Kilmore.

Mike, Manni and I left hurriedly. As we were passing through Heathmont another car honked. Its driver pointed to the posters plastered to the inside of our back windows, and did a thumbs-up. We smiled. We were nervous but positive.

We had waited nearly two weeks for our prayers to be answered. Would Rachel be coming home?

On Canterbury Road, crossing Elgar Road, we received another call from Missing Persons. They asked us who we had in the car. We told them Manni was with us. They were very sorry. But they had made a mistake. We could go home. 'And please *do* go home.'

We did not question them. We went home.

I felt like a small child waking on Christmas morning and see-ing a large colourful parcel with a big red bow on top, at the bottom of the bed. The child, having eagerly awaited Christmas Day, now crawls across her covers to the twitching present. Mum and Dad are peeking in at the door. The child unties the bow, lifts the lid and squeals with delight as she lifts into her arms a Labrador puppy with another big red bow around its neck.

That is how it felt when we received that first phone call. But now, driving home without any prize, I imagined those parents again. I imagined their faces when their child eagerly unties the big red bow on the box, only to lift the lid and find a lifeless puppy, perhaps suffocated or strangled by the big red bow around its neck.

That was how I felt after that second phone call telling us to go home. How would it end for us?

Manni slept in Heather's room that night, but he insisted on sleeping beneath Rachel's favourite cow-print doona. He couldn't be comforted by Rachel's Christmas stocking present, her Humphrey Bear, because Rachel had Humphrey with her. So Manni sprayed his pillow with her favourite perfume. He did not sleep. He lay there breathing in the memories of his dear Rachel.

16

FINALLY FOUND

Day 12: Saturday, 13 March

We took our time on Saturday morning. Mum made us her tomato breakfast specialty, and we sat outside on the back veranda.

Manni asked us if we would mind if he had a cigarette.

'I didn't know you smoked,' I said, surprised.

'Yes, occasionally,' he smiled, perhaps looking a little guilty. 'Not when Rachel's around. She doesn't like me smoking.'

We discussed taking Manni into dance class at 11 a.m. Mike thought it would be good for him to be with his friends, and I knew that Rosa was concerned for him. She would want him home tonight.

We wondered why the police had not called. Why the sudden urgency last night?

Our graphic artist friend David arrived in the morning with another thousand posters. The count so far – five thousand. I thought of that story about the little Japanese girl in Hiroshima and her one thousand paper cranes, and the dreamed-for hope of a life saved. I couldn't bear to think that Rachel was dead.

Mid-morning, somewhere down Riversdale Road on our way to the dance school, the mobile rang.

It was Missing Persons. Where were we?

We were taking Manni to dance class.

What did we plan to do then?

We were going to Prahran to deliver more posters.

The detective told us to take Manni to class and then go home. Directly home. There was a tone in his voice that left no room for debate.

We dropped a worried Manni off at the door. We were being told what to do. It was like there was nothing more we *could* do. We were told not to leave home. It was important we stayed there, and they would contact us later in the day.

Mum was surprised to see us back so early. Concerned when we told her our message.

But Mike encouraged me. 'Elizabeth, the police could be driving up to Kilmore. Maybe they have discovered that Rachel's being held captive.'

'Then why don't *we* drive there? Goodness knows what she's been thinking these past two weeks. Rachel will need us.'

'No, they asked us to stay at home. Let the police do their job.' He put his arms around me, so tenderly. 'Perhaps we may have Rachel home today.'

Michele and Mum sat with me for much of the time in silence. The phone rang many times. Messages were taken. We could not speak.

Rosa and Frank phoned. 'We've heard from Emmanuel. Is there any news?'

Rachel's cousin Tamzin phoned, asking for more posters.

Michelle, the mother of one of Rachel's friends, offered emotional support. I never knew she worked for the Department of Human Services.

Ted rang.

Wendy, another friend, rang.

Junior Connor rang. A Vietnam veteran, and one-time boxer, whom we'd met outside a milk bar on our search. We had spoken to him for a long time. A warm, strong character with a sad past. 'Ring me when you find the bastard and I'll box him out flat.'

Mike went into the garden and began to clean the pool.

The mother of one of Heather's friends rang. She later told us she *knew*. She did not tell. Her sister worked for the police force and had taken a call.

My sister Robbie rang. She did not think as positively as we did.

Barbara, a country friend. Laura, Rachel's long-time school friend. Sheryl, the mother of a dance school friend. Toni, the mother of a friend from Rachel's previous dance school. Erin, another of Rachel's friends. Chris and Debbie from work, and Emmanuel. They all rang.

Neil Paterson from Missing Persons rang and asked to speak to Mike.

Mike came through to us. 'Neil asked if we would be home later in the day. He asked was the tall guy with us. He meant Drew. I told him, no. He asked if family was with us. I told him, yes. He said they would come at six.'

'What did his voice sound like?' I asked.

'Normal.'

'Did you ask him what it was about? Have they found Rachel? My God, perhaps they're going to bring her home. Or perhaps she is in hospital? Please God, let her be alive.'

'I didn't want to put him on the spot,' answered Mike.

'Oh, Michael,' said Mum. 'I'll make you both a cup of tea.'

I was definitely spaced out. I've never been on drugs. I've only been drunk three times. But I might as well have been on everything that Saturday afternoon.

Mike continued cleaning the pool. From the moment of Neil's call, he knew. He cleaned the pool, all afternoon, continually. The motion continuous. Repetitive.

Denial. I was in denial. I savoured the feeling that I still had a living Rachel.

Robbie called again. Mum told her about Neil's phone call. The hardest thing for Robbie was not to show Heather how distressed she was.

Rachel's friend Ellen rang. She had written to the Victorian premier, Jeff Kennett, to ask for his help in bringing Rachel home. She had personally delivered the letter to his letter box.

*

The Missing Persons detectives arrived soon after six. Mike and I both answered the door. Welcomed them in. Shook hands.

Family members retired to the kitchen.

Neil and Steve sat on the couch facing us. Another detective stood up against the wall. I did not take too much notice of him.

Neil said, 'There is no easy way of saying this.'

We held hands. Mike knew. I feared.

Neil said, 'I'm sorry. Rachel has been murdered.'

Silence.

A gasp from the kitchen.

'Who . . . ?' I asked.

'Caroline Reed Robertson. You know her as Caroline Reid.'

Silence.

Mike and I said together, 'Gail is not going to be able to cope with this.'

'Gail?' said a detective.

'Caroline's mother.'

We did not cry. We sat. Numb.

'I wish we didn't know,' I said. 'I wish we hadn't tried so hard. I wish she was still a missing person. Then maybe we would still have some hope.'

'No, you wouldn't,' said one of the detectives. 'The not knowing, you wouldn't want that.'

I looked at the detective standing against the wall. 'Are you from Homicide?'

He nodded. 'Paul Ross.'

I have often thought, over the last three years, and this is taking nothing from our own grief psychologist whom I only have the highest esteem for, but if Paul Ross ever wanted a change in career, he would make an excellent grief counsellor. But then where would the Homicide Department have been without men of the calibre of Paul Ross, who were capable of the human compassion he expressed for us?

We talked of compassion for the Reid family. How terrible for them. Terrible for us, yes. But to know your daughter – your sister, has been charged with murder. The horror for Gail, who saw Rachel grow from nine to fourteen. The horror for her sisters, and her father.

The police told us to have compassion for the Reids if we must. But on no account to have compassion for Caroline. 'She is a cold fish,' they said.

Then, 'How?'

'We have to wait for an autopsy.' Do you know, I can't remember exactly what they said, but we assumed that what she had been killed *with* was found with her body.

'The children,' I said, 'and Emmanuel.'

We could not possibly tell Manni over the phone. We asked Paul Ross if someone could make a home visit to his family. (Emmanuel would drop to the floor, with guttural sobs. His Rachel. Dead. How can this be? They had *promised*. They would never leave each other. First love. Abandonment.)

A car stopped outside. 'You have a visitor,' a detective said.

We both looked. 'Oh Mike, he's here.'

Mike went outside and spoke to the man we had felt necessary to report. He handed Mike some money to help with expenses. I was surprised that Mike accepted. After everything we had been through, and the story I had revealed, I thought Mike would have given it back. But the man insisted. Mike told him the news. Ironically he was the first to hear it outside our family. Much later he told us that he had parked his car at the side of the road on the way home, absolutely grief-stricken.

The police had taken the liberty of contacting our family doctor, who had been dining with friends. She was waiting in the car outside while the detectives spoke to us. What must *that* have felt like?

My mother rang my father's house. Susan took the call. Her reaction? Immediate. She could not contain her grief. My father's reaction? Anger. Ashleigh-Rose's reaction? Shock. 'How can my sister be dead?' Dad and Susan drove a despairing eleven-year-old back to the same address but to a different home. Ashleigh-Rose said, 'It was a long and painful drive. I was very scared.'

But perhaps driving home knowing her sister would not be waiting for her was kinder than the cruel guessing game we allowed Heather to experience. It wasn't until I was speaking to Robbie about the matter nearly two years later that I realised how unreasonable our request to Drew and Robbie had been.

I cannot remember who rang Drew at his blue house on the cliff edge, overlooking the ocean at Harmers Haven. But Drew drove to Robbie at her home in Wonthaggi to tell her. We had requested they not tell Heather as we felt this was our responsibility, but now I think not telling Heather was inept. When Drew took Robbie out onto her veranda she let out a primeval scream. Drew told her we wanted to tell Heather ourselves. Robbie felt this was worse. Robbie wanted desperately to let out her grief, but because of Heather, could not.

Heather hardly said a word. Did she know? Did she weigh up in her nine-year-old mind, over the two-hour drive, what the most likely scenario would be? Robbie and Drew stopped and bought her, uncharacteristically, a can of soft drink, potato chips and lollies. What could they do for this little girl's last two hours of thinking her sister was alive? Robbie said they talked about idiotic things.

When they arrived we whisked Heather into our bedroom and sat her on our bed.

'Heather,' I said.

We sat on either side of her holding her hands.

'You're going to tell me Rachel's dead.'

Robbie was distraught, letting out her two-hour bound-up grief. 'My poor little sister,' she cried, holding me tight. 'My poor little niece.'

'Rachel's with Nanny now, Robbie,' I said. 'Together, with your baby boy.'

Behind the scenes ...

17

A STATISTIC

Every eighteen minutes, every single day in Australia, someone somewhere is reported missing to the police – almost 30 000 reports a year. And in March 1999 Rachel Barber became just one of them.

Among the 6461 missing persons reported in Victoria that year, 3490 were juveniles and 1847 were young women.

But these figures barely scratch the surface of what appears to be a growing problem, and since research is scant, it is also difficult to determine the impact of missing people on families and friends or on the community at large. In 1999 Rachel Barber had been missing less than two hours when her mother first contacted police. Once the official missing person report had been made, it became the responsibility of the officer on the desk at Box Hill police station, and he became the officer assigned to Rachel Barber's case. Later he would have arranged for the family to fill out a standard missing person report: basic information including Rachel's date of birth, sex, appearance, and a brief description of the clothes she would have been wearing – along with the time and place she was last sighted.

The report, along with around thirty other missing person reports made that day around the State, would have been phoned through to the Victoria Police Central Data Entry Bureau, because of Rachel's age, within twenty-four hours.

Once the report was in the system, a regular 24-hour sweep would ensure that it was transmitted to the national network, allowing Rachel's name to show up on police systems in stations throughout Australia.

Missing Persons has strict criteria governing the cases that fall under its jurisdiction. It does not involve itself in simple everyday cases of missing people, only those that suggest foul play, where the disappearance is suspicious – possible abduction, sexual exploitation, people missing for more than seventy-two hours. Such cases are generally potential homicide investigations. Missing Persons also looks into cases where the absence is a significant and inexplicable deviation from established patterns.

The police definition of a 'missing person' covers anyone reported missing to them whose whereabouts are unknown, and where there are fears for their safety. Does *this* definition describe Rachel Barber? Her parents certainly thought so.

But the brief report on Rachel that filtered into the police system a day or so after her disappearance contained no evidence suggesting foul play or suspicious circumstances. There was no undue concern from police in relation to her safety. So the report placed Rachel Barber outside the police criteria, and failed to attract any real attention.

At the time of Rachel's disappearance there were ten police officers staffing the Missing Persons Unit, which operated under the auspices of the Homicide Squad at Victoria Police headquarters in St Kilda Road, Melbourne. One police officer, Senior Constable David dePyle, was an analyst who had the daily task of reviewing the list of missing person reports transmitted to him from police stations around the State. He read the short narrative on each person reported missing during the previous twenty-four hours and examined the brief carefully for evidence of concern that might warrant further investigation. He has no recollection of seeing Rachel Barber's name on his daily list when he logged on the morning after she disappeared. But he would have expected her report to have filtered through the system very quickly.

'In fairness to police members making out initial reports, they are required to fill in only very basic information, like a brief description and where the person was last seen,' says Senior Constable dePyle. 'But if a policeman taking the report gets a bit of a "gut" instinct about a particular case he will often contact his local CIB detectives first, asking for further investigations to be made. Or he might contact Missing Persons asking what we thought about it and what course of action should be taken.'

But only Mike and Elizabeth Barber, and their family and friends, had a gut feeling about Rachel's disappearance.

One of the more unusual unsolved cases that remained part of an ongoing investigation by the Missing Persons Unit at the time Rachel Barber disappeared was that of a woman called Elisabeth Membrey. Elisabeth had also been a student at the dance school Rachel attended in Richmond. She was twenty-two when she disappeared in 1994 from her East Ringwood home, ten minutes away from the Barbers' in neighbouring Heathmont.

Blood specks found on Elisabeth Membrey's carpet and in her car suggested foul play, and police concur that she most certainly disappeared in suspicious circumstances. But extensive inquiries over the past few years have not yet led to a conviction, and her distraught parents live in an endless painful limbo as they wait for new leads. Ironically, Elisabeth Membrey's parents had dedicated a trophy to honour their daughter at the Dance Factory and Rachel Barber had been the third student to receive the award for Most Improved Student. That was three months earlier and now Rachel was missing.

While there was initial speculation among the media that there might be some link between Rachel's disappearance and Elisabeth's, the police say that no connections were ever established.

David dePyle's first recollection of Rachel Barber's case is of hearing his colleague Detective Senior Constable Neil Paterson telling the team 'in passing', of a telephone conversation he had just had with a woman called Elizabeth Barber whose daughter had disappeared on the previous day.

The officer also remembered Paterson saying that he had already received a call earlier that day from a friend who ran a café underneath the dance school from which Rachel had vanished. The friend had rung to say he had given the Barbers Paterson's mobile telephone number in the hope that he might be able to give them some advice on their missing daughter.

Paterson had told the Barbers not to panic because most missing teenagers turn up within twenty-four hours. He also suggested that they compile a list of names since some of Rachel's fellow dance students remembered her mentioning an intended meeting with an 'old female friend' on the evening she vanished. The Unit head, Detective Senior Sergeant Steve Waddell, was informed about the matter.

The following morning, Wednesday 3 March, Neil Paterson, on the advice of his boss, contacted Senior Sergeant Laurie Wilks at Box Hill police station in relation to Rachel Barber, requesting an investigation of the girl's disappearance. Paterson was told that Box Hill police would be contacting Richmond Criminal Investigation Bureau immediately because Box Hill believed Richmond were in a better position to investigate the situation. The missing girl was, after all, last seen in Richmond.

At this stage there was nothing in the Rachel Barber report to suggest that it was a potential case for Missing Persons.

The odds, it seems, are stacked heavily against teenage girls who go missing. They quickly become statistics. Of all the people reported missing in Australia each year, the biggest proportion consists of young women. Most of them are teenage girls. And the police are all too aware, both from personal experience and from supporting studies, that the most typical of these *is* a fifteen-year-old girl.

She often disappears of her own volition, generally with a girlfriend though sometimes with a boyfriend. She goes missing after a family argument or some other parental conflict, more often than not over authority or discipline.

She will choose to disappear on a Friday, in time for the weekend, rather than on any other weekday. And mostly she will disappear from her home, or while travelling to or from school.

Australian research by the National Missing Persons Unit also shows that almost two-thirds of all missing people will be located on the same day, or the day after being reported missing. And half of all teenage girls who go missing in Victoria will turn up, within forty-eight hours, of their own accord. Some are apologetic. Some are not, and will repeat the adventure. And the most effective means of tracing a missing person appears to be 'putting out the word' among friends and social groups.

According to Victoria Police figures, only 10 per cent of missing person cases remain unsolved after one month, 5 per cent after six months and 1 per cent unsolved after twelve. And in rare long-term missing person cases, the subject remains untraced because of a suspected suicide, or because no body has ever been recovered.

Sometimes cases remain unsolved because the person has engineered the disappearance, even though this may be totally out of character. Had Rachel Barber's body not been found, she might well have been deemed to have fallen into this category.

Also highlighted in research conducted by the National Missing Persons Unit is the fact that one-third of all the people who were reported as missing had a history of disappearing.

Rachel Barber had no such history, but her age and sex, and the lack of any evidence of foul play, made it most likely that she would be considered a runaway rather than a missing person. On the other hand, she had not been involved in any family discord. She was happy pursuing her dream of becoming a dancer. She never missed a lesson, even when she was injured.

The day before she disappeared she had been told she could have the kitten she wanted. She had a boyfriend she couldn't bear to be separated from, and even *he* had not heard from her. And she couldn't have run away with a friend because all her known friends had been contacted and were worried about her.

Her mother's fortieth birthday was coming up and she had discussed gifts with her father. And it was her parents' twentieth wedding anniversary the following week.

On top of all that, Rachel was afraid of the dark, uneasy about using public transport – indeed of doing anything alone. She had even persuaded her boyfriend to travel home with her from a recent modelling shoot because she couldn't handle the trip by herself.

So, to the Barbers, Rachel's disappearance *was* highly suspicious. They felt that there was considerable cause for concern about her safety. And they were as bewildered by the response from the local police as they were by their daughter's failure to catch her tram.

It was the Barbers' steadfast refusal to consider Rachel a runaway and the intensity of their ensuing poster campaign and search that brought Rachel's case, one week later, to the attention of the Missing Persons Unit.

18

A VITAL SIGHTING

Senior Constable dePyle had been waiting for his morning train on Tuesday, 9 March – eight days after Rachel's mysterious disappearance – when he first noticed the poster appealing for information on the missing teenager.

It was one of the two thousand posters her family and friends had been busy displaying over the previous holiday weekend as they tramped around bus and train stations, tram depots and a multitude of public venues.

David dePyle remembered the girl from the earlier discussion with Neil Paterson and had a vague recollection of his colleague saying that the family was conducting its own search and putting up posters. But this was the first time he had seen one of the posters bearing Rachel's face.

He remembers being struck by the persistence of the family and, although this was not a particularly unusual case, and it still failed to meet the Unit's criteria for further investigation, he had a feeling that he needed to take a closer look at it.

'It didn't surprise me that there were posters about,' he says. 'Obviously, when a loved one goes missing it is a very worrying, traumatic time for families. But what it triggered in my mind was that this family was very serious indeed. It was a little bit more than the usual level of concern families show when a child disappears. And this was the first time I had ever seen a poster of a missing person displayed on a railway station.'

He again called up Rachel Barber's case on screen. There was nothing of any particular note about it. She'd been missing eight days, and although reports contained in the police computer system are subject to updates as more detailed information emerges, no further updates appeared to have been made to Rachel Barber's file. The narrative was the same straightforward, factual brief that would have been made on the night of her disappearance.

'I just wanted to find out more about this case,' says dePyle. 'Sometimes, as you make inquiries, you just get a bit of a feel for a case and you run with it. Nine times out of ten it fizzles into nothing, but I still thought I would take a better look and just see what I could find out.'

He called the Barbers on the mobile number Elizabeth Barber had given Neil Paterson. They were already at Richmond police station, however, waiting to speak with detectives about the preparation of a press release being distributed by Victoria Police Media Liaison to the print and electronic media. It would be appealing for information about Rachel's disappearance and would include new evidence that had emerged the previous evening.

A young woman who knew Rachel from their days as ballet students together had recalled seeing the teenager shortly after her disappearance on 1 March. Alison Guberek was two years older than Rachel but had known her well. She told police she had been travelling on the number 6 tram from St Kilda to Prahran after 6.20 p.m. on 1 March when she saw Rachel getting onto the same tram with an older girl.

The pair got on in Chapel Street at around 6.40 p.m., said Alison, and although she had not seen Rachel for some time, they made eye contact and it was obvious to her that the younger girl recognised her. But Alison *didn't* recognise the older girl. She said that the pair sat close enough to her on the tram to allow her to overhear a conversation they were having. She'd heard Rachel, who seemed to be talking more than the older girl, discussing her boyfriend, and a cat. Rachel seemed 'excited'.

She'd been wearing black dance pants and looked 'quite

beautiful ... striking in contrast with this other girl, who was plain ...'

Alison assumed that Rachel must have been attending a dancing class, and watched as the two girls got off the tram at the corner of Williams Road and High Street, Prahran. Rachel had given Alison a 'small wave' as she walked along the footpath with the older girl. It struck her as odd that Rachel had been on this particular tram because she knew Rachel lived some distance away, and she had never seen her travelling in this direction before. Alison had no idea that Rachel had disappeared until Monday, 8 March, the day before dePyle noticed the poster at his railway station.

Unable to make contact with the Barbers, dePyle rang a researcher on Channel Nine's national program 'Australia's Most Wanted', to discuss the possibility of airing a story on Rachel Barber's disappearance. The Missing Persons Unit had become a regular contact point for researchers on the show, who would ring one of the officers every couple of days looking for potential material. Often Missing Persons could not provide the sort of visual story the news team was seeking. Sometimes they had nothing mysterious or intriguing enough to make good viewing.

The researcher was very interested in the Rachel Barber case. How long had the girl been missing? Would the family be prepared to talk to them? Would they agree to be filmed?

The police officer offered to seek the family's permission and ask for photographs of Rachel to be sent to the studios in Sydney if they were agreeable. Media Liaison would help coordinate coverage of the story.

When dePyle spoke to Elizabeth Barber she was receptive to the idea of TV coverage and arranged to come to the police complex to answer further questions and supply recent photographs of her missing daughter. Meanwhile the officer discussed the case with his colleagues and a new line of inquiry began.

The Barbers came in late on Tuesday afternoon with the photographs he had requested. There was still no hint of foul play, though Missing Persons were now aware of Alison's new evidence. The press release would be put out in time for the following morning's news. Rachel Barber still might be a runaway. But dePyle, posting his bundle of photographs overnight to Sydney, had a continuing uncomfortable feeling about the case and wanted it solved.

By the time Senior Constable David dePyle boarded his train for work the following morning, Wednesday, 10 March, the Rachel Barber disappearance was already making headline news around the State. Arriving at the office he sat down with Rachel Barber's file again, and together with his colleagues Dave Rae, Neil Paterson and two other experienced detectives, he decided to begin their inquiries at Rachel's former school.

Detective Senior Constable Dave Rae and Detective Sergeant Anthony Thatcher spent a couple of hours at Canterbury Girls Secondary College, where Rachel had been a student for nearly three years. When they returned to their office some time later bearing a hand-made card produced by students who had known Rachel, they too felt that there was something 'not right' about the case.

Studying the giant purple card closely, the police noted that more than two hundred students and staff from the school had signed their names, expressing their concern to the Barber family and hoping for Rachel's safe return. This did not paint the picture of an unhappy girl who had run away. It told police that the girls themselves thought this was out of character for their friend. To all concerned it was strange and worrying that Rachel had not contacted a single friend in over a week.

'This card made the case seem all the more unusual,' recalls Senior Constable dePyle. 'Everything we found out seemed to build up a picture that offered no reason at all for this girl disappearing. If she had been an unhappy girl at school, socially isolated and with few friends, who wanted to run away from her life, that would have explained a little at least. There was none of that here . . . the more we dug the more baffling and mysterious the whole thing became.'

But in spite of the card there was still no evidence that anything suspicious had occurred. Still, Rachel had been missing now for ten days. It didn't *feel* right. Detective Senior Sergeant Steve Waddell left the office with Detective Senior Constable Neil Paterson to pursue further inquiries. They began with a meeting at

Richmond CIB to share their information with the detectives handling the case and to establish the status of the investigation: Waddell informed Richmond police that the Missing Persons Unit would now be assuming responsibility for the investigation into Rachel Barber's disappearance.

Richmond CIB had already conducted preliminary interviews with staff and students at the Richmond dance school a week earlier, closely questioning Rachel's boyfriend, Emmanuel Carella, to establish whether he might have secretly known the girl's motives for disappearing. They had to rule out any possibility that pregnancy might have caused her to disappear. Perhaps her dancing was becoming too punishing? They discovered from another student that Rachel had sat out of dance class on the day she disappeared due to a sore back. Was it possible, the police speculated, that the rigorous dancing routine was becoming too much for her? Was she taking time out from her life perhaps? The police also learnt from dance students that Rachel had mentioned the job interview and had been noticeably quiet during the day.

But what kept rearing its head throughout their discussions was the story of the possible job interview and the prospect of earning a large sum of money.

No one knew a thing about this job. Perhaps it was the sort of work her parents wouldn't have approved of?

The Missing Persons officers also learnt that Richmond detectives had visited the Barbers' home the previous Friday and scoured Rachel's room for any evidence to explain her sudden disappearance. During that search they found a note bearing the words 'running away'. Her parents had later assured police that the note referred to a brand of shoes called 'Runaways'. Their daughter had misinterpreted the name of the shoes.

Then there had been the Barbers' visit to Richmond station to tell police about a man known to Elizabeth Barber who had been effectively 'stalking' her.

And there was the most crucial evidence to emerge since Rachel disappeared: the sighting by Alison Guberek. Yet even this information did not necessarily suggest foul play. After all, Rachel had been laughing and chatting on the tram and did not appear to be in the throes of any sinister abduction.

But she had not told anyone she wouldn't be home that night. She had promised to call her boyfriend and arranged to meet friends for breakfast the following day. Her wallet had been found in her locker at the dance school, containing her ID and some loose change. That didn't suggest someone who intended to stay away.

Later on Wednesday morning Neil Paterson paid a visit to Rachel's dance school in Church Street, Richmond, where he spoke to Rachel's teacher about the girl's disappearance and was struck by her concern about the teenager. He then went to a modelling school in Elizabeth Street, Melbourne, to speak with its head about Rachel's recent modelling and photographic shoot.

Meanwhile, back at the Missing Persons Unit, Senior Constable dePyle continued to make telephone checks to see what he could turn up on the missing girl.

Now aware of the importance of Alison's sighting, Steve Waddell had made arrangements for her to meet Detective Sergeant Adrian Paterson, the officer in charge of the Criminal Identification Squad of the Victoria Police CIB. An appointment was made for the following day.

Later that evening, Missing Persons having now assumed responsibility for the investigation, sent Steve Waddell and Neil Paterson to visit the Barbers' home to discuss the disappearance in more detail. It might not necessarily have meant that there were any obvious grounds for concern about the girl, but they certainly felt it was not a routine missing persons case and wanted more information to work with.

Although the family had previously made two lists of female friends, Missing Persons asked the Barbers to make a third list, this time adding simply everyone they could think of: faces from the past, friends from kindergarten, anyone . . .

The next day a girlfriend of Elizabeth Barber's urged Elizabeth to remember anybody who had lived close to the Barbers at Mont Albert: a face from the past came up, only tenuously linked with Rachel. Caroline Reid's name was included on the list for the first time.

On the following morning, Thursday, 11 March, David dePyle and Neil Paterson began a new series of inquiries – a trace on all calls coming into the Barbers' home the day before Rachel disappeared.

Meanwhile, Alison Guberek helped Detective Sergeant Adrian Paterson to assemble a computerised image of the young woman she had seen with Rachel on the tram. The finished image was circulated to the media for publication in subsequent stories.

Later in the day dePyle received a list of the incoming calls traced to the Barbers' house on that Sunday night. A silent number appeared on the list. Since silent number tracing requires further intelligence work, the police analyst had to wait until the next day for more information. Someone had used the number twice. One telephone call lasting fifteen minutes had been made at 5.24 p.m. and the second call lasting just over twenty-nine minutes followed soon after.

That Friday morning, the photofit of the young woman police wanted to interview in connection with the Rachel Barber disappearance was all over the press. The face was a mystery. And there was still no *concrete* evidence of foul play.

The Barbers had been asked to obtain samples of the sorts of clothing Rachel had been wearing on the day she disappeared, so that detectives could construct a dummy to erect in Prahran, where she had last been sighted.

Rachel Mannequin May Jog Memory, ran the Melbourne *Herald Sun* headline. But by now Missing Persons had the crucial piece of information: the identity of the mysterious caller who had phoned the Barber household the afternoon before Rachel disappeared.

19

SINGLE WHITE FEMALE

The person who had phoned the Barber house that afternoon had rung from a silent number that was listed to a Caroline Reed Robertson. David dePyle spent the morning exhausting his contacts. It emerged that Caroline Reed Robertson was a twenty-year-old single woman living alone in a rental flat in Trinian Street, Prahran, the inner-city suburb where Rachel had last been sighted. As far as he could determine, Caroline Reed Robertson was not known to the police, had no past record for any kind of misdemeanour, and did not have a current driver's licence.

Waddell and Paterson immediately left for the Prahran flat to see if the young woman in question could shed any light on Rachel's disappearance. It seemed at least that she might be responsible for the two mystery telephone calls. And a young woman of about her age had been sighted with Rachel. So the police hoped she would know something of the missing girl's whereabouts.

The detectives were already on their way when dePyle notified them via radio that the young woman they were looking for had changed her name. Caroline Reed Robertson had previously been called Caroline Reid.

The detectives knocked on the door of the tiny one-bedroom apartment in Trinian Street. It was a second-floor flat, around 120 metres from the tram stop on the corner of High Street and Williams Road where Rachel had last been seen. Despite repeated attempts by the police to raise a response, there appeared to be no one at home.

The officers made inquiries at the scene before returning to their office, where David dePyle had more information for them. The young woman worked for a telecommunications service provider in St Kilda Road, where she had been employed in an administrative role since November 1998. The detectives moved on to the young woman's workplace.

But Caroline Reed Robertson was not at work either. The officers talked briefly with her colleagues. Robertson appeared to have taken an unusual amount of sick leave over the past ten days or so – quite out of character for a young woman who rarely stayed away through illness.

But colleagues said that Robertson *had* mentioned the missing girl whose story was across the news. One worker recalled her saying that she had babysat Rachel, and that she was not worried because the girl was always running away. She had treated the disappearance as a joke – Rachel would turn up as she had in the past. But police knew that Rachel Barber had never gone missing before.

Later that morning police went to the offices of Peter Isaacson Publications, where Robertson had worked before starting her present job. The police then went to see Caroline Robertson's father, David Reid, a businessman, and spoke briefly to him about his daughter. He told the officers that she suffered from epilepsy, and mentioned owning a holiday property out at Kilmore, north of Melbourne. If the two girls had run away together, pondered police, then perhaps they had gone there.

Back at the St Kilda office David dePyle, waiting for the Barbers to arrive, had begun a random ring-around of all the real estate agents in the Prahran area in a bid to trace the agent for the Trinian Street flat. His efforts paid off, and the leasing agents agreed to lend the police the spare key to assist in their search for the tenant believed, at that stage, to be on the premises.

In the meantime, David dePyle contacted the Barbers on a mobile phone. They were not far from the St Kilda Road police complex where they were to meet dePyle for lunch. Did the name Caroline Robertson mean anything to them? Try 'Reid'. They knew a Caroline Reid. But Rachel didn't know her particularly well. She would be unlikely to regard her as an old friend.

By Friday afternoon the police were convinced that they were on the verge of finding Rachel. There was still no hint of foul play, but they were quite sure that Caroline Robertson was the 'old female friend' Rachel had told Manni about. They didn't have a motive for Rachel's disappearance but thought, perhaps, that the two girls had decided to run away together.

David dePyle did not want to see the Barbers wandering around the streets searching fruitlessly for their daughter, especially when police inquiries looked like locating her at any moment. Giving them lunch in the police canteen, and obtaining helpful information from them while the officers did their 'legwork' was probably the only constructive thing he could do. As a parent himself he certainly empathised with them, and recognised that they were worn out and anxious from twelve harrowing days of searching for Rachel.

They chatted well into the afternoon, dePyle believing Rachel's return to be imminent: it was just a matter of time before he could give the Barbers some good news. So he urged them to go home and wait.

At 5.25 p.m., dePyle, Waddell and Paterson had made a second visit to the Trinian Street flat. They were joined by Rae and Thatcher who had just completed inquiries with Rachel's family doctor. This time armed with keys, they made several attempts to alert the occupant of the flat by knocking on the door. No answer.

Paterson tried the keys in the lock but the door would not open. It appeared to be deadlocked from the inside, so someone must have been there. Neil Paterson made several calls to Caroline Robertson's telephone number. But on each occasion the answering machine cut in. He left a message asking her to come to the door.

'At this stage I had concerns for the welfare of the occupant of the flat,' said Neil Paterson in a later witness statement. 'I could see that a window was slightly open and subsequently the Melbourne Metropolitan Fire Brigade were called to assist in gaining entry.'

A fire officer put an extension ladder up to the window and was able to open it. He told the waiting officers he could see a female lying face down on the floor of the bedroom. He entered the flat via the window and let Neil Paterson inside. Paterson found Caroline Robertson lying at the foot of her bed. He detected a strong pulse in her neck and shouted to the other officers to ring for an ambulance.

A fire officer began to administer assistance to Robertson, who appeared to be drowsy. Police then noticed a packet of Tegretol, a drug commonly used to treat epilepsy, near the semiconscious woman. They believed at the time that Robertson might possibly have overdosed. As the police waited for the ambulance, they began to check the flat for signs of the missing teenager. They thought that perhaps the two girls were in cahoots, and half expected to find evidence of Rachel's presence in the untidy apartment. Paterson looked around, opened the door to the built-in wardrobe in Robertson's bedroom. But there was no sign of Rachel anywhere.

He telephoned Caroline's father, David Reid, asking him to come to the flat. The other officers continued the search. It was clear that a number of things had been carefully packed away. It appeared that Robertson was moving – packing up to leave, or just arriving. The video and lots of other things were in boxes.

Detective Sergeant Thatcher noticed two packed bags in the lounge room, and what appeared to be a container of hair dye lying on the floor. Caroline's hair showed signs of green rinse. They found a number of notebooks, some apparently blank, lying around, and a bag of size 8 clothes – obviously not clothing belonging to Caroline, who appeared to be quite overweight.

Perhaps the clothing belonged to Rachel? Had she been there then? The clothes were collected to show to the Barbers for identification. Shortly afterwards David Reid arrived. Ambulance officers were giving his daughter medical assistance. He told police it was possible that Caroline had had an epileptic fit.

At 6.55 p.m. Paterson accompanied Caroline in the back of the ambulance to the nearby Alfred Hospital's Emergency Department.

But police were already beginning to wonder what was going on. They had noticed Rachel's name on a number of handwritten documents found lying around the flat. Was it Rachel's hand-writing or Caroline's? They saw a reference to what appeared to be a planned train trip to Sydney. So maybe Caroline *was* about to leave Melbourne – or perhaps both girls might have been planning to leave . . . together. Perhaps Rachel was staying somewhere else, and had already left with her train ticket? Perhaps Caroline was covering for her and planning to join her later? But there was no evidence of that, either. There was really no hard evidence of any-thing at all. And what were all these notes about? There were so many of them . . . and lists. Caroline Reed Robertson was obvi-ously a prolific listmaker.

The detectives gathered up the two packed bags and another bag of size 8 clothes. Later that evening, the Barbers received a call from police asking them to come in and identify a few items, including the clothing which did not appear to belong to Robertson.

The detectives also seized some rubber gloves, a few bank receipts and other items – including the handwritten notes. They took a couple of notepads, some partially filled, others with pages missing. It was hoped that these documents might hold clues to Rachel's whereabouts. But the notes appeared to be of a far more personal nature. Baffling really. They were scribblings *about* Rachel Barber.

20

'ALL THINGS COME TO PASS'

Detective Sergeant Thatcher had the giant rubbish bins at the front of the flats searched, as well as the laundries on each floor. But there was no indication anywhere that Rachel had ever been at Trinian Street. Steve Waddell decided to arrange for an unmarked police car to monitor the region, just in case she was near by. He wondered if she might even be in the vicinity now, perhaps watching activities and waiting for a safe moment to return.

After finding the handwritten document referring to a Sydney trip, Steve Waddell instructed someone to direct police in the Victorian country town of Benalla to halt the Sydney-bound train later that evening before it crossed the border into New South Wales. Just after 8 p.m. local police officers stopped the train. No sign of Rachel.

The flat was secured and remained under police surveillance throughout the coming weekend. Thatcher and Rae remained behind until back-up could be sent from Prahran police station.

The remaining detectives from the Missing Persons Unit returned to the office, taking some of the material they'd found – a couple of notebooks, a diary, and some scribblings on loose sheets of paper. They hoped that these might lead them to Rachel. But all along, dePyle could not help feeling that there was something more to this case than he'd originally envisaged.

The detectives examined the notes more carefully. Among the documents were some partly legible notes referring to Rachel, but they could not be properly deciphered. One appeared to be a carefully charted character profile of the missing teenager, containing personal information such as her date of birth and the name of the hospital where she'd been born.

Then there were other notes about Rachel's family. They struck a particularly uneasy chord among the police. Listed neatly down the page, in impeccable handwriting, someone had noted the full names and birthdays of Rachel Barber's younger sisters and personal background information on her parents, Michael and Elizabeth. The author of the notes appeared to know this family very well indeed. The notes revealed that Rachel's mother Elizabeth was the daughter of prominent Australian children's writer Ivan Southall. She was described in the profile as a religious woman and a 'disciplinarian'.

If it was Caroline Robertson who had written this information, it was clear to everyone she'd been doing her homework. She made mention of Michael Barber's birthplace in England, and noted he was a toymaker and knew something of his work history. The detail suggested an unusual level of monitoring. It charted Rachel's progress through her childhood in the country, describing her romantically as a 'free spirit' who'd run barefoot. It followed her progress closely from her youthful dating habits and dancing to her subsequent decision to leave school in Year 9 to pursue a professional dancing career. It was up-to-date on Rachel's more recent activities too: Rachel's modelling, her love of classical ballet, and her boyfriend.

Robertson wrote in almost glowing terms about her young subject, describing her as a 'strikingly attractive' teenager with a dancer's body, clear pale skin and 'hypnotic' green eyes. Rachel had experimented only recently with hair colouring. The author of the document had noted that too.

There was also the Barbers' home address and telephone number on the bottom. And in the top right-hand corner was another notation: 'Corner Church. Dance Factory Richmond.' Overleaf, there was another even more peculiar list itemising personality characteristics. The police assumed they were those of the missing girl. There was a growing sense that the subject of this romanticised prose held some weird fascination for the writer: she seemed to be almost in awe of her. Rachel Barber, according to the notes, was a 'wild free spirit' who lived life on the edge; a simple yet complicated girl of enormous talent and contradictions. She was a fiercely independent girl who was 'passionate, determined, cheeky, loyal and honest,' with a moody and mysterious personality. She was described as argumentative and difficult, 'eclectic and kooky, crazy, funky and cool.' This was a teenager who didn't suffer fools gladly but had, claimed the writer, a wonderful charisma. It was a list that brimmed with admiration.

But it was then that the police noticed something else. More ominously, in what appeared to be Caroline's handwriting, they saw the words down the bottom of the page, 'All things come to pass.'

'It was fifty-fifty,' recalls David dePyle. 'At that stage we thought Rachel still might turn up at the flat after being out shopping or somewhere else, and maybe this older girl had just developed some unbelievable fascination with Rachel Barber. But then again . . .'

Nothing felt right about this case. The officers studied the notes again. But there were pages missing, and the indentations left behind were too faint to be legible.

Other scribblings listed dates of the month and figures. Scanty handwritten notes, a sheaf of documents. The police began to have a creeping idea that something untoward might have happened to Rachel.

Sitting in the back of the ambulance, on his way to hospital with Caroline, Neil Paterson knew nothing of the notes. He arrived at the Alfred Hospital around 7 p.m. and waited as she was admitted to Emergency. Caroline was conscious and answering questions from hospital staff. David Reid arrived about twenty-five minutes later and spoke to his daughter. After a brief conversation with Neil Paterson, Mr Reid left the hospital, returning a short time later. Caroline had a CT scan of her brain to rule out cerebral bleeding, a tumour, or build-up of fluid around the brain. She was given a lumbar puncture to check for an infection. She had also had an electrocardiograph and chest X-ray by the time her father returned. Neil Paterson then talked to him about Caroline and Rachel.

At 9.45 p.m. medical staff said that Caroline was responding well to questions and that it would be appropriate for Paterson to speak with her. He wanted to determine Rachel Barber's whereabouts, of course. But he was not prepared for what transpired.

'Caroline, can you hear me?' asked the detective.

'Yes,' she replied.

'Caroline, my name is Neil, I'm a policeman. Do you understand that?'

'Yes.'

'I want to talk to you about Rachel, is that okay?'

'Yes.'

'Do you know where Rachel is?'

'Yes.'

'Where is she?'

'She's dead.'

'How did that happen?'

'It was an accident, I killed her.'

The officer, shocked, gave Caroline a formal caution and told her about her rights to communicate with a lawyer. He asked her if she understood her rights and wished to exercise them before he continued speaking with her. She replied, 'No.'

'Are you positive she's dead or can we still help her?' he continued.

'No, she's dead.'

He asked Robertson where Rachel's body was. She said it was up at her father's farm at Kilmore – buried near a clump of trees. She said she'd called a removal van to take it there.

'Who helped you?' asked the detective.

'I can't remember.'

'How did she die?'

'I can't remember – I'm tired.'

'I must again inform you that you are not obliged to say or do anything, but anything you say or do may be given in evidence. Do you still understand this?'

'Yes.'

'Do you want to speak to your father or a solicitor?' he asked.

'I'm tired,' said Caroline.

Paterson left the treatment room, informing David Reid that Rachel Barber was dead. Caroline had said it was an accident.

140

Rachel's body was somewhere at Kilmore. The policeman couldn't imagine what must have been going through David Reid's head, but he appeared shocked at the news, too. He said he knew the location of the clump of trees Caroline had referred to. It was not far from his house on the property – near a place where his children had once buried a dead koala. Mr Reid, no doubt believing the police were investigating an accidental death, went to contact a solicitor for his daughter.

Around 10 p.m. that Friday Neil Paterson rang his boss, Detective Senior Sergeant Steve Waddell, at the Missing Persons Unit, with the news. Waddell immediately contacted the Homicide Squad and arranged for a crime scene guard to be stationed at both the Trinian Street flat and David Reid's farming property at Kilmore.

Caroline was placed in custody. No one except hospital staff was allowed to approach or speak to her without police permission. Hospital security was informed. Later that evening a lawyer went to the Alfred Hospital and spoke to Paterson. The lawyer, Jonathan Mott, had a short conversation with Caroline and left at around 11 p.m. At 11.35 Detective Senior Constable Hamilton relieved Neil Paterson at the hospital, and Paterson returned to the Missing Persons Unit to conduct further inquiries.

By midnight local police officers had been deployed to the Kilmore property, which became the site of extensive police surveillance. Paterson returned to the Alfred Hospital again, this time accompanied by his boss Steve Waddell. At around 1.30 on the Saturday morning, they escorted a dishevelled Caroline Robertson from the hospital's Emergency Department and placed her in the back of an unmarked police vehicle. They drove her to the watchhouse at the Moorabbin police station, where she was placed in the cells at 2 a.m.

21

CHARGED

By the time Neil Paterson resumed duty at 11.45 a.m. on Saturday, 13 March, Detective Sergeant Paul Ross of the Homicide Squad had taken over what was now a murder investigation. Homicide detectives and officers from Missing Persons held a meeting at the Kilmore police station. Forensic experts were already being briefed, as were photographic specialists and officers from the Victoria Police Crime Scenes Department.

Back in Melbourne, Paul Ross took charge of the handwritten material housed in the Missing Persons property store. It had been hoped by everyone on the team that this information would have helped them find Rachel Barber alive and safe.

Neil Paterson joined Thatcher and Ross for an initial interview with Caroline, which was to be videotaped. Caroline had been collected from the cells at the Moorabbin watchhouse and brought to the Homicide Squad offices in St Kilda Road. Thatcher recalls providing her with numerous cups of water but also remembers her continually declining offers of food. She was noticeably quiet.

At around the time the Barbers were leaving their home to drive Rachel's boyfriend Emmanuel to his dancing class in Richmond, Detective Senior Sergeant Steve Waddell had obtained written permission from David Reid to search his Kilmore property. David

Reid had also drawn a map of the region to help police in their search.

The initial videotaped interview with Caroline lasted only a couple of minutes and was suspended to allow her to consult her solicitor, David O'Doherty. She was also allowed to speak to her father.

During the early hours of Saturday morning Homicide detectives had obtained a warrant to conduct a fresh search of the primary crime scene at Trinian Street. It was too dark to begin any kind of search at the Kilmore property until daybreak. The property had been sealed off and placed under guard as a secondary crime scene. But it was possible to examine the Prahran flat more closely. New clues might be found there to build a case against the suspect. So Detective Senior Sergeant Lucio Rovis and Detective Sergeant Ross visited the flat with officers from Police Video Operations and Photographics and began to comb it for evidence.

A number of documents and notebooks were photographed along with a bundle of women's fashion magazines and other items, including an extraordinarily large print of Edvard Munch's famous painting *The Scream*. Samples of hair were collected from the lounge and bedroom along with some from a shoe in the bedroom.

On Saturday afternoon at Kilmore, the team made its way from the tiny police station to David Reid's holiday home, relieving the crime scene guard of his duties and driving up the long track to the brick house on top of the hill. Police cars were parked behind the house. To the north-east there was a gate leading to a dam. On the eastern side of the dam the officers could see a small clump of trees. They made their way to this grove and began an examination of the area.

Thatcher and Waddell saw two small crosses in the ground. One bore the name 'Lucy', which they guessed must have been the pet koala. The other bore the name 'Little Mate', presumably also a pet.

Both officers noticed a strong smell coming from a patch of ground showing signs of increased fly activity. Thatcher's right foot sank into the ground, and as he stood back he saw that the earth had been disturbed and that there were signs of recent digging.

He alerted the other officers and the area was carefully photographed as it was excavated. It became evident to the team that they had found a shallow, crude grave. Shortly before 3.30 the detectives located what appeared to be a human body, lying in a foetal position and wrapped in blankets. The detectives were convinced that they had finally found Rachel Barber.

The entire region, including surrounding bushland, was searched. A shovel and hoe found in a nearby machinery shed were photographed, together with many other items. Two large rubbish bins were searched, as was a 44-gallon drum that had been used as an incinerator. And partially burnt paper with handwriting on it was photographed and collected as well.

As the gravesite was excavated and photographed in stages, it was revealed that the body had been buried with a ligature around its neck.

During the evening Dr Shelley Robertson, Senior Forensic Pathologist from the Victorian Institute of Forensic Medicine, visited the scene and conducted an official examination of the body. She pronounced life extinct and the body was taken away for an autopsy.

Detectives returned to the property again a few days later, when Search and Rescue divers scoured several dams on the property in the hope of finding fresh evidence. A large contingent of personnel from the State Emergency Service also assisted police in an extensive line search. Nothing relevant was discovered.

With David Reid's permission, detectives also searched the house on the property and more items were taken for closer scrutiny.

Back in Melbourne on that Saturday morning, the police began to interview Caroline again. Her lawyer was now present and, apart from confirming her name, age, address and residency status, she had chosen to exercise her legal right to refuse to answer any further questions. That interview was suspended after a few moments. In the interim, Paul Ross was updated on evidence discovered during the search of Caroline's flat. During the night another collection of deeply disturbing writings relating to Rachel Barber had been found. The handwritten notes were sometimes clearly written and easy to read, sometimes scrappy and incomplete. Some apparently innocent and empty notepads may have held vital clues to other missing pages, so these were sent to the Victoria Forensic Science Centre in Macleod for closer examination. Later that Saturday evening Paul Ross seized more items from the flat, including forensic samples, receipts, clothing, a telephone answering machine and assorted books on the occult.

It appeared that the suspect did indeed harbour some sort of unnatural interest in Rachel Barber. Why though? It hardly seemed credible. Caroline was just twenty years old and had no kind of criminal record. But the evidence suggested a sinister scenario beyond the comprehension of even the most experienced Homicide detectives. More disturbing still was the discovery of an application for a birth certificate bearing Rachel Barber's details, apparently in Caroline Robertson's handwriting. And there were notes recording very personal observations on Rachel and her family.

It appeared to the officers studying the notes that some kind of plan might have been formulated by Robertson to lure the young girl to the flat.

The police were keen to speak further with Caroline. They wanted to ask her about her movements on the day of Rachel Barber's disappearance. And they wanted to question her about the handwritten notes. She had already volunteered a confession in hospital, but today, as was her right, she was saying little more.

At 1.19 p.m. on Saturday, Detective Sergeant Ross turned on the videotape and began a second interview, during which Caroline admitted that she had changed her name by deed poll. But this was the only question she answered. To everything else she responded, 'I don't want to answer any questions.'

After Ross had suspended the interview he received a telephone call telling him that a body believed to be that of Rachel Barber had been discovered buried on the property at Kilmore.

Later that afternoon he recommenced the videotaped interview and again it was suspended to allow Caroline to speak to her lawyer. By 4.54 p.m., when the interview was recommenced for the final time, Caroline had developed a headache and had received medication. She was told that Rachel's body had been found at Kilmore and was asked if she had anything to say about that. Her response was the same: 'I don't want to answer any questions.'

Paul Ross had shown Caroline samples of the handwritten documents seized from her flat. He asked if she had seen them before. He asked who had written the notes in the diary planner. Who had filled out the birth certificate in Rachel Barber's name? Who had made the jottings and lists about Rachel Barber? Was that her handwriting? He showed her the size 8 clothing taken from Trinian Street. Did she know anything about these items? Did she know Rachel Barber's mother's maiden name? Had she ever rented a post-office box? Caroline refused to answer.

The detective ended the interview, telling Caroline she was the suspect in a murder case and warning her that she was shortly to be charged with killing Rachel Barber. He then requested permission for the police to obtain samples for forensic testing. These would include fingerprints, together with samples of hair, dental impressions and blood samples taken in the presence of a doctor of her choice.

Caroline asked to speak with her lawyer, though it had been explained to her that as she was a suspect in a murder case, police could obtain a court order forcing her to comply with the request.

After being cautioned in relation to the pending charge, she was allowed a brief discussion with her lawyer. Permission was given – for the fingerprinting only, not the biological samples.

By evening, Caroline Reed Robertson had been formally charged with the murder of Rachel Elizabeth Barber and remanded in custody at the Fitzroy police station to appear in court on the following Monday morning.

PART TWO

Murder

I must say after many, many homicide cases one has seen, I have certainly not come across a more frustrating or more irrational taking of a human life.

DEFENCE BARRISTER COLIN LOVITT, QC

22

SUNDAY

Early Morning, 14 March

I woke around 4 a.m. The doctor had left Temazepam tablets to help us sleep. The family had insisted we take them. But I was awake, lying beside Mike and two sleeping daughters.

Rachel, I thought. Rachel, come home.

We had said prayers for Rachel. The Salvation Army had been present because Lindsay and another Captain had tried so hard to find our lovely girl. They'd offered to say prayers and everyone had sat in a circle, even those who were not Christians. And we'd prayed for Rachel's soul. We'd thanked God for bringing her home. Only Ashleigh-Rose had left the room; she'd busied herself arranging flowers.

And then John Blacker, a priest friend of my parents who hadn't seen me since primary school, came too, and had said prayers.

I lay there in our bed, thinking and not thinking. Lying with my eyes closed. Lying with my eyes opened in the dark room, shadows slowly becoming distinguishable.

I got up and walked down the hallway. I opened Rachel's door. My mother rested in her murdered grand-daughter's bed.

I quietly lifted the corner of the doona and slithered in.

'Roll over,' came a soft voice.

I rolled over, my mother protecting me in her arms. We lay together, looking at Rachel's night sky.

'Oh, Mummy,' I cried, 'I've lost my baby.'

'I know,' she said. 'I know.'

We sat on the back veranda. It was about eight or nine in the morning. Our search really had come to an end.

My sister Robbie came out with her smoke and coffee, pen and paper.

'The press will want to see you,' she said.

'Yes,' answered Mike. 'I never thought we'd find ourselves in such a bizarre predicament.'

'I don't know what I can say,' I said, 'apart from saying thank you to everyone who helped.'

'I've put together a statement,' said Robbie. 'It says everything you've expressed in the last twenty-four hours. I hope you don't mind.'

'No, I don't mind, Robbie,' I said. 'Don't you realise how much we need to depend on you?'

Robbie doesn't like to accept compliments, so she ignored my comments. 'How does this sound . . . ?'

Statement for the Media by
Robbie Glover (Aunt of Rachel Barber)

Elizabeth and Michael are endeavouring to bear the unbearable. They are being supported by loving family and friends. We have all been devastated by the death of their beloved daughter Rachel.

Elizabeth and Michael want the family of the woman charged with the murder of Rachel to know that they feel nothing but compassion for them.

Rachel's burning light has been dimmed but will burn bright in our hearts for ever. She will always be young, beautiful, happy, smiling and dancing in our hearts.

We would like to thank Elizabeth and Michael's family and friends; Emmanuel, his parents, brothers

13. The funeral, 24 March 1999. Outside St Hilary's Anglican Church in Kew, Melbourne. From left to right - Elizabeth, Ashleigh-Rose, Heather, Mike, Domenic Carella, Rosa Carella.

14. Victoria Police photograph of Caroline Reed Robertson's flat in Trinian Street, Prahran.

15. Caroline Reed Robertson being led from the Supreme Court after changing her plea to guilty. October, 2000.

16. John Spooner's court drawings of Caroline Reed Robertson: the first, after her arrest in 1999; the second, a year later at the Supreme Court at the time of her plea.

17. The Barber family - Mike, Heather, Elizabeth and Ashleigh-Rose, outside the Supreme Court after sentencing in November, 2000.

18. Aerial view of the property at Kilmore, indicating the location of the burial site.

19. Homicide detectives locate a shallow grave in a grove of trees on Saturday, 13 March 1999.

20. The murder weapon – a double-knotted slip ligature prepared from a telecommunications cable.

and family; students and teachers of the Dance Factory; shopkeepers of Richmond; Rachel's school friends old and new; the Salvation Army; the Missing Persons Squad and Homicide Squad; the Crime Department of Victoria Police; our friends David and Cathy and everyone who helped with posters; and the street kids of Melbourne.'

'That's just perfect,' said Mike, getting up and giving her a cuddle.

She started to cry. But could she have realised how caring we had found our family? How supportive? How ready they were to pick up our pieces? To take phone calls, to arrange house cleaning, arrange visits with the funeral director and the ministers? Our family organised our lives for us.

Ian, my cousin, organised the bills. Little things we had never thought of. Little things which would have developed into big things, like the run-in I had with the credit card lady . . .

'I'm sorry I haven't paid,' I tried to explain. 'I forgot.'

'What, for two months?'

'My daughter's been murdered.'

'So, that's not my problem. I just want you to pay.'

Some time in the afternoon the phone rang yet again.

Mike answered it and after a short while came out saying, 'It's Jeff Kennett.'

This Sunday afternoon was such a haze that I can't remember Mr Kennett's exact words. But the Premier of Victoria said how devastated he and his wife Felicity were for our family, and wanted to express their sympathy. They had been following Rachel's story in the press. If there was anything they could do for us, just ask, and Mr Kennett would see if they could help. We could contact him by ringing the Chief of Staff at his parliamentary office.

This was a caring phone call from another empathising parent. It meant a great deal to us.

When I told my sister Robbie she became very animated. 'Did he really say that?'

'Yes,' I said.

'Do you know what you need him to do?' She grabbed a pen and an exercise book. 'You need to ask him for funding for a special police liaison officer to be attached to the Missing Persons Unit to help parents from *day one* when their children go missing in suspicious circumstances.'

'Yes,' responded Mike enthusiastically.

We were not concerned with internal police politics, not then. It is something we have come, in time, to learn about and accept. But on that Sunday all we could think of was, yes, that's it. That's where we can help. We didn't want other parents to encounter similar struggles with the local police. So Robbie contacted Jeff Kennett's Victorian Parliamentary Chief of Staff who conveyed our thoughts to the Premier.

The next few weeks were a blur of funeral arrangements. We had to cope with two cancelled funeral dates because the coroner's office required further autopsies. We had DNA tests to prove we really were the victim's parents. This was because, firstly, Rachel's dental records were not up to date and, secondly, because we were strongly advised for the sake of the trial not to view her body.

In between the horror of '*life with no meaning*' and readjusting to the absence of the person who really was the dynamo in our family, we discovered that the world really *did* revolve around Rachel Barber. 'Rachel, the world does not revolve around you,' said Mike when she was in one of her demanding 'notice me' moods. But the truth was, she really was the organiser of events – the centre of daily concerts, the reason for outings to the city. And now she was gone.

23
_____

BURIAL

The third week of March

We were driving past the old Lilydale Cemetery in the foothills of the ranges east of Melbourne, looking for somewhere for Rachel's burial. *Burial.* An odd-sounding word considering the activity was going to involve one's dynamic fifteen-year-old daughter.

'Why don't you go and look at the new cemetery in Lilydale?' my mother had said. 'A friend of mine was buried there recently. It has a lovely outlook.'

So my brother Drew drove us, with Robbie and Ashleigh-Rose, to the cemetery. We drove past the crematorium, past the lawn burial sites which were marked with simple loving flat plaques. Past the ornate miniature mausoleums, past the lawn burials with headstones, and on to the cemetery office.

A short while later a woman led us to a new area where there were only two or three headstones in the row. The headstones bordered native gardens that were watered by underground hoses. I noticed that a 28-year-old man was buried near by. So she'd be close to another young person, I thought.

'There're not too many people here,' I said. 'She may be lonely.' An odd thing to say, but we were in an odd situation.

'It's a growing business,' the woman replied. 'She won't be lonely for long.'

I laughed nervously.

'What do you think, Ashleigh-Rose?'

'There's a lovely view through to the mountains,' she replied.

'Yes,' said Robbie. 'And that will be nice for you when you visit.'

'And when we're old we can sit in that gazebo or shelter from the sun.'

'Yes, it's a lovely spot,' said the cemetery woman.

It felt as if we were making a land purchase. Small as it was, I suppose we were.

'Would you like the plot to be one deep, two deep or three deep?' the woman asked. 'Often when young people die we find parents like to buy a three-deep plot so they can join their child. After all, you are going to be your daughter's only family.'

Until my 96-year-old grandmother died about ten years earlier and was buried on top of my grandfather in the same grave, I had always had the impression that people were buried individually.

'And if you wish,' she went on, 'other family members who have been cremated may be interred here as well.'

It almost sounded like one of those sales on television where you hear a voice-over: 'But wait, there's more. Order now and receive a free set of . . . ' interments?

'Three-deep,' I said, looking at the spot, feeling peculiar. The sensation was something I had never experienced before and hopefully never will again. It was like a birth – in reverse – only more painful, and a pain shared by Mike who held my hand.

'You know, Mum and Dad, Rachel wasn't afraid of dying,' eleven-year-old Ashleigh-Rose said.

'Pardon?' said Mike.

'Well, Rachel said that I should never fear death. She said when we die Jesus is there to look after us, even if we die as little children. She said so in one of our sister chats. You know, when we used to sit with our legs crossed on our beds.'

I thought, good on you, Rachel. Bravo. That's my girl. It was as if she was already speaking from the grave.

'Well,' I said, 'even though Rachel said she wasn't afraid of dying, I think she would have preferred to have lived a lot longer, but isn't it lovely she had the opportunity of sharing this thought with you?'

We selected the only plot of land Rachel will ever own and looked across the sun-parched valley which, in years to come, as we stand before our daughter's grave, will change. An eagle flying high in the sky came to rest on a gum tree. The same gum will probably grow twice the size, be struck by lightning, and be bulldozed with two dozen others to one day make way for a housing estate. Wasn't Burwood cemetery once surrounded by pasture and apple orchards? And now it is in the middle of suburbia. Everything changes, I thought. Everything.

We were conscious that a lot of young people would be present at Rachel's funeral and that for many it would be their first experience of a funeral. We didn't want them to be scared, and directed one of the ministers of St Hilary's to help us create a funeral that would celebrate Rachel's short life rather than centre on the heartbreak. Let her friends choose some of the music, I suggested, and please involve the minister from Balwyn who had known Rachel for four years.

I deliberately chose not to wear black at Rachel's funeral. Sometimes I have regretted this decision, but we wanted it to be a beautiful service in memory of a beautiful person.

The greatest honour Ted did for Rachel was not to wear his cap to her funeral. I do not think he realised how much I appreciated this display of love for her. Over the seventeen years we have known Ted, and out of all the visits we had shared, I had not once seen him without his denim cap.

Many friends of Rachel knew she was a spiritual girl. A minister who had first met Rachel while teaching her religious instruction in Grade 6 said in his condolence letter:

> . . . A few years ago the son of a friend of mine died and he said that Michael left behind a sweet fragrance. At the time I thought it an odd thing to say in the midst of grief but now that we have been thinking of Rachel every day and remembering the part of her life we knew, I am beginning to understand what

he meant. She was such a sweet child and there is a fragrance in recalling her personality . . .

Then she began going to St Hilary's and one consequence of that was the loveliest memory I have of her: kneeling and leafing through my prayer book. She said she thought that with the help of some friends she could start an evening youth service at St Augustine's: a band, with catchy choruses just like St Hilary's, with Rachel pulling focus somewhere up front. I was very encouraged and I loved her optimism. It was easy for her to believe that it could happen. I would hate to think it hurt her that this particular plan came to nothing. I rather think she simply moved on to other things.

My lasting memory of Rachel is of an adolescent who showed no awkwardness with older adults. She always seemed genuinely pleased to see my wife and I, on our afternoon walks, and there was never a sign of an inward sigh that said, 'Here come those wrinklies again.' She was on the level we knew her, easy, humorous, polite and very smiley . . .

And then there was a youth group leader at St Hilary's who said, 'Rachel had this ability to make people she knew feel so special and through her hugs, huge smile and open nature she made me feel very close to her, and really loved . . . Over the last week as I prayed for her and you both, and (like so many others I'm sure) spent time driving the streets of Prahran at night looking for her, I was able to reflect on how special Rachel is to my life, and how vividly her many qualities came flooding to mind. Please be constantly reminded of the joy and friendship she gave to so many, including me.

'As I remember how tightly Rachel used to hug me, I love to think of how much tighter God has his arms wrapped around her right now . . . '

The funeral was somewhat of an anticlimax because it took so long to happen. We even withdrew from our family to Harmers

Haven the weekend before the funeral, where we took long walks. There was time for private reflection – and I screamed across the ocean from the edges of the rockpools.

It was Ashleigh-Rose, the voice of Rachel's eleven-year-old sister, who most effectively seemed to capture our family's situation at the funeral itself . . .

The night before the funeral, people were allowed to go and see Rachel's coffin at the funeral parlour. I cried my heart out. Mum, Dad, Heather and I were able to go in by ourselves for a while. Heather wanted to try and lift the coffin lid to see if it really was Rachel inside. Mum freaked, and said she hoped it was nailed down, because Heather really tried to give it a hard tug. But Mum and Dad had said Rachel had been dead too long and that was why we couldn't see her. I thought, in the movies, relatives get to see the dead in their coffins.

I was almost on top of her coffin. It was very difficult, especially when everybody came in and said, 'Oh, I'm so sorry, it must be hard for you.' I was very annoyed because they had no idea what it felt like. Some did, like her boyfriend Emmanuel Carella, his family and all of Rachel's friends.

It's hard to believe Rachel is dead, and it's different because she was murdered. I didn't get to say goodbye or tell her how much I loved her. It's harder still because I didn't even see her the last day. I said goodnight to her the night before. She said, 'Love you, Ash.'

When a grandmother dies of old age or of a sickness it still hurts but at least you know it's coming. I didn't know this was coming and that's why it hurt even more. I don't think I'll get to sleep for a long time. I don't ever want to sleep by myself again. I'm too scared to.

Rachel's friends gave the funeral man letters and poems to put in Rachel's coffin. Mum and Dad took photocopies of these. I gave Rachel a letter as well. This is what I said:

> *To my dearest sister Rachel,*
> *I love you a lot and I will never not love you. It was not your time and we all know that. It's no*

one's fault that you died, only Caroline's fault. You had a long time to go if Caroline had not been born. I wish I never knew her sister because if I had never known her, Caroline would not have met you, and you would still be here.

I miss you a lot and I wish you were still here but you're not, and I will have to live with that. Everyone loves you and will always miss you. I will never forget you, Rachel, and I hope maybe one day you will visit us. I hope you will never forget me and the family.

I hope you didn't go through any pain when you died.

Love always,
Your little sister, Ashleigh-Rose.

We went to Rachel's funeral in big white cars. When we got to the church I saw the press. I did not like the press on this day because they took my parents away from me even before we got into the church. This was just so all you people out there could know what was going on. I'm sorry, but if you wanted to know then you should have come to the funeral.

I didn't care that they were filming the funeral because I couldn't see them and they didn't take me away from my parents.

I was okay during the funeral until the song 'Finally Found' came on. I started to cry then because I tried to sing it. This song makes me sad because it was the song Rachel dedicated to her boyfriend Emmanuel the year before. They told me I could kiss her coffin but I didn't and I'm very sorry I didn't. I didn't even blow a kiss.

We sat in the front car for a long time after the funeral, while people talked. People came to our car doors. One of my friends handed me letters from friends from my old school. Rachel's car moved in front of us and as a long slow trail of cars left the church I opened the top letter and read it out loud:

Dear Ashleigh-Rose,
I am really really sorry for what my sister did. I still want to be your friend even though I know that

158

you don't want to be mine. I want to tell you something that my dad told me. 'I still believe that she is dancing with the fairies.' Rachel was a beautiful fairy. She danced like a dream. I'm just glad that she had you in her life.

I still can't believe that my sister killed someone that I knew. It just seems like a dream. In my dream Caroline is in hospital after having an epileptic fit and Rachel is probably out shopping or something. I know how hard it is. I know because I'm going through this too.

Love from your (maybe) friend,
Catherine
P.S. Remember, she is dancing with the fairies.

Ashleigh-Rose never replied to this letter, the letter written to her by Caroline's youngest sister. After hearing Ashleigh-Rose read it, the driver said, 'How do you cope with all this?'

Ashleigh-Rose folded her letter. 'Shouldn't I have read the letter?'

I looked at the insecurity of my daughter and thought, well it probably wasn't very good timing. But I said, 'No, it's fine, Ashleigh-Rose, don't worry.'

The pain, I thought, the pain.

About a month after the funeral, I became aware of my fear of forgetting 'the Rachel within'. I didn't want to lose touch with her essence. So I decided to write letters to her as if she was still living. It was then that I began a journey of letters and poems.

deep beneath the soil
your body rests
clothed in rosewood
surrounded by letters and poems
toys and shoes
ballet shoes and Spice Girl shoes
dressed in lace underwear
and your last solo costume

you lay there
bones and dried flesh
even so, beautiful would your skeleton be
a beautiful skeleton
dressed in seashells
dancing feet resting their dancing toes
buried beneath nine feet of cold earth
killed by a cold heart
a cold fish

the warmth of your smile
your being and serenity
can never be frozen from recognition
when people think of Rachel Barber
memories remain vivid
vivid as you were – as you are
energetic with life
full-on yet also shy
timid of things new
I am so glad you were found – in your shallow grave
and brought home to those
who loved their dear sweet Rachel
always remembered
forever in their memory – their hearts

LETTERS TO RACHEL –
EXTRACTS FROM THE FIRST YEAR

The first letter . . .

24 May 1999

My darling Rachel,

I don't even know what day you died on, or whether you died in pain. I'm sorry. Deeply sorry, from the depths of my soul, we were unable to save you. I do not understand. I will never understand. Fifteen years old. Only fifteen.

We have shifted worlds. Somewhere your family has taken a right-angle and ended up in this surreal world. Caught out, unable to reach the real world left behind. Somewhere our world continues around us, abandoning us in this living nightmare. But then, there is yet another world. Your world.

I am comatosed. I don't know why this is happening to you. I have no answers, but pray you are safe in God's heaven, wherever that may be. I pray you didn't grieve too long for Manni, or for us. I pray you have settled in to your new world, for surely your heaven must feel as surreal for you as our leftover world does for us. I pray we are not tearing your spirit apart. Let your spirit dance, sweetheart.

I think Caroline may have been fifteen when we first met her, perhaps younger. Poor girl – broken girl, a girl with a broken soul to take someone so loved. Did she know love as you do? As you still do? I don't know. I fear this stems from *her* feeling of abandonment. A feeling of loneliness. But to murder? And why you?

I didn't think you were dead. Didn't feel it, and that's why my faith in God has not been broken. You are still living in spirit. I thank God that Jesus died on the cross. I thank God that Jesus wept. Jesus wept. For you, as I do.

Do I ever want to grow old? I don't think so. But your father and sisters need me. I must stay. But to think I won't see you until I am old. Rachel . . . Rachel . . . it is so hard to accept you are no longer here. I need your warmth, your love, your cuddles, your dance, your smile. Yes, even those times you were cross with me, and I with you.

I'm sorry you struggled through school. I'm sorry I didn't protect you or allow you to be courageous when you believed you were wronged at a past dance school. I'm sorry I nagged you about looking for part-time work. But I didn't know of any impending evil plotting against you. You were, at last, so happy. And then . . . oh, it was all so sudden.

Everybody misses you, Rachel. You are loved by so many people. You have so much to give, so much loving to share. I grimace at thinking of you in a past tense. You will always be real. Every day from your birth I have thought of you, even if not in active thought, I have always been conscious of your being. The same for your sisters. Why then, just because someone stole you from our physical lives, should I not think of you still, in this new present tense, every day? I still have three daughters.

Stop. I'm going to wake. This pain must go away. My heart is broken.

I failed you. Didn't teach you enough awareness of the dangers in this world. What did she lure you with, what lies did she tell? Evil and wickedness festering, waiting to slaughter our angel. But you were only robbed of your earthly life. I am so sad. So deeply sad. My beautiful, vibrant, bubbly Rachel.

We picked up the kitten I said you could have the day before you went missing; four weeks after you went missing,

Humphrey became your parting gift. I haven't been too impressed by the way he claws up curtains, but still, he is a lovely kitten, and he is your kitten. You would have liked him.

I always taught you to respect the police force and now I have lost trust in them. They let you down. They let us down. How many others are let down?

Rachel, I want to hold you in my arms, to kiss you, to stroke your hair. There is no justice in your death. I grieve and need comfort but do not know where I can turn. I need to share my grieving. To cry in someone's arms. To be cradled and comforted and be allowed to cry, to share tears, to share grief and not be strong. I am not depressed. I am grieving. I have lost you. I gave birth to you, nursed you, sang and danced with you, even in the rain. Ran up sand dunes and walked along the beach. Played games and read to you, even spanked you and shouted at you. I sewed clothes for you. Sang 'Silent Night' to you. Drove you to dance classes and took you to the theatre. Watched you dance in the State Theatre aisles. Journeyed through school days and church days with you. Birthday parties and concerts and ballet exams. Phone-call-too-long fights and radio-too-loud fights. I laughed and cried with you. I watched you sleep, and felt you safe.

I never dreamt we'd lose you so young. You always gave me cuddles and kisses. Even at fifteen, you always kissed me goodnight.

I cannot believe you are dead. I cannot believe you were murdered. An ugly word for our beautiful first born. I love you, Rachel,
    Love, Mum.

25 May 1999

Dear Rachel,

I'll be transferring this into a journal shortly. I've decided for as long as I live I am going to write to you, daily, even if it's just a note. This way I will keep in touch – even when I am an old, old lady. Sometimes I'll write about you and what happened to you. Sometimes it will be about me. Other times I'll write to you as if I am posting a letter to a penfriend in a faraway country, filling you in with all the local gossip. Maybe then when I'm too old to make sense – you'll write *me* a letter. Don't I wish. You are my dearly loved daughter. My somersault baby.

13 July 1999

Dear Rachel,

Well, I worked all day today, for the first time since I went back to work part time, five weeks after your disappearance. I'll now be working three full days a week. I don't want to. I really don't. But I'm all right when I'm at work. It's the traffic and the driving I have the problem with.

How am I going to live without you?

It is so cruel. Cruel to you and cruel to us. Cruel to me. My beautiful Rachel, I didn't protect you from an unseen enemy.

How could I have done?

14 July 1999

Rachel,

Death is like a book with many final chapters. Your death still continues for us. The headstone went up today and that's another finality. Then the plants will go in on Saturday and that is closing another chapter. Yet for us there are still many chapters to come because of the nature of your death. Such as writing a card of acknowledgement to Gail for the flowers and her letter. Going to the committal mention, hearing and trial. Placing the final date and photo on your headstone. Receiving your death certificate and going to an inquest.

But your death can never really be closed for me. It is an open wound, your physical death, even though I know your soul lives and this gives me peace of mind . . .

Rachel, at secondary school, you had a poor self-image but darling, we are all different and have natural talents we can choose to develop when and if we wish. You worked extremely hard with your dance. You needed discipline, concentration and

164

aptitude to do what you did. You needed belief in what you knew you were good at, and you had that.

Maybe you felt you had to prove yourself to me work-wise, and I know I did pressure you about work, but I thought this was for your good: for your independence. Yet you should have known any work you went for should have been okayed by one of us first.

I should have told you to slow up in your clear thinking. Taught you to be more aware. I thought you were always careful about where you went. So Caroline must have really set you up good. And I am so angry with her, and sorry for you, and sorry for us.

The girls saw their counsellor after school and I think this is helping them.

I'm finding the hours long at work. I look at mothers with their teenage daughters and think of you . . .

20 July 1999

I wish I'd had longer conversations with you, Rachel. I know we used to talk but I wish I had listened more. You were a fun kid, and an entertaining teenager to watch. There was a gentle quality about you, underneath the noisy teenager. You were too trusting.

There's no going back. Gail's daughter cannot undo what she did. Gail and David's daughter. Caroline killed Elizabeth and Michael's daughter. Daughter. Daughter is such a lovely sounding word. It is a word said with pride.

I nearly collected a truck today which went through a red light. I couldn't believe it. I saw it coming, in slow motion, and I looked at the traffic light which was a firm green. The other cars had seen it and stopped. God willing we didn't connect.

God willing. God willing, could your physical life not have been saved?

I need to know what time you died. I need to know so many things. I want to know what Caroline has done with your earrings, your two necklaces, Manni's ring, your black jazz shoes, your Humphrey Bear and your Bloch dance bag. I want to feel angry all the time but I can't, and can you appreciate how *annoying* that is? I am angry towards Gail and David's daughter, but I am not angry towards *them*.

6 August 1999

Dear Rachel,

Again today, I was really upset in the car on the way home from work. Work all seems very bewildering at the moment. I've been making little mistakes and don't usually do that.

Rachel, I went to see Nanny Joy in hospital, after work. Remember I'd told you she'd had a hip operation and then she'd developed blood clots? And to tell you the truth, if she had died, I'd have thought there would be only one small positive and that was that she would see you. And for a moment I felt jealous of this. I don't believe Mum will die. She is still needed very much here.

Is this futile, writing to you every night? I really do hope you can *feel* these letters. I know I should read them to you, and if you can't read my mind, then maybe you are sitting beside me and reading as I write.

Paul Ross, our Homicide detective, spoke to your dad on the phone today, and he said he would possibly call around Monday evening. I want to speak to him about the details of your death without your sisters being present.

Oh, the agony, Rachel. I so desperately want to hold you. At work today I just imagined you bursting through the back door, and saying, 'I'm home, God's let me come back.' And Rachel, for a moment I really believed it could happen. It didn't matter that I knew you were buried nine feet underground, surrounded by mementos with a headstone above you. It was like God could say, 'Yes, Elizabeth, I'm giving her back.'

I can't imagine I'm ever going to get over this.

Love, Mum.

12 August 1999

Paul Ross came this evening and filled us in on some of the details of your death. Until now we only knew some of it. You poor dear, how frightened you must have been, and what a bitch Caroline was.

He said the case is unique and bizarre, and there will be a lot of press coverage. I am amazed. Amazed that Caroline believed she could actually get away with it.

It was a comfort, however, to know your body was not disturbed by animals. Yes, they do have photographs, but Paul says he will not show us photographs that will upset us. I still cannot – no – I do not *want* to believe this has happened. And it wouldn't have done if not for Caroline, a girl with no friends.

Michael Clarebrough, my counsellor, rang me at work today to let me know the name of the person who did your autopsy. It is a comfort, in some strange way, to know a woman carried out the autopsy . . .

When all this has finished, Rachel, if we wish, we can obtain copies of the police reports, the coroner's reports and trial proceedings. And I do want these.

14 August 1999

Dear Rachel,

Your dad worried me yesterday morning by saying he was beginning to feel that death is the end to it. Final. No more. That there is no spiritual existence. He doesn't believe he will ever see you again. I said to him, 'You know that is not true,' but he just looked at me with his all-knowing 'I'm right' expression.

Sometimes I wish he wouldn't express that thought. If this was absolutely the case then life wouldn't be worth living – at all. No point to any of it. I really want to discuss these thoughts with a minister of the clergy, but no minister is forthcoming. I've thought about attending a local church, but is that fair to them? Kew is so far away, and although a pastoral carer has visited us, how can I tell her I need a priest? So I wait. Sometimes I feel even they feel it is easier not to visit me, so they are not so confronted by the cruel manner of your death. It is easier to say, 'There is a reason for everything and God has his reason.' But I do not hold God responsible for your death. God's protection for you was there for your soul.

I struggle now with all those warnings that seemed to occur before your death. The few I have discussed with Michael Clarebrough he feels are coincidental. But I cannot deny that they happened:

Daddy saying to himself, at the beginning of the year, how lucky our family was never to have had a tragedy.

Me thinking, while processing books at work, what on earth would I ever do if Rachel was not here?

You telling me, in the car this year, that you thought sometimes you would only have a short life and me laughing it off because everything was going so well for you, and you agreeing.

Me, sitting on your bed, while you were laughing and dancing with Manni in our living room (only a few weeks before your murder) and you sounding so excited that I thought, 'This kid's not going to make it through her teen years. I must warn her to slow up.' I never did.

You sharing with our friend David – only a few weeks before your murder – a nightmare you had about someone trying to push you into an open grave and a person in a dark cloak and scythe standing above you both, encouraging you down. Dad knows these details better because David told Dad after your murder. It was the same dream you wanted to tell me about – only I said, 'Tell me later.' And of course you never did.

Manni saying a few weeks before your death he put your photograph on his bedside table in the centre of a circle of candles. His mother telling him off because in their family this is what they do for people who have died. Manni's answer was, 'But she looks so pretty surrounded by a circle of candles.'

You telling Manni you had seen an elderly woman in his bedroom – either the week before your murder or the second weekend before your murder, and then you sharing this with Rosa. Rosa telling you the woman you described sounded like Manni's grandmother – the one who had died – and how you had *insisted* on Rosa taking you to her grave.

The last morning, the Thursday, that I dropped you off at the corner of Riversdale and Tooronga Roads so you could catch your tram, and me watching you wave in my rear-vision mirror, and me thinking it could be the last time I ever see you do that. It was.

These all happened close to your death this year. But what of the time I took you to the Opera in the Park at Prahran? And how I had parked the car in Trinian Street, down the end where Caroline's flat was to be only a few years later. I remember when we left the Opera about midnight, how you carried on about how much you hated the street, going on in your over-the-top way, and hurrying me on. You wanted us to get out quickly.

So many clues and I ignored them all. I didn't make any connection. Why would I?

Your sisters' counsellor Catherine saw Ashleigh-Rose and Heather last night. Ashleigh-Rose wants to go to the trial but I do not want her to go. It's not a suitable place for a twelve-year-old, even a thirteen-year-old, as she may well be by then. Now I am not sure if your dad has conveyed my feelings, but Catherine is apparently going to ring Paul Ross to see what the situation is. I must say I was cross when I discovered this and told your dad so. Ashleigh-Rose immediately told me it was *her* life (where have I heard that before?) and she would go if she wanted to. Dad got cross with me then, and said that I did things he didn't approve of either . . .

12 October 1999

The following is not a letter to Rachel, but was written as a grief statement.

When your children are alive not a day goes by when you don't think of them. When your children die not a day goes by when your mind is not consumed by them. When a child is murdered not a day goes by you do not suffer, consumed by the 'what ifs' and the 'whys'. Not a day goes by when I don't think of the total cruelty of the evil act that senselessly robbed Rachel of the highs and lows – of grandchildren that may have been. Not one child is murdered but generations are murdered. Only a parent who has lost a child can grasp any real understanding of the grief experienced and in the case of a murder that grief is exacerbated.

We are supposed to die in our old age surrounded by children and extended families – that is the fantasy of life. In reality some parents experience the grief of watching terminally ill children slip away – some parents suffer the anguish of losing children in a sudden accident. And some parents suffer the agony of being told, 'Sorry, there is no easy way of saying this. Unfortunately your child has been murdered.'

Murdered. Can you believe it? And for a time you choose not to believe it. But when your beautiful child continues not to run in through the door, when she continues not to contact you and you know deep down it really was a funeral you attended, and it really is a cemetery you visit each week with a headstone engraved with your daughter's name – you know deep down that life has dealt her and yourselves an evil blow.

Into the next year . . .

10 January 2000

Your dad and I went to see the new film *Cider House Rules*. There was one scene where a dead man was being unceremoniously taken from a house on a stretcher covered in a white sheet and put in a van to be taken to the mortuary. Your dad said later, all he could think of at that moment was you. He feels the police should have told us you were found at Kilmore so we could have gone with them. I said they would not have wanted hysterical parents interfering with the crime scene. Even so, your dad feels we were left right out of the picture. I think he feels the same as I do – that we let you down. We should have been with you at some stage – even before Forensics saw you. You are our daughter and it was our right. Of course, at the time neither of us could think straight. We couldn't even think bent.

Paul Ross is right though when he explains why we couldn't go, because we are possible witnesses for the trial.

This is a living nightmare . . .

17 January 2000

Did I tell you I've changed the formal living room around? I've brought my desk out to encourage me to write. I can also see your photographs and feel comforted and inspired.

I wish your daddy could feel inspired – or interested in anything. Life has no meaning for him. He says he just lives one day to another, living a boring existence until he dies. He says he is not happy. It is amazing how quickly one's life can change.

24 January 2000

I have no interest in life. Your dad's views on the universe are beginning to rub off on me. It seems easier now to be uncomplicated by life's complexities, such as friendships. I do not wish to be a sideshow.

I fear for the girls because I am no longer challenged by life. You, my darling Rachel, were always given opportunities to extend your creativity. But I am being hard on myself. For Ashleigh-Rose loves playing the flute and has done so for four years, and she enjoys her pottery. And although Heather seems to have lost interest in singing – she is still musical. But I do not want to do anything. It is easier to sit at home and do nothing than even to go for a walk in the park, and I fear I will bring your sisters up not to enjoy the company of others . . .

I am reading Grandad Ivan's book *Ziggurat* again, published in 1997. It is the story of Knut who went missing one night without trace. Life has so many odd coincidences.

I rang Paul Ross today.

Yesterday, the vicar from the church we now attend would have read out our statement about your death at the Sunday services. Rachel, the parish folk have not known about you, and neither did the vicar for the first few months. The girls said they felt normal going to a church where no one knew about their sister. I had to respect their wishes. But this will change next week with the committal hearing. So with the co-operation of the vicar we thought this was the best way of telling people at the church. It has become a responsibility.

We went to Grandad Ivan's. We labelled all Ashleigh-Rose's workbooks and sewed up her hems. The girls *will* stay with Grandad while we go to the committal hearing . . .

Your sisters don't like to see me cry. I need to know that I am loved. You loved me. I feel you loved me, dearly. *Yet* I was unkind to you, too. There were times I smacked you, and times I yelled at you. But, Rachel, I was scared for your future. I didn't want you to grow up struggling for money. It is probably because we struggled for money that you now find yourself dead because I kept on at you about looking for a job. If we'd earned more money, just maybe Caroline would not have been able to entice you away with that so-called story about making lots of money.

I need a holiday away from all of this nightmare, Rachel. It's a shame I couldn't come on holiday and see you. But then, if I did, that would be a permanent holiday and I would grieve the loss of your sisters because I would be in heaven and they would be on earth. No, I'll have to learn to accept what has happened but I find it hard to believe almost a year has gone by.

This time last year you only had five to six weeks to live – yet possibly they were some of the happiest weeks of your life.

What will happen to your sisters, Rachel?

Love, Mum.

29 January 2000

Dear Rachel,

Yesterday Paul Ross rang.

The barrister for the prosecution, Robert Barry, has said he doesn't want your father and I to be present during the committal hearing. As you can imagine I was distressed by this development. Paul said the reason for this is to do with the documents I saw a little of when we were making a police statement at the Homicide office on 14 March last year.

Apparently there are a lot more entries made by Caroline

before she killed you. In fact, if I am right, I think he said journals to do with the nature of the obsession Caroline had with you. Paul used the word 'bizarre' again. He said, 'The girl depicted in Caroline's journals is not the Rachel we know.' I said to Paul that I hoped this didn't mean your name was going to be muddied in the courts. He said, no that's not what he was expressing. However the barrister doesn't want us in the hearing because he doesn't want the defence to say we have been prejudiced because we are witnesses for the trial. I told Paul that he wouldn't get your dad in the witness box. He said, 'We won't worry about the trial now, just the hearing.'

It is doubtful that it will be made known how you died at the hearing because the forensic scientists have not been called. I told Paul that I at least wanted to go for a short while at the beginning because I wanted to *see* Caroline and more importantly I wanted Caroline to *see* us. Paul said okay, but to be aware it may only be for a few minutes because when the evidence is given we have to leave. The same goes for Manni. He said he trusts we will leave the court room when he nods to us. We will wait somewhere in the Magistrates Court.

This is all over for you, sweetheart, but for us this is still a nightmare. I am very worried for your dad and I am worried for us. He said he is *not* going to be a witness and will just disappear. Now I don't think I want to put that to the test. He said it wouldn't pay them to get him in court because he would just get angry.

Paul Ross is going to ask family not to tell us what happens although we may read some of it in the papers.

Your father said, 'Every day is the same – a nothingness – a blankness just to be lived through.'

We are now off to Manni's to let him know how you died.

Love, Mum.

1 February 2000, 4.04 a.m.

Dear Rachel,

The first day of the committal hearing was yesterday and now I find I have been dreaming of you, glimpses of the hearing and the coming trial – fading memories in dreams I do not wish to remember. So I came out into the living room about 3.30 a.m. and watched the video 'Rachel and her sisters'. Now I have just turned on the funeral video. I have wanted to watch it for some time but the opportunity has just not occurred until now. Your dad and a recovered Nanny Joy are asleep and Ashleigh-Rose and Heather are at Grandad Ivan and Granny Susan's place.

I need to watch the video to connect yesterday's committal hearing to you. It is as if you have been distanced from this, although Nanny Joy said that, being in the committal hearing, she definitely felt connected to you. We, as you already know, were not allowed to be present at the committal but I did convince Paul Ross to allow us to be present in the court room until the evidence began. And because of an unexpected hitch, Caroline was there for about twenty-five minutes before we left the court.

I'm now listening to Mendelssohn's *Midsummer Night's Dream* at the beginning of your funeral.

The court network cleared a space for us because it was a full court and they sat me next to a man I didn't recognise. He said, 'Elizabeth, I'm David Reid. I'm sorry you have to sit next to me.' I answered, 'I didn't recognise you. Thank you for introducing yourself.' I thanked him for his sympathy letter, adding that I could not reply because there was no return address. He said, 'I would like to speak to you when all this is over.' He meant everything. He then pointed out the man standing beside Caroline as her psychologist. Paul Ross then interrupted and reminded us to leave shortly because we were trial witnesses.

When we left the courtroom we went and sat with a court networker in the network family room. I needed to feel close to what was happening, Rachel.

Humphrey your cat is playing with an old cane Christmas decoration. He's a scatty cat. You would have loved him.

I'm now listening to one of the funeral sermons and it is a great comfort.

I am so hot I think I have a fever.

The court announced how you died, Rachel – revealed in full horror the bizarre act and how Caroline kept notes about you and plotted to murder you.

The Balwyn minister is now speaking. He was truly fortunate to know you as a child. He likens you to a butterfly that has been released into the limitless love of our Lord. And he asked, for now, that God forgive those whom we cannot forgive because of our pain and agony.

The film screen has now come forward and they are about to show video clips of you. My darling Rachel. What can I say? You were a delight.

The film has now finished and the final hymn, chosen by Rosa, 'What a Friend We Have in Jesus' is being sung. Even Rosa knew how important Jesus was to you. Your Grandad Ivan, Uncle Drew, Cousins Shaun and Ben, Uncle Graham, and your beloved Manni are carrying your coffin through the church to the tears of your family, friends and teachers.

5 February 2000 (I think.)

Dear Rachel,

What I thought would happen has. This week has been so distressing I haven't kept writing letters to you, but I wish I had because now I won't be able to recall the moments as they occurred. I have lost the feelings of the present.

I think sometimes these letters are as much for myself as for you, and also for your sisters, for when they are old enough to understand.

Going back to the second day of the committal hearing. Let's see if I can recall . . . It was the 1st of February 2000 . . .

Mike, Nanny Joy, Grandad Ivan and myself drove into the city with Susan. Chris went in by train. I probably should not have watched the funeral beforehand but I really needed to. Then I had a long and very hot bath and walked to the service station to buy the newspapers. Like the day before, the committal hearing was reported in all the newspapers. I almost feel I should list the headings the newspapers used, as Dad had in his novel *Ziggurat*:

Murder notes found
Murder plot in writing, court told

Accused kept notes of kill plan, court told
Family friend plotted to kill teen, court told
Police hunt two more over death
Woman for trial on dancer death
Babysitter faces murder trial

So, Rachel, Caroline was committed to trial on murder. It had been seen from her medical file that she had shown no indication of mental impairment. She simply committed an evil and wicked act.

Back to the events of the day . . .

Susan dropped Nanny Joy, Dad and I off at William Street in the city, so we did not have far to walk to the Magistrates Court. We met your second cousin Lindsay and Aunty Babe in the court, and Chris arrived soon after. We went to the court network room and refreshed with a glass of water. When we went down to the courtroom it was still closed, and we found ourselves sitting opposite David Reid, Caroline's father. Her parents are in an impossible position, and I pray for them, for if the role were reversed I feel my soul would be destroyed. How much must one suffer when realising one has given birth to someone who could so wilfully take another's life?

Inside the court, Aunty Babe, who has emphysema and cannot walk for long periods, came through in her wheelchair and sat in the aisle alongside David who tried to make her feel more comfortable. 'I don't need any help,' she snapped. 'I'm het up enough as it is!' I felt sorry for him and almost apologised but they were on the other side of the court. All he was trying to do was help her. She must remember, as I need to, that it was not David who killed you. Gail came in and sat in the back row. And then Aunty Babe got up and walked! What must the man have thought? She went and sat next to my mother.

Then Caroline came in – no, not that quickly – her barrister had not arrived when the magistrate had, so he left and didn't appear for another fifteen to twenty minutes. So I got to look at Caroline all this time.

She started to write down notes as everybody had said she had the day before, and in view of the revelation from the previous day regarding her notes and premeditated plots, I couldn't help thinking she was very good at recording everything. She seemed cool and calm – not agitated – perhaps looking self important. Once or twice her eyes gazed over in our direction but she made no eye contact.

I noticed a document being handed over from the prosecution solicitor to the prosecution barrister which was an application for a birth certificate in your name, but not in your handwriting. I wonder if she ever knew you were left-handed. Perhaps she is left-handed herself. I should have noted. We were required to leave soon afterwards.

We only just managed to reach the court network room before I broke down, uncontrollably. Your dad held me in his arms for a long time before we both sat down. The time in the court had affected Dad as well. Writing now, I find it difficult to express our emotions, only to say they were ones of loss – like a *new* bereavement. It was then, yet again, that the drawn-out procedures of the court brought it home to us that we were still very much in the funeral stage of your death. We can never hope to be further along until the trial is over.

I looked out the window and noticed police cars had numbers on their rooftops. I'd never noticed this before and I stopped crying.

When we calmed down we went downstairs to the Salvation Army who said we could use their photocopier to copy some letters we had received from your teachers and friends after your murder. I thought these would personalise you for the prosecution solicitor.

Everything finished about noon and we were suddenly overwhelmed by family, who came in insisting that the trial would be May 1st, and wasn't that great – exciting, in fact, because it meant we wouldn't have long to wait. I tried to tell them this would be the arraignment date but they didn't understand.

Paul Ross and barrister Robert Barry, together with our prosecution solicitor Matthew directed us into a quiet room and said, as we had rightly assumed, that May 1st represented the arraignment date. The trial will probably be some time between August and October.

Later, your dad told me he had started to panic and was shaking.

When we left the court we dropped into the Salvation Army to say goodbye and found Gail Reid there. She was nervous about leaving the court and Lindsay, the Salvation Army officer who had helped in your search, offered to walk her to Flagstaff Station but she did not take him up. They suggested she call a taxi but she wouldn't do this either. It was odd standing there with her. I didn't feel any hostility towards her and I wasn't feeling stressed by the situation. A bystander would never have imagined that her daughter was accused of murdering our daughter.

My God, Rachel, she was on her *own*. I felt so much pity for her, but I cannot take on her welfare any more. Last time I did look where it all ended. I can pray for her though, and pray some friends stand by her, for her sake alone.

We were waiting for Susan at the Salvation Army, but she just hadn't appeared so we went outside. Still no Susan. She had gone to collect her car, perhaps half an hour earlier, and before long we were being photographed and filmed. I was asked what I thought of the 'Not Guilty' plea. I didn't want to jeopardise the trial. I didn't want the defence to have any reason to say 'unfair trial', so I answered, 'We'll just have to wait and see. We were not in the committal hearing because we were not allowed to be. We sat in the court network room. It has been very hard. Could you please respect our privacy?' We were followed to the end of the street but not harassed. We turned around and walked back in the direction of the court. I noticed Gail walking directly towards us, quite oblivious of our presence so I turned away because I did not think it prudent for the press to photograph us together.

Your father and I felt totally drained, my darling, because we had not had any idea how premeditated your murder was. I have begun to understand why Paul Ross said we were required as witnesses.

Your dad, Chris and I had a quiet afternoon, although by the time we got home it was already three o'clock.

I asked Chris if she was resilient enough to hear the poems I

178

had written to you, explaining they were not properly constructed poems, more thoughts on paper. After a while she was sobbing, and I said, 'Oh Chris, I shouldn't have put you through this.' It was quite thoughtless of me really, considering she had sat through the committal hearing. But she said, 'No, no, go on.' But after a few more lines we decided to get some fresh air out on the front veranda . . .

Rachel, I want to go on now because I feel it important to record this, but it is 1.25 a.m. and I am *so* tired, even though all I have done today is go to church, watch a video with your dad and sister and then literally sleep all afternoon. This week of the committal hearing has really whacked me, and my heavy cold has not helped. But I will continue . . .

By the time Chris and I were leaning against the front veranda I was crying too. As we were trying to compose ourselves a red van rolled up and a man got out holding a clipboard. He looked very official. I said, 'Oh no, do you think he is a journalist?' Chris answered, 'No, he looks like someone from the Salvation Army.'

This was all in slow motion. It felt like we should have said, 'Is it a plane? Is it a bird? No, it's not Superman but a man of some variety.' Now, don't get me wrong Rachel, but in all the grief and trauma of the past two days of the committal hearing, what was about to happen was like a Monty Python sketch.

Our eyes were bloodshot and teary as this poor man walked up to the veranda completely ignorant of the events of our day.

He said, 'Good afternoon, would you like your roof retiled and we'll give you a free check.'

Chris stopped in her tracks and said, 'Now's not the time for roofing. There has been a tragedy in the family.'

And I said, 'Well, the tragedy happened a year ago and it's just been renewed.' (Silly thing to say, really.)

Then Chris laughed, and I did too because 'renewed' sounded such a ridiculous expression.

He was about to leave, looking disconcerted.

I said, 'No, wait. What do you mean by "you'll retile our roof and then give us a free check"? Do you mean a free check C-H-E-C-K or cheque C-H-E-Q-U-E?'

'Oh,' said Chris. 'He means C-H-E-Q-U-E.'

179

'No,' said the man, very carefully, obviously now aware of our reddened eyes and smudged make-up. 'What we do is give your roof a free check C-H-E-C-K, then if you wish we will retile your roof and then *you* will give *us* a cheque C-H-E-Q-U-E.'

Well, we started to laugh and cry at the same time. Not crying as a result of a spillover of laughter, but real crying from the events of the day.

He gave us his name and phone number and left.

Chris and I were then surprisingly refreshed and returned to the poems. After this Mike and I drove Chris home and on the way back treated ourselves to Chinese takeaway, but ended up throwing half of it away because we really didn't have any appetite.

Writing back on this week, a week later, I do feel the raw emotions of the moment have been lost. When I write these letters to you, Rachel, they are an expression of *that* point in time. When I read back on them I am reflecting just as much on the pen and ink, and the flow from the hand connected to my thoughts.

Wednesday morning we did a small amount of banking and shopping. People were pointing at us.

Michael Clarebrough came about 12.40 and stayed until five. We have been so shocked by all the events revealed in the media that it left us feeling winded. This was a turning point for your father, who now concedes the need to see a counsellor.

After Michael Clarebrough had been we drove to the cemetery and on to Healesville to collect Heather and Ashleigh-Rose. On the way home we visited Mum and later collapsed, totally drained of everything.

Thursday.

Ashleigh-Rose was only at school an hour when my friend Chris, who also teaches at her school, rang us up. Things had not gone well for Ashleigh-Rose and she had gone to the office looking for Chris, who was fortunately teaching today. Their social welfare counsellor is going to bring her home.

I'm done in, Rachel.

Love, Mum.

The other story ...

25

MURDER MAKING HEADLINES

Caroline Reed Robertson made her first appearance before the Melbourne Magistrates Court on Monday, 15 March 1999 – a twenty-year-old office administrator appearing briefly, charged with one count of murder.

Word of her arrest had come to newsroom staff late on Saturday evening, shortly before her appearance in front of a duty magistrate who formally remanded her in custody until Monday morning. It was sensational stuff, but the media knew that Robertson's pending court appearance was likely to last only a matter of minutes. And since police investigations were ongoing, and no autopsy findings had been released positively identifying the cause of death, news coverage of the case would undoubtedly be limited by legal constraints.

This case would, no doubt, involve a high-profile trial since few defendants ever plead guilty to the serious charge of murder. And because Caroline Robertson was not required to enter a plea at this stage, any revelations about the alleged murder would have to wait until the committal hearing.

'Missing Teenager Found Dead' reported the *Sunday Age*. 'Missing Dancer Found Dead' echoed another paper, announcing the fact that an autopsy was due to be conducted later on Sunday. In fact, the autopsy was carried out that morning, but because of the decomposed state of the body it was difficult to establish either its identity or the cause of death. Forensic tests later showed that it was indeed Rachel Barber and that she had most likely died about twelve days earlier, very shortly after her disappearance. Probably the same night. It was determined by the pathologist that the probable cause of death had been ligature strangulation.

On Monday morning the story made national headlines. The *Sydney Morning Herald* covered the syndicated story of the senseless killing, the family's search, and the accused killer's expected court appearance. And, as all this news was breaking, Robertson was led under guard into court, where she appeared dazed and distressed. She cut a bizarre figure as she sat, rocking and swaying, breathing heavily, dressed in a blue T-shirt and still with traces of bright green dye in her bedraggled brown hair.

When the magistrate ordered her to stand for the single murder charge to be formally read out to her, she staggered to her feet and gripped the edge of the dock to steady herself.

She shot a quick glance at her lawyer, who acknowledged her with a very slight nod of his head. She was then asked to confirm her name, age and address. No application was made for bail and she was remanded in custody to reappear in court on 25 March.

Robertson's lawyer, David O'Doherty, told the court that forensic procedures such as blood-testing and taking DNA samples were still pending, and that he would require notice for permission to carry out those tests. Outside the new court complex he told journalists his client was 'very unwell at the moment', and had received medical attention while in custody. But they would have to wait for the results of the autopsy and the findings of toxicological testing on the dead girl.

For the time being, the extraordinary details of the crime itself remained a mystery to everyone.

In the street there were emotional scenes among friends and relatives of Rachel Barber. Her boyfriend Emmanuel, still too upset to speak to waiting camera crews, huddled with his family and wiped tears from his face. Elizabeth Barber's cousin, Michele, also wept.

'We had to be here for the parents today,' she told journalists. 'They weren't strong enough. Her mother wanted to come today, but she couldn't. We had to get her to stay at home.'

Caroline Robertson's father also attended the hearing but left quickly, carefully avoiding the cameras and media posse in the street.

Amid all this publicity 'Australia's Most Wanted' went to air with the story that David dePyle of the Missing Persons Unit had suggested to the program. It went to air on the day of the court hearing, two days after Rachel Barber's body had been found. Two weeks too late.

The show updated the story, explaining the tragic outcome. Police were still appealing for information from witnesses who might have seen a white van Robertson initially claimed to have hired to transfer Rachel Barber's body from the flat to her country grave.

But the real story, in the eyes of the media, was the link between the mother of the victim and the mother of the killer. They had been friends. Both were mothers of three girls. The two elder daughters were involved here – one charged with the death of another, a girl she had once been friendly with, once babysat. Press coverage abounded. There were character profiles of the bewitching, talented young dancer who had dreamed of being a big star one day. Elizabeth Barber's grief-stricken account, told in a broken voice to reporters the day after the discovery of Rachel's body, was seized upon by the media and aired repeatedly on TV and radio broadcasts: 'I just thank God that we had her for fifteen years. I would rather have had her for fifteen years than not have had her at all.'

Community concerns were voiced, sympathising with the family's plight. A letter in the Melbourne *Age* expressed sympathy for the Barber family, saying how 'doubly cruel' this crime had been for Rachel Barber's parents and sisters. 'Snatched from them at such a tender age and by such inexplicable violence.'

A week later, a letter in the *Sunday Age* from the family of one of Rachel's school friends demanded to know why this case had not been referred to Missing Persons sooner. Why had there been such an apparent lack of support for the Barbers from the appropriate authorities at the time of their daughter's disappearance? 'Why', ran the letter, 'is it that missing children are immediately branded as miscreants and no credence is given to parents' concerns about abduction and foul play? Why is there no support for such families if immediate police action cannot be taken?'

At this very early stage police were still compiling evidence against the young woman in custody. They had the documents seized during their searches of Robertson's flat. But pages from the suspect's notebooks had clearly been ripped out, perhaps destroyed. The torn pages were certainly not found around the flat.

It was clear from Robertson's carefully compiled lists that she was a methodical, well-organised person. After all, she'd made detailed handwritten observations on the victim and her family. And the enormous creepy 'Scream' print dominating the tiny lounge room only added to the detectives' general feelings of unease.

They could offer no concrete motive at this stage – though they had their suspicions. There was Robertson's earlier confession to Neil Paterson at the hospital, though she maintained that Rachel's death was an accident. After that, she had refused to co-operate at all. What could Robertson have said to Rachel in those two lengthy phone calls the night before their secret rendezvous? Identifying a motive would offer some explanation – rational or otherwise.

But the case had been adjourned now, until 25 March, and the committal hearing was several months away. Caroline Reed Robertson was remanded in custody to the Metropolitan Women's Correctional Centre at Deer Park. Her lawyers had begun work, and now there was time for police to collect witness statements. Time to unearth more evidence.

26

A FRIENDLESS NOBODY

On Wednesday, 24 March more than 850 mourners gathered at Rachel Barber's funeral in St Hilary's Anglican Church, Kew, including all her friends and instructors from the Dance Factory. There were friends from her former dancing school, past schoolmates and teachers, together with family friends. There were supporters from her local church group, boys she had grown up with like Macca, Anthony, Hugh and Ben – some of whom had put up many posters in the days when Rachel was missing. And of course there was Rachel's boyfriend Emmanuel, who was supported by his entire family. Elizabeth's employers and friends from the bookshop where she worked also attended and closed their business for the day.

A moving video depicting Rachel with Emmanuel was shown during the service by the Carella brothers. It showed Emmanuel's sixteenth birthday, with Rachel and Manni's brothers, and Rachel's sisters; Rachel dancing solo in concerts; dancing with Manni; a Christmas party with Manni's family and friends. Rachel Star. The 'little butterfly that has been released into the limitless love of our Lord', as the minister described her. Rachel waving at the camera, smiling broadly . . . and mouthing the words 'bye bye'. The little butterfly and her flowers were later taken away for private burial at the Lilydale Memorial Park.

As news crews swelled the crowd at the teenager's funeral, Caroline Robertson was preparing herself for a second appearance at the Melbourne Magistrates Court. She had been on remand and was required to appear in court again for the prosecution to provide information on the status of the case.

Prosecutor Scott Johns told the court the following morning that the Homicide Squad was now in the process of preparing sixty witness statements. The police brief, including forensic test results, would be extensive and looked likely to take at least three months to complete.

No application for bail was made on Robertson's behalf and, given the amount of paperwork to be undertaken and the seriousness of the charge, Deputy Chief Magistrate Jelena Popovic remanded the suspect in custody again. With the media focus now on the funeral, Robertson's court appearance warranted barely a mention in the news.

'Free Spirit who Lived to Dance,' ran a headline in the *Herald Sun,* which described the service for the fifteen-year-old 'vivacious spirit' who, her family said, would 'dance on in their hearts for ever'. The newspaper also reported a proposed meeting between the family and the Victorian Premier, Mr Kennett, at which they would ask for a liaison officer to be attached to the police Missing Persons Unit to help parents worried about missing children. Meanwhile, the *Age* carried a story under the heading 'Friends and Family Remember Their Beautiful Butterfly.'

Within weeks of the funeral, a date was set for a conference between the Barber family, senior police executives and a Victorian government representative. The conference was held at the Victorian Police Centre in central Melbourne to give the family an opportunity to raise their concerns about not just police involvement in Rachel's case, but about the role of police in investigating missing children in general.

While the expected government representative did not attend, the Victoria Police Chief Superintendent and Chief of Staff, Paul Hornbuckle, was present. He was joined by a Victoria Police Media Liaison Officer, representatives from Homicide and Missing Persons, and the Manager of the Victims Advisory Unit, Rob Read. Mike and Elizabeth Barber were supported by Elizabeth's sister, Robbie.

Elizabeth, Michael and Robbie read to the meeting a lengthy statement which they had prepared together. Earlier the Barbers had received a formal apology from the Victoria Police by Chief Superintendent Hornbuckle. He expressed remorse for the difficulties experienced by the family following their daughter's disappearance, but pointed out that the circumstances of Rachel Barber's disappearance and murder had been unique and bizarre.

At the meeting, for the first time since Rachel's disappearance, the Barbers learned of the investigations that had been carried out by Richmond police, though the family had been unaware of them at the time.

Discussions followed about the predicament of families faced with a missing child; of the restrictions facing local police; of the need to keep relatives fully updated on the status of the case as it progresses. Protection of parents, explained Elizabeth Barber, simply added to their distress. Then there were questions. Why, asked the Barbers, had Richmond police told them it was not possible to trace incoming calls, when Missing Persons had done exactly that? They were told that Richmond police had been correct – it was not possible for local police to access incoming telephone records. It was in breach of the privacy act. Even in cases where there is evidence of foul play, protocol requires that an application must be made through proper channels.

On a more personal note, the Barbers compared the caring attitudes shown to them by detectives from Homicide and Missing Persons with what they considered to be indifference from other officers. This difference in attitude, complained Elizabeth, was confronting to the family at a time when they most needed support. Perhaps Homicide and Missing Persons officers were more experienced in dealing with emotional parents and hysterical families. She had a solution. Perhaps all missing persons should be handled by a central missing person agency, separate to the Homicide Squad. Cases could be handed over to Homicide only when there is enough evidence to suggest foul play. But she was told this was not practical. Every local police station, explained the executives, is different. Its officers respond differently to individual community demands and experience varying problems in each local region.

So, given the complexities of Missing Persons and the unique nature of each case, executives felt that a uniformed officer being assigned to the Unit would not be appropriate. The most practical response, in the absence of any evidence of foul play, was still believed to be through the local police station. In Rachel's case there had only ever been a gut feeling. 'Gut feeling,' responded Elizabeth Barber. 'It was probably the nagging gut feeling of the Missing Persons Unit which prevented an almost perfect murder slipping through the hands of the police.'

One result came from that meeting between the Barbers and the police. A new clause was added into the Victoria Police Manual in relation to the investigation of missing persons, stating that members of the police force should be aware of the need for sensitivity in dealing with family members of missing persons and ensure they are informed, where appropriate, of relevant police procedures and investigation processes.

Over the coming months there were a number of adjournments as witness statements were prepared. Caroline Robertson's case was finally listed for a committal hearing before Magistrate Frank Hender at the Melbourne Magistrates Court on Monday, 31 January 2000 – ten long months after her victim's death.

Although Robertson's lawyers had talked with her on a number of occasions in jail, their interviews had produced very little material to help them build a strong defence case. Indeed, Robertson's barrister Colin Lovitt, QC, was later to tell the Supreme Court that his client's apparent amnesia as to the details of the murder had made the case frustrating and difficult for everyone attempting to assist her. This shortage of any real information meant that the defence team had to make its own inquiries on Robertson's behalf.

Her lawyers managed to trace the pizza shop where she and Rachel Barber had ordered pizza on the evening of Monday, 1 March. They also talked to another person who, Robertson told them, had given her a lift back to Melbourne from Kilmore. She had told her lawyers she had hitchhiked home from the country property, but was unable to tell them any more except that she had buried Rachel Barber there – at the suggestion of others.

Her tale about possible accomplices assisting in the crime

remains unclear. Until ten weeks before her final plea hearing, Robertson maintained the story that she was *involved* in the offence but was not the sole perpetrator. She insisted that she had been involved with two others who had abandoned her: Caroline was left to take the blame for the killing.

Robertson's first few weeks in prison had been a nightmare for her. Greg Sneddon, a Buddhist monk who had spent twenty years working with women accused of serious crimes, said that the new prisoner was pointed out to him shortly after her arrival at Deer Park. He recalls seeing her around the jail, and noting that she appeared 'vulnerable and at risk' from the other more seasoned criminals. During that early period of incarceration he made a point of speaking to her, even if only in passing, each time he visited the prison. He often observed that she had black eyes and other unexplained injuries.

In fact Robertson, in her depressive state of mind, was a regular and serious self-mutilator after Rachel Barber's death, spending time in the prison hospital having treatment for self-inflicted injuries, mostly slashing injuries to her forearms and wrists. At around that time her epileptic seizures became more frequent.

Michael Crewdson, a clinical psychologist appointed by Robertson's father, David Reid, to treat his daughter in the days following her arrest, was well aware that the accused was suicidal during that time. Crewdson had the task of helping to keep her alive. He had been given a bundle of documents and letters written by Robertson over a seven-year period, beginning when she was just thirteen, and these helped him compile a psychological profile of her.

While she was in custody, detectives from the Homicide Squad were building their own profile of Robertson. They had already begun to interview her colleagues at Austalk Communications and former workmates from Kompass Australia.

Detective Sergeant Paul Ross said it was a striking feature of the case that no one knew much about Caroline Robertson. Her only associates appeared to be the people she worked with, and they said she kept very much to herself. None of her former colleagues described themselves as a friend of hers, nor were they aware of the names of any of Robertson's friends outside work.

Information from Rachel's sister Ashleigh-Rose confirmed the possibility that the suspect had developed an unusual interest in the young dancer at least three months before her disappearance. Ashleigh-Rose told police that Caroline had telephoned their home in the summer holidays before Rachel was murdered, asking for the dates of birth of each of the Barber girls. Ashleigh-Rose gave Robertson her own details, and those of her sister Heather. But she had to call to Rachel in the backyard swimming pool to check on her birth date.

Elizabeth Barber had asked why Robertson needed this information. So Ashleigh-Rose asked the question and was told it was for her university project. Police suspected that this was the data Robertson needed to enable her to apply for a birth certificate in Rachel Barber's name. They also knew, from information the dead girl's parents gave them, that a couple of years earlier Robertson had taken a series of photographs of thirteen-year-old Rachel, claiming it was for her VCE project.

Another incident that now seemed relevant had occurred three years before Rachel disappeared. It had taken place in the front garden of the Barbers' old house in Mont Albert when Rachel was just twelve. She had been playing in the street with another girl when Caroline approached her, asking if she could be her friend. Rachel, uneasy at the prospect of being 'friends' with a girl so much older, had retreated indoors.

Four days after Robertson was charged with murdering Rachel Barber, Detective Sergeant Paul Ross from the Homicide Squad interviewed the suspect's supervisor at Austalk Communications, Cathryn Felstead. Miss Felstead, then the dealer support manager, said in a sworn statement that Robertson had been a good worker who was efficient, punctual and self-motivated. A quick learner, she had been with the company since November 1998 as a sales co-ordinator, liaising with customers and internal staff. She got on well with everyone, but did not reveal much about herself. People knew Robertson was a vegetarian. And most of those who worked with her were aware of her background of family disharmony. She did not get along with her mother, and did not like her stepmother, claiming that her father's new wife supposedly preferred her two younger sisters.

Robertson regularly spoke about her father. She had left her flat in St Kilda to live at his home in Toorak while she looked for somewhere else to live. She told Miss Felstead that her father had asked her to leave because she had arrived home late one night. After that she moved to her flat in Prahran. She also told her boss about a property her father had, north of Melbourne, where she had spent time with her family in younger days. She used to swim in the dam there.

Robertson claimed that she generally went to bed early on Friday nights, woke around midnight, got dressed up, and went out partying and clubbing with her friends. But the police could find no friends to interview. At her later plea hearing, Robertson's barrister confirmed that she was, in fact, a lonely girl who appeared to have no friends or social life.

Once she told a former workmate about a male friend who shared her interest in motor racing and with whom she had spent a weekend. But she did not name him or mention him again. Another time she spoke of an ex-boyfriend, but again did not identify him.

Police learnt that Robertson had told her Austalk supervisor and her former Kompass workmates that she had a circle of friends in the theatre. Then she claimed they had moved to Sydney. One, she told everyone, was in television commercials.

One Kompass colleague, Josephine Fsadni, elaborated on this, saying that Robertson had told her of a boy she knew who was in the TV industry. And she mentioned a friend called Christian who had moved to New South Wales.

Robertson's Kompass colleagues Carmel Rosendale and Sarah Dean were surprised when she told them about her show business friends and the theatre group she had once belonged to. Robertson had confided in Carmel that she wanted to obtain theatre work, perhaps working backstage. She said she had done it before on a voluntary basis.

Her Austalk supervisor also expressed surprise when Robertson revealed this interest to her, and admits she was taken aback when Robertson talked about her acting circle. 'She didn't appear like someone who would be involved in that area,' recalled Miss Felstead. 'She seemed very interested in the Internet and spoke of it several times. I thought she was more inclined to the telecommunications industry than the arts.'

In fact it seems that Robertson probably *was* serious about wanting to join a theatre group. But then, nobody really knew her at all . . .

The only person Caroline appeared to know who had a performing role or belonged to any kind of showbiz circle was Rachel Barber. Talented, slim and pretty, Rachel was popular. She really *did* have a boyfriend. And other friends. Lots of them. Many were dancers and performers. She had been modelling and, as Robertson noted in her later writings, had moved to a new dance school. Rachel Barber seemed to have a promising life ahead of her.

But if Robertson was depressed about herself and her life, it was not apparent to colleagues. There was little hint of inner pain when Robertson first met her new Austalk colleague Donna Waters, back in November 1998.

To Donna, Robertson seemed 'a friendly type of person' who appeared to have no trouble talking to her. But she quickly became aware of Robertson's family problems. Donna recounted a conversation in which Caroline Robertson claimed that her mother, Gail Reid, had taken out a restraining order on her and that her father didn't talk to her. No mention of a restraining order was ever made in court, however, and it would have been relevant to the defendant's prior character if it had existed. When police at Missing Persons conducted their background search, nothing of the kind showed up on the police computer.

Donna Waters said she would often go for lunch with Robertson, along with another colleague, Sally Arthur. But neither of the girls saw Robertson socially or visited her new flat.

Donna did, however, recall meeting Robertson outside the block of flats two days after Rachel Barber disappeared on Monday, 1 March 1999. She had been asked to return some money lent to her by Robertson a couple of weeks earlier. Robertson had written a cheque for $320, and agreed that the money could be repaid after their mid-March payday. But then she suddenly rang Donna on Tuesday, 2 March, asking for the money back. She said she needed it to pay a removalist who was coming first thing the next morning to take some property from the flat to her father's country house. On the Monday Robertson had left a message on her supervisor's voicemail, stating that she was sick and would not be coming to work. This was unusual for her. She had only telephoned in sick once before, in early February.

Robertson had gone to work the day after Rachel had disappeared, but looked decidedly pale and unwell. She was unusually quiet and her boss, concerned about her health, drove her home to Trinian Street, dropping her off outside the flats.

Then, later that day, Robertson phoned Donna Waters on her mobile asking her to repay the money she owed. She rang Donna again very early the next day, checking that she was bringing the money around. Donna drove to the flat to find Robertson waiting outside in the street. There was no sign of a removal van, which she thought odd. She gave Robertson $100 before driving her to the nearest ATM, where Robertson took another $100 from her. Donna promised to repay the remainder before the end of the week.

On the way back, Donna asked where the removalist was. Robertson said she had left the back door open for him in case he arrived while they were out. Again, there was no sign of a van on their return to the flats. Robertson then told Waters she was moving furniture to her father's holiday house without his knowledge and intended to store it in a shed there.

Robertson's supervisor at Austalk, Cathryn Felstead, recalled Robertson mentioning the case of the missing girl in passing when the story was first on the news. Robertson said she knew the girl, but she wasn't concerned because, she said, the girl had done it before. She implied that it was a bit of a joke.

When police spoke to some women who had been workmates of Caroline Robertson's at Kompass, they all remembered Robertson as the girl who had changed her name from Reid in 1998 when she was living with her father. Sarah Dean recalled Robertson telling her that the name change came about because she had been having problems with her father. Sarah described her as a manipulative young woman who liked to gossip. She also appeared to lack confidence and blushed easily, especially when the women talked about sex. Josephine Fsadni and Carmel Rosendale saw Robertson as an 'acquaintance' rather than a friend. Josephine, who had helped Robertson find her earlier flat in St Kilda, recalled Robertson mentioning her father's property at Kilmore, as did the others, and her saying that she sometimes visited by train because she couldn't drive.

Everyone remembered Robertson's conversations about her family and her failure to get along with either her mother or stepmother. Sarah Dean said Robertson seemed resentful because of her stepmother's obvious preference for her younger sisters. She told Sarah she thought her mother was 'mad', and wanted to have nothing to do with her. The relationship with her father seemed strained, said Sarah.

Colleagues remembered Robertson saying she was looking for a flat, claiming her stepmother didn't want her in her father's house. 'I remember Caroline told me about her father getting married to her stepmother,' Sarah Dean told detectives. 'She made preparations for the wedding by buying new shoes and clothing. While she was preparing for this wedding she told me that her younger sisters were going to look gorgeous as they were young, slim and pretty.'

Kompass colleagues told police no one had ever been to the new flat in Trinian Street where Robertson lived, though Sarah and Carmel had been to Robertson's former home in St Kilda. They said she had occasionally invited people around, but no one ever went.

Sarah recalled going to the St Kilda flat on several occasions during 1998 to use Robertson's electric hot water shower during a time of gas restrictions. Carmel said she had accompanied Robertson home on an occasion in 1998 after she had suffered an epileptic seizure, which she blamed on stress. The workmate said, though, that Robertson was generally a calm person.

Robertson resigned from Kompass in 1998, saying she could not cope with the added pressure of her work. After leaving, she continued to stay in touch with some of her former associates, mainly by telephone.

Strangely, during the first week of March 1999, in the days after Rachel Barber disappeared, Robertson rang Josephine Fsadni out of the blue, asking if she would like to move in with her. Josephine, who was considering moving, said she would get back to Robertson on this. She had no idea Robertson had only a one-bedroom flat.

The women who had visited the St Kilda flat were later able to describe to police a blue throw rug they had seen draped across a couch there. Their descriptions matched that of the rug wrapped around Rachel Barber's body when it was found.

Carmel Rosendale also told Homicide detectives how she had received a strange email from Robertson the week Rachel Barber disappeared. 'It started, "Where the fuck are you!"' said the woman. 'This was a bit of a shock to me, as it was unlike Caroline to use terminology like this on an email.'

After reading of Robertson's arrest in the media, two of her former Kompass workmates, Michelle Batselas and Denise Harris, wrote to her in the Deer Park prison, sending her a stamped self-addressed envelope. She responded, inviting them to visit her on remand.

She told the women she had been sick from her epilepsy and claimed there were people who wanted to visit her 'out of curiosity'. She also told them not to believe everything they read about her in the newspapers. This letter was subsequently handed over to Homicide Squad detectives.

On Saturday, 17 April, the two women went to Deer Park to visit Robertson, spending over two hours with her. She discussed her pending court appearance but declined to talk about the case, claiming the interview room was 'bugged'.

Neither women asked her about the case but noticed that her hair had recently been dyed blonde. When asked why she had done this, she responded that she wanted to get rid of the green dye that had been in her hair at the time of her arrest. She said she had no idea why she'd had green hair in the first place.

She then accused her mother of ringing a newspaper to volunteer 'her story'. Robertson told the women she would not allow her mother, or stepmother to visit her.

After the visit Michelle Batselas continued to write to Robertson, but never received a response.

OBSESSION

Detectives building a case against the suspect on remand were intrigued by the meticulous observations contained in the hand-written dossier Robertson had carefully compiled on her chosen victim. A victim she perceived to be perfect.

Though the document bore no date, it was obvious from the detail in the character study and background history that the suspect had shown more than a passing interest in Rachel, and had been closely monitoring the girl for at least twelve months. The general opinion among the detectives was that this crime stemmed from some powerful fascination with the victim. She appeared to be a girl who had been targeted over a long period of time.

To the Homicide Squad the dossier, collected along with other equally mystifying writings from Robertson's flat, suggested almost an *admiration* for Rachel Barber. The romanticised list of the younger girl's qualities catalogued in a neat, orderly fashion down the page certainly seemed obsessive. This was not, though, a hate list. On the contrary, there was no mention of any ill feeling towards Rachel. It was only Robertson's closing statement, 'All things come to pass', that sounded warning bells.

The unhealthy interest was not confined to Rachel either.

Robertson's writings showed that she had done some detailed background work on the entire family.

Her research tracked the Barbers from their early days in England together, to Elizabeth's work in a castle, and followed them to Australia and the large country house they'd struggled to sell. She even noted the Barber home was 'one filled with joy'. She'd studied the victim's uncle Tony, and Rachel's grandfather, the prominent Australian children's writer, Ivan Southall. Living opposite Rachel in Mont Albert, Robertson would have been fully aware of the family's creative talents. Rachel's mother Elizabeth was a writer, her father a toymaker and designer. Rachel's step-grandmother Susan was a photographer and artist, her Uncle Drew an artist and author. Ashleigh-Rose had taken up the flute and little Heather, with her beautiful singing voice, was musical too.

It was not surprising that Rachel had been born with an artistic streak. It had been obvious to everyone, from very early on, that Rachel's talents lay in dancing. She danced almost as soon as she could walk. Robertson, a heavy, plain girl, could well have been envious of this slightly built dancer. She would have observed Rachel running in and out of her house in ballet outfits, hopping into the car for constant lifts to her latest performances. She'd also been fascinated by a photographic portrait of Rachel that hung in the Barbers' lounge room, commenting on her graceful neck.

Still, nothing in this profile gave police the faintest idea why Robertson had chosen Rachel in particular. And the lack of any explanation by the suspect after her arrest, and her refusal to answer further questions, left everyone baffled.

Police had sensed that there was something extraordinary about this crime. And as the committal hearing loomed, and the pile of information grew, they were able to throw more light on Robertson's character and her choice of prey.

The pile of paper was sent to police forensic scientists. Some of the notes were intriguing. Other documents made little sense to the untrained eye. Seemingly useless, innocent sheets of blank paper left in notepads where pages had been ripped out were closely scrutinised for information. If useful evidence had been destroyed in the missing pages, the forensic experts would soon find it. Using special electronic equipment, the scientists quickly discovered that these

blank pages were loaded with vital clues. They were able to reconstruct fresh notes from the missing sheets of paper – interpreting
indentations made by the writer's pen as much as six pages below.

A forensic comparison of handwriting samples was conducted
to identify Robertson's handwriting. Almost all the writings, concluded forensic scientist Dr David Black, were penned by the
killer. They were compiled into a legible transcript for Homicide
Squad detectives. And what they revealed was startling indeed.
The scientists had uncovered a blueprint for Rachel Barber's murder. In her own hand, Robertson had written down details of a
complicated and bizarre scheme to lure the teenager to her
death. It was a grim plot that involved drugging, killing and dis-
figuring her, then dumping the girl far away. Her body, concealed
in an army bag, was to be disposed of at a place only the killer
knew.

Detectives now believed that Rachel Barber's death could not
possibly have been accidental, as Robertson had originally
claimed. On the contrary, the crime had been very deliberately
planned, a cold-hearted murder that had involved considerable
thought. Crown Prosecutor Jeremy Rapke, QC, would later tell the
Supreme Court hearing that this was the premeditated and cruel
murder of a totally innocent, harmless child by the older daughter
of a family friend.

Detectives speculated about the length of time Robertson had
been planning the crime. How far back was it that she had begun
cataloguing her intended victim's movements, her physical characteristics? A fixation this powerful must have taken a long time to
germinate.

The documents included endless 'action' lists. Things to be
done, places to go. They seemed very precise and methodical,
checklists ticked off in order. Always organised. Among her plans
was a trip around Australia for the weeks immediately following
Rachel Barber's disappearance. There was also a note about a train
ticket from Melbourne to Sydney, and another about a ticket to
Queensland. Since Robertson could not drive because of her
epilepsy, train transport made sense.

Police also found an application for a bank loan, made out in
Robertson's name just two days before her arrest. She had applied

to borrow $10 000 for a new car. The application was rejected, of course. What *did* she want the money for? Travel perhaps.

In other lists Robertson recorded items she wanted to buy. Household items. Lists of cosmetics and clothing. And repeated notes on plans for cosmetic surgery. Expensive procedures: a nose job, liposculpture. Would $10 000 cover this? Strangely enough, though, Robertson had not made a single mark in her diary for the day Rachel Barber disappeared. Or during the weeks after the teenager's disappearance. Not a single note on a single day during the first two weeks of March. It seemed out of character for such an organised and careful thinker, one who had even prepared a careful countdown for the day leading up to the murder: plans for showering, dressing, calling in sick, even what she would have for breakfast.

And Robertson *had* taken extreme care to compile a priority list of the things she would need to do immediately after killing Rachel Barber in order to conceal her death. It was a checklist of all the things police later concluded she had done in the days after the murder: things like checking a farm, a reference to a bag, trashing stuff, going to the Grand Prix and arranging the loan. Then there was the name Jem Southall – Byron Bay, Bondi Beach.

Now *this* name was a bit of a puzzle to police. Southall, police already knew from Robertson's writings, was Elizabeth's father's name.

Another thing that struck the police as even stranger was that Robertson had also appeared to have completed research on missing persons: questions were listed such as, did they still have rights; and for how long? What about applying for things like birth certificates; and was there a list that enabled follow-up checks to be done on missing people? She considered the prospect of private detectives, writing in brackets the words 'six years'. Was she wondering, perhaps, how long someone might search for a missing person before giving up? Then she wrote of a plan to rent a box 'so Rachel can't be traced'. Undoubtedly this was a reference to Rachel Barber and the police assumed the box she wrote about was some kind of post-office box.

More concerning still was yet another peculiar action plan, an orderly checklist which seemed to prioritise her week. It began by repeating the mention of a farm, then on Tuesday she would arrange the bank loan; then a moving van. She'd allocated a night to disguise her hair and thoroughly clean her house, including a steam clean of all the carpets.

So, she didn't intend Rachel Barber to be found? Or perhaps *she* was intending to go missing herself? After all, she'd taken the trouble to dye her long brown hair green. And only recently too. Had she cleaned her carpet to remove any evidence that would have revealed Rachel had been there? Police thought this possible since they had found another note planning 'to fix everything', including cleaning the carpet. It also revealed plans to sleep in nearby parklands on the Friday evening, but she was arrested hours before this could happen. And since Rachel had been missing twelve days by the time Forensics moved into the flat, there would have been sufficient time for her to erase any incriminating stains or other evidence.

Detectives gathered from the telephone call trace, revealing Robertson's two lengthy calls to the Barber household the night before Rachel's disappearance, that this was when she had put her murder plan into action. This was when she offered the naive young dancer $100 to take part in the so-called 'highly confidential' psychological study she had written into her plan. This, the Crown speculated at Robertson's final plea hearing, was the bait she laid for the unsuspecting girl, a plan that was headed 'Rachel Southall' rather than 'Rachel Barber'.

In that carefully constructed plan, Robertson refers to the final phase of the fictitious psychological study. It's clear she'd given this some detailed thought because she instructed Rachel to pack a small backpack, as if she were running away. She also told the teenager to bring her wallet, her ID, photographs and clothes. Even her teddy and ballet shoes. She stressed the confidential nature of the study: 'you can't tell anybody about this,' she writes.

It appears from the plan that Robertson had intended to meet Rachel Barber outside Melbourne's Flinders Street station, but this idea is punctuated by a query about cameras in the area. The motive behind the secret meeting then becomes apparent: Robertson reveals a plan to lace a pizza with 'drowsy powder' before going through some relaxation techniques. 'Then toxic cloth over mouth – use army bag,' continues the plan. It appears she'd already contemplated dumping her victim's body far way, concealed in the bag that police assumed must be some sort of body bag. But the last line of the plan puzzled everyone. 'Dump bag separately – then I'll drive you home.' Drive *who* home? Since Robertson had no driver's licence she wouldn't have been able to drive anyone anywhere.

The tale Robertson spun must have been very convincing, and Rachel obediently kept the study secret. She did not tell her parents about this highly confidential work; even Manni just got a vague story about a job that would earn her 'heaps'. To Rachel, eager for her first pay cheque, $100 was a huge amount. She'd already earmarked the money for the shoes her parents could not afford, and she would soon be wearing them. So Rachel went along, and in keeping with the secret nature of the study, she did not mention the name Caroline Reid. She was just an 'old female friend'.

Rachel, court evidence later revealed, was 'somewhat shy and reserved' with strangers, and was more comfortable and talkative around those she knew. Because Caroline was no stranger to Rachel, she had no reason to suspect the older girl of ill intent.

Despite Robertson's lack of assistance in police inquiries, investigations revealed that after leaving her dance friends in Richmond, Rachel walked a short distance to a toilet block on the corner of Lennox Street, where Caroline Robertson was waiting for her. The older girl had earlier caught a taxi from her flat in Prahran to Richmond, walking from Erin Street – not far from Rachel's dance school – to the appointed meeting place. Rachel followed the instructions she'd been given, taking along her dance bag, ballet shoes and the teddy bear she took everywhere with her. She was also wearing the commitment ring Manni had bought her at Christmas, plus tiny diamond earrings and two gold necklaces.

The girls caught the tram to Prahran, as Robertson intended, with Rachel excitedly telling her about the new kitten and her boyfriend. But Robertson had not counted on the presence of Alison Guberek. Her sighting of the two together was to prove more than a hiccup in Robertson's scheme to commit the perfect murder.

After reaching Prahran the two girls ordered pizza and went off to Robertson's flat, Rachel probably being keen to get on with the study and head off home with her $100.

Robertson's murder plan mentioning the toxic cloth over the girl's face and lacing the pizza with 'drowsy powder' was probably designed to render the victim unconscious so that the rest of the plan could be executed without attracting attention. Robertson could carry out the disfigurement she wrote about before putting Rachel's body into the army bag she had prepared. She would dump the body and Rachel's belongings in different remote locations.

Whether she actually used 'drowsy powder' to dope her victim is unclear. But toxicological tests conducted on Rachel Barber's body twelve days after her death revealed traces of diphenhydramine in her system. This antihistamine compound found in cold and flu preparations has side effects of drowsiness and impaired mental alertness. Rachel was also found to have a blood alcohol reading of 0.05. This reading, said the pathologist, could have been a result of biological changes in the girl's body after death, though she could not rule out the possibility that Rachel had drunk alcohol beforehand. Robertson did recall buying alcohol for them to drink at Trinian Street, but Rachel, she claimed, had declined. There was no obvious explanation for the antihistamine. Rachel's family told police she had not been sick or on any medication at the time she disappeared.

In fact, despite her handwritten reference to 'drowsy powder', Robertson strenuously denied carrying out this part of the plan when questioned by Buddhist monk, Greg Sneddon: 'Jee, if I'd wanted to make the girl drowsy, I mean, I could have easily stolen it [drugs], just easily got pills from my mum's place, much more powerful pills than something like that.'

Mr Rapke, for the Crown, told the subsequent plea hearing that while it was 'not possible to say with any degree of certainty' when the prisoner murdered Rachel, forensic tests showed that the girl most likely died very soon after her disappearance on 1 March. He said that some helpful information could be gleaned from a report by Robertson's treating psychologist, Michael Crewdson, which detailed a conversation Crewdson had had with the killer. 'Caroline has given me an account of the way in which Rachel

Barber died, but was only able to do it reasonably recently. Caroline told me she had asked Rachel to do some meditation exercise . . . she told Rachel it would help with unpleasant things and told me she had been in a daze and did not want to do it. "I was in so much trouble now, I had to."'

Robertson told the psychologist that she had strangled Rachel Barber with a piece of telephone cord from an obsolete handset, then kept her body hidden in the bedroom wardrobe for two days, the cord still around the neck. When her father visited the flat the following day, he noticed that she took an 'unusually long time' to answer the door, and that the door to her bedroom remained firmly closed. Robertson later told Mr Crewdson she had shut the door to discourage her father from entering and perhaps finding the body.

Mr Rapke, in his later summation of the case to the Supreme Court, was to say that this killing had been executed 'in a particularly cruel and callous fashion. Manual strangulation seldom leads to instantaneous death. It requires an application of some force, applied at close quarters for some seconds or minutes'.

Even more distressing to the Barber family was the revelation at the plea hearing that Rachel might have had some forewarning of what was to happen, pleading with her killer just before she was strangled, 'Please, please don't.' Robertson had volunteered this information when talking to her psychologist in prison.

Though it is unclear when Robertson actually carried out the strangulation, Steven Granger, an occupant of the flat below, said he had been woken early on Tuesday morning by crying and sobbing coming from the bathroom area above his flat. He thought it was a young female, possibly a child, having 'a furious tantrum'. He said he lay awake listening to the wailing for about ten minutes before falling asleep again with the noise still going. The Crown later concluded that while the sounds possibly came from Rachel, no one could exclude the possibility that they were the cries of her murderer.

The day after the killing Robertson went to work as usual, but was notably quiet. Police investigations revealed she telephoned the Victorian Transport Corporation twice that morning from work, and again the following morning from home. Oddly, at 9.48 that morning when Robertson was at work, her workstation telephone was used to call her own home number. But it did not answer.

Subsequent police checks on Robertson's telephone line showed that on Wednesday, 3 March she had made calls to a local taxi truck company, though no record of them was ever found at the company itself. The Supreme Court was later told that it was reasonable to conclude that the prisoner transported Rachel's body to Kilmore that day.

In spite of the 'cock and bull story' Colin Lovitt, QC, said she had originally given to her lawyers about having help with the actual killing, it transpired at the Supreme Court that she had acted alone. Mr Lovitt said that once Robertson had decided to 'come clean' she'd even admitted that her earlier version had been 'bullshit'. She then admitted to hiring a truck and telling the driver that she wanted him to help move a statue, or sculpture, to the Kilmore property. He probably had no idea that the figure wrapped in blankets and concealed in an army bag, lifted out of her wardrobe and into the truck, was the body of a dead girl. At Kilmore, she instructed the driver to drop the bag off next to the house. She told Crewdson she then dragged it to the clump of trees, burying it 'in a hastily dug shallow grave'.

The van Robertson claimed she had hired was seen by neighbours at the Kilmore property on that Wednesday afternoon – two days after Rachel's death. It was sighted near the clump of trees where the girl's body was later found. One neighbour claimed she saw the faded white older-style van in the grounds late that afternoon. She had been driving to collect her children at a nearby pick-up point just before 4 p.m. that day, when she noticed the van moving away from the clump of trees. She described seeing two people walking alongside the van, apparently talking to one another. The van was moving, she said, so a third person must have been driving it.

Of the two walking people, the neighbour claimed, one was short and stocky with dark shoulder-length hair, while the other was taller and thinner, with shorter, fair hair. But she was unable to tell, given the distance, whether that person was male or female. When she returned a short while later the van was still at the property.

Another neighbour also reported seeing the van, but because it was moving she could not see who was driving. Later investigations failed either to identify or locate the driver, or the third person supposedly sighted in the area at the time.

On Friday, 5 March, four days after Rachel Barber's disappearance, Robertson appeared to have recovered from her alleged illness. Using some of the free tickets handed out around her office, she attended a practice session for the Formula One Grand Prix. This was the same day the Barbers had attempted to visit the event as well, looking for their daughter.

Two days later she telephoned the Barbers' house and spoke with Rachel's uncle, Andrew Southall, for fourteen minutes. He recorded her name and number on a notepad along with those of other callers that day and, though he cannot recall what they discussed, he feels sure he would have informed Robertson – who gave him her old name, Caroline Reid – that the family was out, still searching for the missing girl.

On Thursday, 11 March and Friday, 12 March, Robertson left messages at work saying she was still sick and would not be coming in. But when the supervisor rang her home on the Friday requesting a medical certificate, there was no answer. Robertson had already left by cab for the city, probably to make arrangements for her train ticket out of the State. She was still in the city when detectives from Missing Persons first called at her flat during the morning. Returning home at around lunchtime, Robertson telephoned Donna Waters. She wanted the rest of her money, this time for a 'musical session'. She rang Waters again that afternoon, just two hours before the police returned with the keys to her flat.

Robertson's semiconscious state when the police found her in the flat was thought to have been the result of an epileptic fit induced by their forced entry. Manufactured symptoms could not be ruled out, however, said Mr Rapke at the plea hearing.

At the final plea hearing Jeremy Rapke told the court that in considering the mental and emotional state of the defendant at the time of the killing it should be remembered that Robertson had shown some degree of clarity in the days following the murder – chasing up money, working some full days, and her visiting the Grand Prix, where her employers observed her to be 'in good spirits'.

'If she'd been struck by immediate remorse or regret for what she had done, she was able to suppress such feelings to an extent that she was able to function normally and efficiently, even ruthlessly', he said in his closing speech. 'Her conduct after the murder was, therefore, particularly cold-hearted and calculating. She had set about creating the impression that she was leading a normal and unremarkable life, while having the body of a child that she'd murdered in her cupboard and planning and executing its disposal. And at the same time attempting to gain funds, presumably to assist her in her own escape from justice.'

Caroline's profile on Rachel, her methodical death plan and the orderly checklists of a killer intending to get away with murder certainly added up to damning evidence. And the police, armed with this information for the Crown, were well prepared by the time the suspect's name appeared on the committal hearing list.

A much thinner Caroline Reed Robertson arrived at the hearing before the Melbourne Magistrates Court on Monday, 31 January 2000. She was handcuffed to two prison officers. This was her first court appearance in several months. Her depressive illness combined with the stress of the pending court case had undoubtedly contributed to her weight loss.

For members of the Barber family, it was their first opportunity to glimpse the young woman accused of killing Rachel. They filed into court to ensure that Robertson felt their presence. But because the Crown intended calling them as key witnesses in the trial, still many months away, Elizabeth and Michael Barber were not allowed to hear any of the police evidence that would be aired over the coming two days.

It was at this preliminary committal hearing that the bizarre story of Robertson's blueprint for murder emerged for the first time. It had all the elements of a thriller – and the media seized upon it. A weird, obsessive girl, hatching a macabre plan to kill a pretty young dancer. A contrived plot, reconstructed from old notes. Evidence penned by an apparently ordinary young woman from a middleclass family living in an affluent suburb. A quiet office administrator, a former babysitter.

Prosecutor Robert Barry outlined the strange case, calling witnesses to support the contention that this was a cold-blooded killing executed by a callous murderer. He called Robertson's work colleagues, the neighbour who had heard the early-morning sobbing from the flat above, neighbours from Kilmore who had seen the van, scientists, pathologists and police.

Robertson sat quietly throughout the hearing. But her defence lawyer, still armed with her earlier yarn about her two supposed accomplices, took care to explore this possibility. It was corroborated by the evidence of the Kilmore neighbour who was convinced that she had seen *three* people at the Reids' holiday home.

A forensic psychiatrist, Dr Helen Parker, called by police to assess Robertson's ability to answer questions, told the court she could find no major physical, intellectual or psychological problem with the accused that would prevent her from pleading to the charge of murder.

At the close of the hearing, Robertson formally pleaded not guilty to the murder of Rachel Barber. Magistrate Frank Hender determined that there was sufficient evidence against the defendant to support a possible murder conviction, and ordered her to stand trial in the Supreme Court. As Robertson was handcuffed and led away, back to Deer Park to await a trial date, police issued an appeal for more information about the van and the 'two other people'. But they did not believe for a moment that anyone other than the suspect was responsible for the death of Rachel.

Caroline Reed Robertson's trial was listed for September 2000 at the Supreme Court in Melbourne. She was still maintaining her innocence.

But a week before the case was due to be heard, the family received an unexpected telephone call from Paul Ross at the Homicide Squad, informing them that the hearing date had been postponed again. They were given no explanation, but it looked as if paperwork for the defence case was still outstanding. The waiting game began again. The case was eventually relisted for trial on 10 October before Justice Frank Vincent.

Witness subpoenas had already been issued when the Office of

Public Prosecutions was notified of a significant and unexpected development. A last-minute bombshell: Robertson wanted to change her plea to guilty.

Detectives at the Homicide Squad greeted the news with sighs of relief. Paul Ross was later to say that while police had strong evidence and had always been confident of securing a conviction in the case, they had anticipated that the trial would be a prolonged and painful affair for the Barber family. A guilty plea meant that the family would be spared the distress of hearing fabricated stories from Robertson – a manufactured, sanitised version of their daughter's death that would only have compounded their anguish. Now they would be spared the trauma of having to give evidence. And it would mean that the Crown did not have to call witnesses to prove what Robertson's writings had already told them. That she was the killer.

Since her change of heart there would be no need to prove the case beyond reasonable doubt. No trial by jury. No agonising wait while the panel of twelve men and women considered a verdict. The case was relisted for plea mention the following morning.

The sudden change of plea took the media by surprise. The press bench was virtually empty, save for a sole journalist from one of the daily newspapers.

At the brief hearing Robertson's barrister Colin Lovitt, QC, told Justice Frank Vincent that his client had given him 'quite firm instructions' that she wanted to change her plea from not guilty to guilty. Later it would be revealed that Robertson's change of heart had followed 'a tempestuous period of internal turmoil'. This led to her terminating investigations which had produced material Justice Vincent claimed might have 'greatly assisted her legal situation'. But now she'd told her lawyers to formally abort all outstanding investigations.

The defendant, who had to be guided past the press bench and up the staircase into the heavily oak-panelled dock, was escorted by prison officers. She was asked to stand and was arraigned before the court, formally entering her new plea. Mr Lovitt told the brief hearing that a weekly visit from a private psychologist had been necessary to keep Robertson alive, and he informed the judge that further evidence would be called at the full hearing to show that the defendant had been a desperately discontented person with an unhappy family background.

The case was adjourned for a two-day full plea and mitigation hearing at the Supreme Court before Justice Vincent on 25 October. Since there was no longer to be a trial, the only witnesses called would be those giving evidence on behalf of the killer.

28

A New Persona – Total Revhead

'Jem Southall – 16 years – Total revhead' ran a note presented in evidence at the Supreme Court on the first day of Caroline Reed Robertson's plea hearing on Wednesday, 25 October 2000.

The handwritten documents had not made much sense to detectives originally studying them. But this note, combined with the application for a copy of Rachel's birth certificate, raised a new suspicion. And at the Supreme Court in Melbourne, on a miserable October morning, what already promised to be an exceedingly strange murder case began to take on a new dimension.

An incredibly bizarre twist seemed to be emerging from the investigations, and it gave the Crown a possible motive for murder. Robertson, it appeared, had not just planned to *kill* Rachel Barber, she had wanted to *become* her. Or at least somebody closely resembling Rachel Barber, with all the admirable qualities and physical characteristics she perceived in the young dancer. Somebody far removed from the '*nobody*' Caroline Reed Robertson considered herself to be.

'It seems from the prisoner's handwritten notes, that she intended to adopt the name "Jem Southall",' stated Mr Jeremy Rapke, QC, opening the Crown's case at the two-day plea hearing. 'She even constructed a short personal history of Jem Southall which contained fictitious details of the parents of the new persona,' he said.

Robertson described her new alter ego as sixteen years old and a 'total revhead'. She was going to reinvent herself as someone younger, more dynamic, different. A real go-getter.

Another document confirms the existence of this extraordinary identity-swap scheme. In this one, Robertson begins scribbling Rachel's name in capital letters, slowly renaming her Rachel *Southall* as she goes down the page. Then Rachel's name disappears and a new signature emerges – *Jem* Southall. She doodles the new name repeatedly as if this new identity is slowly evolving from her imagination, the new person subtly replacing Rachel Barber, whose name has vanished. 'Jem, Jem, Jemmy', she scribbles. Then, 'Oh Baby, baby, how was I supposed to know'. She signs off with 'Cool Bananas', punctuated with a heart.

More puzzling is the sudden appearance in her writings of the international racing car celebrity Jacques Villeneuve. Police knew from Robertson's conversations with friends that she expressed some interest in Formula One racing. She had, after all, gone to the Grand Prix in Melbourne just two days after disposing of Rachel's body at Kilmore. Perhaps Villeneuve's name featured in her fantasy of becoming someone new because of his glitzy lifestyle – the lifestyle she may have dreamed of having. In other writings Robertson refers to the Australian entertainer Dannii Minogue, Villeneuve's love interest at the time and a self-confessed chameleon of 1990s transformation herself. Alongside the 'Jem' signatures Robertson had also written, 'Jem Southall Year 11 – 2000', suggesting that in her fantasy she was already projecting herself a year ahead, into the new person whose identity she planned to assume.

Rachel Barber, like the new persona Jem Southall, would have been a Year 11 student by the year 2000 if she had not already left school to pursue dancing full time. If the undated document had been written before Rachel had even left school, it would explain Robertson's assumption that the girl would be in Year 11 by 2000. And this meant that the crime could have been germinating for more than eighteen months.

It was plausible, said her defence lawyer Colin Lovitt, QC, that the crime *had* been motivated by the killer's desire to become Rachel Barber – or at the very least to reinvent herself in an image resembling that of the girl who possessed all the wonderful qualities she lacked. A talented, loved, pretty, popular child who had the makings of a big star.

'Rachel had everything going for her, and she had nothing going for her,' said Mr Lovitt. 'So, it seems, she [Robertson] ultimately decided, in the most illogical fashion that it beggars belief, that she would take the life of a child, because she could then, in some way, become that child, or at least have the qualities of that person as she perceived them to be.' It was baffling to all concerned, especially to Robertson, he explained. Everyone trying to help her had all 'drawn a blank' when it came to offering a reliable explanation for what had occurred. Mr Lovitt said 'her motivation we can only guess at'. He found it totally irrational: 'and I must say after many, many homicide cases one has seen, I have certainly not come across a more frustrating or more irrational taking of a human life'. The last-minute change of plea, he said, illustrated Robertson's remorse for her crime. It resulted from the passage of time, her conscience and her friendship with the Buddhist monk now supporting her in jail.

The Crown concurred with the defence that the material before the court did not give 'an entirely reliable picture' of the motive for the murder – though, if it lay anywhere, it appeared to be in the killer's jealousy of Rachel Barber's attractiveness, popularity and success, in the desire to emulate the successes of the girl with whom she had become 'infatuated'.

'The writings of the prisoner show an abnormal, almost obsessional interest by her in the deceased,' said Jeremy Rapke, QC. 'Her writings are replete with references to Jem Southall and one is driven, almost invariably, to the conclusion that it was the plan of the prisoner, after killing the deceased, to assume a false identity – more than likely that of Jem Southall.'

So what slowly emerged during the course of this two-day hearing was a deeply disturbing portrait of a plain, depressed young woman who, like Rachel Barber, was the eldest of three daughters, and who had once lived with her family in the house across the road. But it was a warped mirror-image Robertson saw reflected from the happy Barber household. Robertson had little in common with Rachel and her loving close-knit family. Robertson was the first-born in a crumbling, unhappy, though well-off family on the brink of divorce. Rachel, charming and apparently blessed, might not have been well off, but she had beauty, recognition, love and happiness.

When Robertson set out to obtain a copy of Rachel Barber's birth certificate, she had already rented a post-office box presumably to avoid detection. But when she filled out the application, she ticked the box indicating that she would pay for it by cheque. Presumably a personal cheque in her own name, which was certainly a major slip-up in the carefully planned scheme.

In Caroline Reed Robertson's unhappy mind, her fantasy had found its focus. And as in all fantasies, everything was perfect. *She* was perfect. Jem Southall was young and beautiful. Her notes about cosmetic surgery suggested a plan to reinvent herself into the 'total revhead' of her dreams. She would do this, she wrote, through liposculpture for a new slimline figure. She would achieve flawless skin, perfect white teeth through bleaching. She would dye her hair different colours, just as Rachel had.

Robertson also made comparisons in her notes between Rachel and the young Hollywood actress Claire Danes, who played the lead role in Baz Luhrmann's *Romeo and Juliet*. 'Nose job as per Rachel Barber/ Claire Danes/ Juliet,' she wrote. She had collected dozens of coloured photographs of Claire Danes, and others of another Hollywood actress, Katie Holmes – teen heroine of the American TV show, 'Dawson's Creek'. 'Smile and talk to one side (like Katie Holmes/Jewel) – clear big open eyes (like Katie Holmes/young CR)', Robertson wrote. The 'Jewel' referred to an Alaskan pop singer who has the same luminous, angelic wide-eyed look as Claire Danes, Katie Holmes and Rachel Barber. The initials CR possibly referred to a young Caroline Reid – perhaps as a young girl she had found herself more attractive.

Robertson had already noted Rachel's large hypnotic green eyes, and her habit of smiling and chatting with her head to one side: she had been watching Rachel very closely indeed. Elizabeth Barber remembers being shown the collection of photographs of Claire Danes by detectives who were suspicious that the young woman in the photographs might in fact be Rachel. Since neither Elizabeth nor the police followed show business with the same devotion as Robertson and other young girls, these pictures remained unidentified until after the murderer was sentenced. Yet they fit perfectly the image of the new Jem Southall persona Robertson intended to assume. The groovy, fresh-faced teen chick who was to live in Bondi Beach or Byron Bay, where beautiful people *should* live.

During the plea hearing Caroline Reed Robertson, who had been led through the packed courtroom into the dock, sat quietly between two prison guards. Now almost thirty kilograms lighter than she had been at the time of her arrest, Robertson was a fragile-looking figure. She appeared downcast throughout the proceedings, visibly distressed at times, and not once casting a glance at her mother Gail Reid, who sat a noticeable distance from Robertson's father David, at the back of the public gallery. She had already spent 627 days of pre-sentence detention in custody. And as her barrister Colin Lovitt was to tell the court, her last-minute change of plea meant she already accepted that she was facing a very lengthy term of imprisonment for a crime she seemed to have only vague memories of.

As newspaper artists sketched the figure in the dock, Rachel's younger sister Ashleigh-Rose stared hard at the back of Rachel's killer's head. This didn't look like the overweight older girl she remembered from their old house in Mont Albert. This didn't look like the girl who once took her to the movies. This girl was a shadow of the dazed suspect who had first appeared before the Magistrates Court nineteen months earlier.

For Ashleigh-Rose Barber, accompanied in court by her counsellor, the day's court proceedings had been stressful. She was still upset by an earlier encounter which had taken place in the ladies' toilets earlier in the morning when she had unexpectedly bumped into Gail Reid. Ashleigh-Rose, who closely resembles her older sister, had opened the door as she left the ladies' toilet block, walking straight into Gail, who appeared equally uneasy in her presence.

The brief confrontation had been followed by an embarrassed silence. What do you say to a little girl whose sister is dead because your daughter murdered her? What do you say to the mother of the girl who strangled the big sister you loved? Ashleigh-Rose, a little girl taught to respect older people, was flustered. 'Oh . . . hi,' she stammered anxiously. Later she declared angrily: 'I didn't *want* to have to speak to her. Ever. I *hate* Caroline.'

Mr Rapke, QC, had already canvassed the possible motive behind one of the most bizarre murders in Victorian legal history. He had detailed the murder plan, the infatuation Robertson developed with her victim, the highly confidential 'study'. The disappearance, the 'drowsy powder', the disfigurement and death. He'd covered the sobbing in the early hours, the body in the wardrobe, the telephone messages. Lists and more lists.

Justice Frank Vincent, presiding, noted that it was 'an act of incredible destruction in which there were two people to be destroyed, the victim, and herself.' And he added that this 'curious' scheme had developed out of an 'abnormal almost obsessional interest' in her victim. The photographs Robertson had taken of Rachel Barber as far back as 1997, and her telephone calls during the summer of 1998–99, indicated that Rachel already held 'some level of fascination' for her.

But in Robertson's defence, Colin Lovitt stated that his instructions, 'for what they are worth', were that Robertson was 'genuinely unable' to recall the events surrounding Rachel Barber's death. She could offer no explanation at all for the murder, and was herself so traumatised by the crime that she was still suffering amnesia about what actually happened at Trinian Street. 'Whether my client has deliberately or unconsciously suppressed what has occurred, or is just refusing to tell us what occurred, it is impossible to say,' he said. He added that it was unlikely anyone would ever know why this fixation should have led to murder – because Robertson had not let anyone in on it. 'She just took her [Rachel's] life away. We can't explain that and so far – *she* won't.'

What Robertson's writings did illustrate, said Lovitt, was that even as a thirteen-year-old girl – a full six years before the murder – she had compiled endless lists about transforming herself. In 1993, in large childish handwriting, the already dissatisfied Robertson wrote of a personal and physical reinvention. It was given a title page: 'How to Change in Nine Weeks'. Then Robertson acknowledges that undergoing some magical reinvention in such a short period of time was unlikely – but it was a starting point. She reaffirms her goal of transforming herself and says her action plan will provide the foundation for her new life. However illogical this unrealistic goal might seem, to the desperately unhappy young girl it appears to be the answer to all her problems. She tells herself that while the value of a nose job as a remedy to such extreme unhappiness might seem questionable, she is in no doubt that it is a 'minor foundation' that will bring happiness and give her the strength to 'keep going and succeed'.

As well as this letter from 1993, there was also a plan headed 'Wilsons Prom' which appears to have been compiled while Caroline was on holiday. It details ideas on how she might achieve the proposed transformation. Then in another list she writes her priorities for change, beginning with a nose job, weight loss of around fifteen to twenty kilograms, 'almost flawless skin' and her goal of getting a main part in the school's Year 7, 8 and 9 productions. She also lists jazz and drama as her main interests. Being organised seemed very important to her. She was methodical and apparently needed to feel in control.

Throughout the hearing Robertson could be heard sobbing intermittently, her body shaking uncontrollably at times. At one stage in the process her distress attracted the attention of Justice Vincent, who told the defence: 'Your client has had enough,' and called for a brief adjournment to allow her to regain her composure.

Colin Lovitt said there was no doubt that while his client was unable to 'explain what had been going on in her head' at the time she killed Rachel Barber, there was 'some clear obsessional background' to the crime. Her written work revealed volumes about the disparity between her life and the life she perceived to be perfect – Rachel Barber's. He said that while Rachel was a happy girl, Robertson was depressed and experiencing 'some difficulties' within her family, especially after her parents' marriage breakdown in her mid-teens.

In closing, Colin Lovitt said this notion of becoming Jem Southall, or Rachel Barber, seemed 'an awfully obscure and irrational belief' on Robertson's part. 'How can you *become* someone else?' he asked. 'She [Robertson] is still going to have all the things she perceived about herself, about her body and face and so forth.' It just didn't make sense.

A revealing glimpse into Robertson's mind emerged during the expert testimony of forensic psychiatrist Dr Justin Barry-Walsh, who had written a seven-page assessment of the defendant in Deer Park. He said he had found nothing in the writings to support the view that Robertson had actually been *obsessed* with her victim. But she certainly had some 'abnormal interest' in the girl, who in her eyes symbolised perfection. He said that during his conversation with Robertson she had described Rachel as '*a white picket fence*' to illustrate her belief that Rachel was perfect and had, in her eyes, a perfect life. 'She acknowledges that Rachel was a bright, attractive girl whose life had everything,' he said. Robertson had used the same metaphor to describe Rachel to her treating psychologist.

Though Dr Barry-Walsh said he had found no evidence to support the Crown's case that Robertson was obsessed with her victim, he admitted that he had not been shown the documents she had compiled on Rachel Barber and her family – or the murder plan. He agreed that he could not say for sure that an obsession had *not* existed.

'What is inescapable though,' said Dr Barry-Walsh, 'is that she planned this offence and deliberately chose the victim. The victim seemed to represent all those qualities and ideals that she wished to attain for herself and could not. Thus, in the act of killing, she destroys an object in which she has invested qualities that she can never attain and towards which she may have felt profound animosity and anger because of her own self-loathing . . . It is possible that she thought she could somehow magically reinvent herself in the image of the victim.'

But Justice Vincent said the proposed disfigurement of Rachel Barber suggested the crime was more likely to be about destroying her chosen victim. While no evidence had been aired to prove that disfigurement had taken place, due to the advanced decomposition of the victim's body, if any mutilation had been inflicted by the defendant, then it would have other connotations. 'That's not simply an attempt to reinvent herself through that other person. That's got a real element of hatred about it,' said the judge.

Dr Barry-Walsh said that, since the killing, Robertson had been 'completely mystified and appalled' by her actions and was still unable to offer any motive. And she was now regretful of her inability to fully recall the events at Trinian Street. He added that although Robertson's crime showed 'a considerable degree of planning and foresight', he believed the trauma of executing such a terrible deed had caused the partial amnesia surrounding the circumstances themselves.

This lack of recall was likely to be genuine, in his opinion, and research showed that amnesia, or partial amnesia as in her case, was common among those committing serious crimes.

He said there were many reasons why people suffered, or claimed to suffer, from amnesia in these circumstances. It often persisted long after sentences were imposed, so could not always be regarded simply as an excuse employed to avoid punishment. In false cases of amnesia there were often variations in the defendant's account of events. But Robertson had consistent gaps in her recall, which supported his belief that she probably was partially amnesic about the murder and continued to be haunted by it.

The Buddhist monk Greg Sneddon, now Robertson's support in prison, had attended court to speak on her behalf. He too believed the amnesia was genuine, agreeing that she found her lack of memory upsetting and frustrating. It was Mr Sneddon's work with Robertson that had brought about the sudden change of heart and subsequent change of plea. He said her final admission of guilt and her acknowledgment that she had lied to her lawyers followed discussions in prison on accepting moral responsibility for taking the life of another. At the time when he first encountered Robertson, during her initial period of incarceration, he said he was aware that she was depressed and at a high risk of suicide. Though they often spoke briefly, she had little to say to him.

Then, while Sneddon was holding classes for other women offenders of serious crimes about accepting responsibility for their crimes, another inmate suggested that Robertson should speak with him. Initially, he said, she repeated the same story she had given her lawyers about the accomplices and how she had acted on the instructions of others.

'Upon questioning, the previous story fell apart,' he stated. He had suggested that Robertson might like to speak again when she felt able to reveal something 'closer to the truth'. But when she returned to speak openly about Rachel Barber's murder, she suffered an epileptic fit and was sent to the prison medical centre. Later, she was 'determined to continue', telling him what she could remember about the killing, which was very little since there were significant gaps in her memory.

Mr Sneddon said she was 'extremely sorry' for the murder and he admitted being moved by 'the depth of her remorse' which left her living with the 'terrible knowledge' that she had killed another person. Her acceptance of killing Rachel, he said, culminated in the dramatic change of plea. She alone had killed Rachel and could not begin to explain why.

'My feeling is that she didn't have a complete understanding of what it means to kill somebody the way we take it for granted in our society that children are educated, you know, with the number one principle, respect all life. And I would question whether Caroline has had a comprehensive education on that subject,' said Mr Sneddon. 'It became clear to me that it was somewhat of a surprise to her, the implications of taking another's life, not in prison terms, but just in terms that it's not a normal thing, that it's not what you do if you have a problem, or it's not the way it is on American TV.'

The admission of guilt appeared to offer some relief to Robertson, he told the court. She now seemed happier and less depressed and had stopped self-mutilating. She was undertaking study and had finally begun to grieve for her friend Rachel. At this, Rosa Carella, her face undeniably angry, left the court comforting her son Emmanuel who had become visibly upset.

Mr Rapke was later to say in his closing remarks that if Robertson harboured feelings of regret for killing Rachel Barber, it did not apparently 'impel' her to acknowledge her guilt for about seventeen months after being charged with the crime.

29

TORTURED SOUL

Caroline Reed Robertson's overwhelming desire to erase the over-weight, unworthy girl she perceived herself to be was clearly festering away for many years before she finally made her fatal move on Rachel Barber. In an agonising letter to her father, presented in evidence to the Supreme Court, Robertson complains that she feels like a misfit in a world filled with perfect people. She repeatedly apologises for her inability to live up to anyone's expectations, especially her own.

In despairing words, she sadly acknowledges that she'll never be the skinny, pretty girl of her dreams. She harbours thoughts about her physically flawed appearance and remains convinced that everything will always be wrong with her – from her head to her toes. She feels that nothing will ever improve, claiming fatal-istically that she will 'never fit into the world because I am what I am'.

But the depressive tone which marks the start of this letter makes way to words of rage. In a litany of fury she seethes with resentment about having to behave nicely in front of other people: she hates having to use 'acceptable language' around her younger sisters and claims she feels furious when she doesn't get her own way. Robertson hates life and everything about it. 'I hate what I hate with a passion,' she says, then quickly apologies for expressing such feelings.

This extraordinary letter was just one among a pile of frightening hate lists and letters penned by a profoundly disturbed Robertson and handed to her defence barrister by her father David Reid shortly after her arrest. It is painful material to read, and offers a significant insight into the extreme paranoia and rage of a girl who described herself as a 'misfit': a social outcast, a family outsider, a weird, ugly, fat girl, marginalised at school, bullied and turned into the butt of jokes by her friends. A girl who hated life passionately. And most of all, a girl who hated herself.

'She hated a lot of things,' said Colin Lovitt, handing over pages and pages of disturbing lists that Robertson had compulsively begun compiling as far back as 1993, when she was just thirteen years old and a Grade 8 student at Camberwell Girls Grammar, where she had been awarded a partial scholarship.

Hour after hour, sometimes in the middle of the night, a deeply unhappy Caroline Reid would scrawl wild, self-denigrating letters. She catalogued, again methodically, all the qualities in herself that she hated most. She would revile herself with intense venom before moving on to all the things she hated in those around her. No one escaped these hate letters: not her father or sisters or school friends who'd taunted her; and certainly not her mother Gail, whom she scorned and insulted with astonishing fury.

Robertson seems to have spent a considerable amount of her spare time ruminating on perceived slights or injustices – raging, furious thoughts about a world in which she saw herself as an innocent victim. She felt herself to be badly mistreated always. She poured her heart out with angry words on paper – page after page of them. Long before she turned her attention to Rachel Barber, she had begun to develop a weird and warped view of her world and everyone in it.

Many of these lists too were organised and orderly. On one page she listed her school friends, dividing them tidily into columns according to how kind they had been to her. Those who had been downright cruel; those who were followers; those who were nice. Then she gave them points in the form of fractions, prioritising them into a vengeful list with their scores reflecting how she perceived their treatment of her.

223

Back then, Caroline Reid's life appears to have taken a wrong turn into poor self-image, low self-esteem, shattered confidence. Before this, at the age of twelve, she had written an introductory letter about herself, a type of personal profile. It has a cheerful tone, and demonstrates her pride at winning a scholarship to Camberwell Girls Grammar, where she is enjoying school. She even had *likes* in that period of her life. She talks about her family, at that time still a unit, and extra drama classes. It is a normal-sounding letter from a girl whose idol is Kylie Minogue, who has posters of pop stars like Michael Jackson and Madonna on her bedroom wall. She loves the new TV show 'The Simpsons', and playing guitar and piano. In that letter Robertson mentions the Gulf War and how she enjoys reading. She's clearly interested in life. Perhaps there's one note of foreboding: at that very early age she announces her love of Agatha Christie thrillers and prides herself on watching horror movies 'without getting freaked'. The only hints of dislike in the letter relate to homework – and her view that she is ugly.

By the following year, however, *ugly* is a tame word in Robertson's abusive vocabulary. Just one year later, by the time she is thirteen, things have changed so dramatically that she holds herself and her life in absolute contempt. She hates everything, especially herself, and cannot find a single positive thing worth writing about. Over the coming six years, a desperately unhappy, lonely little girl matures into an angry, friendless, depressed adult. Throughout her teens she hates school, and by adulthood her only contacts, outside her family, appear to be with her colleagues at work. By now we see a deeply damaged young woman, brimming with intense self-loathing. Little wonder that she wished for transformation. In one of these disturbing, undated letters to her father, in childish handwriting, she claims apologetically that she's facing the end of her life. Burdened with so many bad things, she finds nothing positive to make her life worth living. 'I'm sorry I can't stop the end of my life,' she says flatly, explaining that 'everything' has ended it. There is a pervading sense of isolation and hopelessness about the letter as she says that nobody understands her pain, a pain most people couldn't even begin to imagine. She acknowledges that people think she is immature, but swears 'till I'm dead that today was the end of my life.'

In another similarly worded letter, Robertson's desperation is evident even in her style of handwriting: her enormous scribbled uncontrolled words almost spilling off the pages as she again pleads for understanding, and asks him not to be angry with her for saying her life is over.

A photocopied bundle of these writings was presented to Justice Vincent to illustrate how prolific an author of lists, letters and notes Robertson became during those early formative years leading up to Rachel Barber's murder. Seven long years of venting her rage on paper.

In one letter she says she finds it difficult to discuss her feelings with her family, preferring to put her thoughts on paper as a safe outlet for them. 'I heard a saying ages ago, "Paper is more patient than man". I suppose it's real.'

Most of the writings appear to date back to Robertson's very early teen years which Lovitt claimed were 'disastrous'. And the majority refer quite dramatically to her relationship, as she perceived it, with her mother Gail Reid.

Among these documents were the letters from as far back as 1992 when Caroline Reid would have been only about twelve years old. Some of these too indicate the despair she felt about her family and her life. In a letter written late one evening during the school holidays of April 1993, Caroline tells her father she has spent the entire break feeling horrible. She repeats bitterly the belief that she'll never achieve anything worthwhile in life and lashes out in distress, claiming everyone yells and 'bitches' at her. 'I'm so sick of everything!!!' she writes angrily, before adopting the same persecuted tone in which she states school life is hell and she's tired of being a victim. Then she denigrates herself, saying she is viewed as an ugly, weird girl who'll never fit in.

Then in September 1993 a miserable fourteen-year-old Caroline Reid drew a portrait of herself. She called it 'Misfit' and surrounded her sketch with a list of adjectives summing up her appearance and emotions. Of all the writings tendered to the court, this picture of intense self-loathing speaks most eloquently of the turmoil in her mind. She brands herself an idiot, funny in the head, calls herself 'Spotty Dotty', and claims to have a brain tumour. She believes she's boring, weird and jealous. She even writes some verse down the side of the drawing: 'If the plastic surgeon lived overseas, what a good swimmer Carrie would be!' Her desire to remove herself from the person she most hated – herself – was clearly very strong indeed. There is also an earlier drawing from 1992, where Robertson has smothered her face with hundreds of dots representing her pimples, not neat pin-point dots created with a steady hand, but marks made by the apparently frenzied jabs of a sharpened pencil.

She writes in one undated note, 'I get yelled at and hated . . . I don't let people get close to me . . .' Faintly, at the top of the note, are the words 'I Hate Caroline Club – President; Caroline.'

In another deeply disturbing letter, entitled 'School is Hell', Robertson writes of her childhood dreams of becoming an actor. Written in giant, simple, childish print, it begins almost apologetically, saying she doesn't want to burden her father with more 'childish crap'. But she reveals pathetically that she is haunted by a particular problem that has been 'pissing her off' for some months and she needs to share it with someone.

She then details an incident in which she has told her friends about her secret dreams of becoming a singer or an actor, and how she is humiliated when they respond by laughing at her. Crushed, the teenage Robertson notes that her friends have always been more 'striking, more unusual and more attractive' than she is. 'I just keep dreaming that one day everything would be almost perfect (as perfect as things can be)', she concludes.

By the time Robertson reached her mid-teens she had become a totally frustrated and unhappy young woman, stated Colin Lovitt. She writes of her feelings and problems in a barrage of 'outpourings' tinged with despair. Some of the letters she asks to be thrown away or burnt; others, including diary entries, she wrote to herself and kept. Occasionally, after writing, she would mention her intention to destroy the document, stating that putting her feelings into words relieved her despair.

There are indications in the writings of intense anxiety about herself and her future – and grave concerns about achieving many of the often impossible goals she has set for herself.

In a sad letter riddled with enormous anxieties, she expresses the constant inner turmoil and confusion that dogs her life. It's clear, from the struggle Robertson describes, that she's now finding it increasingly difficult to express her feelings to anyone, or even to understand them herself. The letter is loaded with concerns for her future and is marked by a depressive perception of what life is likely to hold for her. By now it appears she is recognising that perhaps a nose job may not provide her with true happiness. But she replaces this goal with an equally unrealistic one. This time, she claims, becoming an actor is the only thing that will bring relief and a happy life. Then she cries for help, saying, 'What am I to do?' She is so far away from reaching her goal that it seems almost unattainable.

In another tragic letter, under the heading, 'Life is Torture in Its Purest Form, aged 14', she repeats the following negatives about herself: 'Funny in the head, ugly, deformed, stupid, doormat, loser, dickhead' and again claims to have a brain tumour.

Two psychologists and a psychiatrist assessing the defendant told the court that they had read the material, which gave them a helpful and very revealing glimpse of Robertson's disturbed thinking. Mr Lovitt stated that though the court might reasonably hold the view that these were the typical scribblings of adolescence and expressed the sentiments of many young people, there was something far more troubling about them that should be considered when examining the background of the case.

One particularly unsettling letter demonstrated this, he said. The letter, which Robertson signs 'Spotty Dotty', is indicative of the despair that now tinged every aspect of her life.

By the time she wrote that letter, life had deteriorated into a black trough where she was questioning how much longer she could survive with her overload of intensely bad feelings and thoughts. 'I don't know how I have survived this long,' she writes bleakly, hinting of suicide. She can't envisage a happy future any more and says death might be her only escape from a horrible existence in which she feels embarrassed to be alive. In this letter her prolific lists which itemised the reasons for her negative thoughts have by now disappeared. She abandons any attempt to explain her thought patterns. Life, she says simply, holds no hope.

The most troubling aspect of these teenage scribblings is the mounting sense of detachment which surfaces repeatedly. She is flawed, different, less worthy, more loathesome and totally unlovable. All these negative beliefs appear to add momentum to her growing sense of 'otherness'. In Robertson's mind she's become a 'troubled, tortured soul' thrown into an alien environment 'full of angels'. She can't even communicate her feelings any more . . . except from her letters. 'Life for me sucks,' she says.

While many of Robertson's letters carry the same depressive trademark of hopelessness and helplessness, others can barely contain the mounting sense of rage she feels towards a world that has apparently abandoned her. Many open with a torrent of self-directed anger about her physical flaws. Others are outwardly angry – her giant writing dominating the pages of her notes. She tells herself it's because she's fat, weird, unattractive and stupid that she attracts victimisation and is an outsider at school. A lonely girl, she cries through her words that nobody understands or cares about Caroline the victim. Yet amid the barrage of illogical rantings she vaguely acknowledges that her mother has attempted to organise counselling for her and that her school teachers have repeatedly tried to talk to her about her moody withdrawal. She describes them asking if she's okay, but seems hostile towards their approaches.

By now she feels out of reach. 'All of the feelings and horrible things everybody says about me bottle up,' she wrote, 'and I have nowhere to explode everything.' But with such powerful feelings even a disturbed teenager like Caroline Robertson noted that she wouldn't be able to contain such angry emotions for ever. Murderous thoughts may not have been on her mind back then, but in a chilling prediction of the overspill of rage that would eventually erupt six years ahead, Robertson foretold the explosion inside her would get bigger and bigger, 'until there is nothing left inside me.'

The reports written by doctors assessing the prisoner in jail support the difficulties Robertson had in relating to her parents, and they to her. Her relationship with her father, while apparently close at times, was often strained, and in several letters she directs her anger at him. In others it is focused on her mother, who had apparently suffered post-natal depression after Caroline's birth. In her writings Caroline describes her as weak, powerless and dependent. Mr Lovitt said that in the defendant's perception her relationship with her mother had broken down 'many, many years ago'.

In one letter to her father, dated 11 November 1996, Caroline acknowledges in a defensive tone that she knows she's rude and a 'bitch', but claims that these are defensive mechanisms. Again she expresses her desire for a happy life and laments that she is feeling isolated because there is nobody who understands 'what it is like in here'.

Among the writings tendered to the court as part of the defence case was an extract from a letter in different handwriting from Robertson's. It appeared to be written by Gail Reid to her estranged husband, expressing her concern for Caroline: 'It is for my Carrie that I cry, she is so unhappy.' In return, Caroline fumes about her mother in her writings and accuses her of carping criticisms – of telling her she could never do some things like dancing. 'She said I was awful at ballet.'

At fifteen Robertson begged her father to let her move out of home. But she was clearly emotionally vulnerable and immature at that time, and he refused. Her repeated references to her parents' marriage breakdown in her letters to her father make mention of his dealings with lawyers. These notes, said Mr Lovitt, paint a vivid picture of the trauma she experienced as she battled to cope with her parents' divorce. In many of her letters Robertson refers to her parents by their first names, and she occasionally spells their names backwards.

These letters of misery escalate in intensity as the years pass and, though bizarre and disturbing, they do bear some degree of eloquence, depicting a literate and intelligent, if somewhat immature, author. As Caroline Reid matures, the entanglements in her unhappy home life cause her to resent both parents. She portrays herself as 'the blame thing' in one of her letters, and complains yet again that the pressures on her are 'so numerous I just can't humanly possibly cope with life'.

Her simmering anger seems to grow following her parents' separation when she is sixteen, and is further magnified when her father embarks on a new relationship and later remarries. The disruption to Robertson caused by this family breakdown, said Mr Lovitt, was profound.

All of this highlighted the glaring disparity between Robertson's unhappy life and that of her victim. Robertson was shattered, experiencing 'severe difficulties' with both parents – particularly her mother. She refers in one of her self-hate lists to having no family and in distancing herself from her parents she already appears to have begun the slow process of dissociating herself from the Caroline she loathes. She refuses to address her parents as 'Mum' or 'Dad', signing off in names other than her own. Even back then, in 1993, there were indications that the awfulness of her life, and her intense self-anger, had begun to manifest itself in a strong desire to escape what she described as her 'blue cardigan life' – by being someone else. She signs off her letters often using different names: sometimes she's Rebekah, sometimes Charley Robertson, sometimes *Reid* Robertson. Occasionally she uses the signatory 'Spotty Dotty' or the 'Hellraiser'. In her own mind she is now no longer Caroline Reid. And then in 1998 she actually does change her name by deed poll, retaining the name Reid but changing the spelling and becoming Caroline Reed Robertson.

In one of the few optimistic letters tendered to the Supreme Court, Robertson says that it is time she moved on in her life. She appears in this brief notation to have had some glimpse of a more positive future, saying it is time for a fresh start and expressing a desire to move to a new home in a new suburb. She will start a new school and take up new hobbies. But the hint of wanting to be a whole new person is still very much in evidence, even in this letter. She ends the letter angrily, stating she is still 'harping on' about wanting a new name. Caroline, or 'Carrie' as she calls herself, is a product 'of the shit'.

Robertson's treating psychologist, Michael Crewdson, said she saw herself as 'the bad kid' in the family, failing everyone's expectations. In revenge, her aggression was directed back at her family. She stole from them and lied. David Reid, one doctor noted, described her as a manipulative, sometimes frightening girl. Rapke, for the Crown, told the plea hearing that although no application had ever been made for bail on Robertson's behalf, any such application would have resulted in David Reid lodging an objection – on the grounds that five other women would have feared for their lives.

Crewdson wrote that Robertson felt alienated and perceived a sense of unfairness permeating her life: 'Others seem to have good lives – Caroline has shit. She once painted and hung a portrait of herself, which was completely black.'

This black mindset coloured Robertson's teen years completely. She lashes out at her family for not being the 'perfect child' she claims they wanted her to be. In another furious letter to her parents, she apologises to her mother for having been born, stating that she wishes she'd been aborted before birth. Her punishment for living, she says, is to live the life of a 'cursed alien'. She writes about an alien-like force inside her that compels her to commit despicable and objectionable acts like cheating, lying, stealing, swearing and screaming. She claims these feelings were there at her birth. Now, even as she verges on adult life, she perceives herself to be an older version of the same angry, confused child.

Then, in a pathetic apology, she professes to feel sorry for her parents and vaguely acknowledges the hurt and pain she is causing to her family. 'I'm sorry I'm not a perfect kid,' she says. 'I'm really, really sorry.'

In the Supreme Court, Justice Vincent asked the defence a question: 'What, if any, response was made to these various calls by her?'

Mr Lovitt responded: 'It would seem very little, Your Honour . . .' But this was only Robertson's perception of events, he said, that when she cried out for help, none was forthcoming.

'One has to differentiate between things that she says as being true and things that she is believing were true,' said Lovitt. 'It is clear that the disruption to her family had a profound effect on her in a way that clearly we can happily say doesn't normally occur but certainly has in this case.'

Little wonder then that, filled with such self-hate, Robertson's depressive state of mind would spiral downwards over the years to a point where she would plot and scheme to leave it behind for ever. That she would create a fantasy in her mind in the form of a new persona – one that she would create through cosmetic surgery, weight loss and disguise. One that she would kill for.

By her mid-teens Caroline Reid described her life as a living hell – if she could magically change herself, then she and her life would be perfect. Being perfect meant she would finally be happy.

One of her letters talks about her aspirations to achieve total perfection and she fantasises about a distant scenario where she would one day appear on TV and amaze all her old acquaintances with a fabulous new persona. She refers to a segment on 'The Oprah Winfrey Show' in which old friends are reunited with people from their past. The segment, with the title 'If You Could See Me Now' appears to have captured her imagination and in her writings she had already projected herself into this fantasy scene where she'd reveal herself as a transformed star. This, she pondered vengefully, would be fitting justice for all the people in her life that had ever insulted or underestimated her determination and talent. The newly invented Caroline would be a million miles away from the 'little deadbeat scum bag' they remembered. She would show everyone.

Robertson, it appears, pursued this fantasy of becoming a famous somebody with tragic desperation. She blamed her parents for her own lack of achievement in life. When she became a parent, she says, she would ensure everything was 'set up perfectly' to help her children achieve their dreams. She wrote of her plans to do this; by recruiting an agent for them; by organising dancing classes, acting courses and singing lessons. She would do everything in her power to make sure her children made it.

These letters were written five full years before she found a symbol for her fantasy. That symbol was Rachel Barber, according to Caroline – the perfect girl.

All of this evidence then seems to beg the question: was Robertson mad when she killed Rachel Barber? Mr Lovitt argued that while she might not have been legally insane at the time she murdered, her writings nevertheless showed that she was profoundly disturbed. Experts assessing Robertson agreed: there was no evidence of any recognised mental illness. They were divided on the subject of whether she had been actively depressed at the time of the crime, but agreed she'd been significantly depressed following her detection and arrest. All agreed she now suffered from a major depressive illness.

'She could tell me that she felt the worst she'd ever felt and she described feelings of helplessness which you often see in someone who suffers a major depressive illness, a psychiatric illness,' said Dr Barry-Walsh. But he said that while he could find no other symptoms to support the diagnosis that she was suffering from an identifiable psychiatric illness at the time of the offence, he couldn't discount it either, just that he believed it was *possible* that she was actively depressed. 'I couldn't put it higher than that,' he said.

'I think the two most striking things are her recurrent self-denigratory comments, and just the sort of avalanche of them,' Dr Barry-Walsh continued.

'The other thing that struck me was her relationship with her father, someone that she had problems relating to, but nevertheless she clearly very much wanted to have a relationship and saw it as being very important. But the theme of self-esteem just recurs, just its content and prevalence through the writings.'

In his opinion the murder of Rachel Barber was the product of a disturbed, dysfunctional woman with a 'marked disorder of personality'. Robertson's belief that she was a misfit among her peers had been reinforced, the court heard, when she developed epilepsy in her mid-teens, heightening her feelings of abnormality and 'otherness'.

Barry-Walsh said that while many of the fits were genuine epileptic seizures, some of the evidence suggested that others might have been subconsciously precipitated by stress. He agreed with Justice Vincent's observations that some of the episodes could have been 'pseudo-fits', but this didn't mean she was 'faking' them. They could have been anxiety-induced: her subconscious was seeking temporary escape from stress.

Like the other experts, however, he conceded that Robertson had been fit to plead to the charge of murder and knew right from wrong when she killed her victim. She was not, he said, legally insane.

However, a clinical forensic psychologist, Mr Jeffrey Cummins, later stated that her disturbed state of mind at the time of the killing raised questions about her ability to appreciate her *blameworthiness* for her conduct. He said her writings, her mental state in her mid to late teens and her unhappy family background had contributed to her 'extreme and bizarre' behaviour at the time of the crime, leading him to form the view that she was 'in part out of touch with reality'.

But quite unexpectedly, Mr Cummins's testimony led to fresh evidence emerging that offered a new explanation for the cause of the defendant's psychological state.

Justice Vincent told Mr Cummins he wanted to explore a previously unaired issue that had not received much attention during the hearing. Directing Cummins to a section of his report on Robertson, the judge asked if there was any 'real substance' to the defendant's claims that she had been the childhood victim of some past sexual trauma. His Honour said that *if* there was any truth to these allegations, it might explain Robertson's low self-esteem and self-hatred from a young age.

'At the end of the day, I have to consider what sentence is to be imposed upon this young woman,' Justice Vincent said. 'It is one thing to regard as inexplicable the development of an intense degree of self-hatred, an intense degree of animosity towards others and jealousy and envy and so forth, and a preparedness to destroy – not only her own personality, but the life of someone else as a consequence. That's a very difficult scenario to contemplate in a variety of senses,' he said.

But if these behaviours, he continued, were placed in the context of a young woman 'abused from a young age, and badly' then the existence of such a background history might explain her warped frame of mind, her low self-esteem and make her writings 'entirely consistent' with a history of sexual trauma. What otherwise appeared to be an inexplicable murder might then be better understood.

'The white picket fence references, and all that sort of thing,' Justice Vincent asked, 'are all, of course, very easily integrated into that kind of scenario?' Justice Vincent said everyone had been 'very coy' about discussing the issue and was aware that Robertson herself had not wanted the alleged sexual abuse story raised in her defence. This placed her barrister in a difficult position, constrained by his client's instructions. And he said that while he accepted Mr Cummins's refusal to breach doctor-patient confidentiality by elaborating on the prisoner's alleged past, the question of whether she had truly been the victim of sexual abuse was relevant when considering rehabilitation and sentencing.

'What is presented before me is a history of childhood sexual abuse which, of course, to my observation and experience, over many years, can produce enormous personal damage and lack of self-esteem in young teenagers,' said the judge. 'How prominently do you perceive that consideration as featuring in your analysis of her situation?'

'Very significantly, Your Honour,' responded the witness.

Mr Cummins said he didn't believe Robertson had concocted the story to attract sympathy, since she would then have raised the issue much earlier in her assessment and insisted on having it aired in court to assist her. Instead she had refused to allow the matters to be raised, or even explored further, which was of no benefit to her at all.

Cummins agreed though, that Robertson had told her story only *after* being probed about possible abuse. He said he would raise issues of sexual abuse routinely in such cases, agreeing that he had already read about her claims of abuse in Crewdson's report. During his assessment Robertson gave more details but said she didn't want them repeated.

Robertson, he said, was now more psychologically at ease than she had been in years. He said it was his view that she was now exhibiting symptoms indicative of reactive agitated depression, thought to be a response to immediate stressors such as the court case and her present incarceration. Mr Cummins said he, like Mr Crewdson, had also identified a number of aspects of her presentation which were consistent with Robertson possibly having a borderline personality disorder, though he was more inclined to say that her negative ruminative thinking, low self-esteem and self-doubting were more consistent with major depression.

Justice Vincent then took an unusual step. He decided to call Robertson's treating psychologist, Michael Crewdson, into the witness box. This was the man who, many speculated, offered the greatest insight into the prisoner's behaviour. He had seen her every week since her arrest and knew most about her. Surprisingly, he was the only medical expert who had not been called as a key witness for the defence.

'It is not the practice for judges, nor is it appropriate for judges, to be calling witnesses who the parties have decided not to call before them on a plea,' said Justice Vincent. 'But in the particular circumstances of this matter, and because of personal concerns which I experience in relation to the way in which I have to go about dealing with this matter, I decided that it was appropriate for me to do so.'

The judge wanted to explore further the possibility of sexual abuse. 'I don't know how far I can take it,' responded Crewdson, referring to professional doctor-patient confidentiality. He did, however, confirm that the details of Robertson's alleged abuse, while limited, appeared to cause 'an immense amount of distress' to her. If the statements were true, he said, they provided the court with a clinically demonstrable track through the self-esteem issues, the depression and the teenage years themselves – explaining the crime as 'an acting out of internal conflicts'. But whether the prisoner's story was founded in reality or not, her eventual act of strangling the young dancer, and her mental state leading up to the killing, illustrated a 'common joining together of issues', he said.

Justice Vincent said his parole board experience had led him to read 'vast amounts of material' relating to victims of sexual abuse and stated that everything about the prisoner's history was consistent with that picture. 'There is nothing that jars,' he said. But, if it *were* untrue, it could indicate the basis of some other psychological disturbance underlying Robertson's behaviour – right up to the present time. And *that* would provide an entirely different basis for the 'horrendously tragic action and killing'.

Mr Crewdson told the court that he believed Robertson was suffering from Post-traumatic Stress Syndrome. Though more usually an illness suffered by victims of violent crime, PTS was an illness that could affect the perpetrator of an offence too. He explained that Robertson was so traumatised by the murder of Rachel Barber that this form of dissociation was likely to be the cause of her amnesia. He said that in spite of this post-traumatic 'distancing' from her crime, being apprehended and incarcerated provided some catharsis as Robertson attempted to internally resolve her guilt and shame. Ironically though, the fearful prospect of being sentenced remained a barrier to any further recall at present.

He said he had no reason to doubt Caroline Reed Robertson's story that she continued to be 'haunted' by her actions – plagued by repeated memories of them at night when she tried to sleep. But she was not a young woman facing trial for an awful murder, he said. For her, at a fantasy level, she was still a young child in trouble again, where revelation of her motive brought the prospect of even more fearful punishment.

30

THE SENTENCE

Three weeks elapsed before Justice Frank Vincent announced a date for sentencing. He had already warned lawyers representing both parties at the plea hearing that since his burden of responsibility was 'heavy,' he would have to think long and deeply about the evidence.

The Barber family learnt on Monday, 27 November 2000 that the judge had made his decision. Robertson would be sentenced on Wednesday at 10 a.m. and attending media would be issued with a written statement outlining his decision.

Caroline Robertson, looking pale and distant, filed into the Supreme Court through a side door for the final time. Escorted by two uniformed guards, she was led past a watchful and cramped press bench to her seat where she stayed, head bowed, avoiding the eyes of her estranged parents who sat well apart in the public gallery behind her.

Barristers for both sides, shuffling black robes and paperwork, and whispering among themselves, their grey wigs still glistening with raindrops from the downpour outside the historic building, took their places in the bowl of the court. The Barbers, joined by the Carella family together with friends, relatives and many of Rachel's fellow dance students, sat in a nervous silence. And waited.

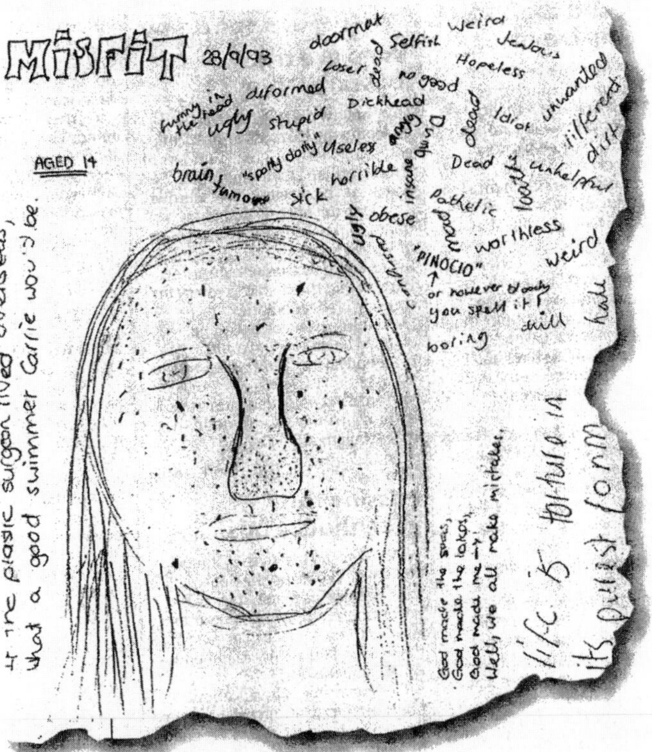
MISFIT
28/9/93
doormat
Weird
Selfish
Jealous
Hopeless
Loser
no good
funny in the head
deformed
Dickhead
ugly
stupid
dead
Idiot
unwanted
different
AGED 14
"spotty dotty"
Useless
brain tumour
horrible
insane
Dead
dirt
unhelpful
sick
obese
Pathetic
loathe
ugly
confused
mad
worthless
"PINOCIO"
or however bloody you spell it!
weird
dull
boring
hate
If the plastic surgeon lived overseas, what a good swimmer Carrie would be.
God made the stars, God made the lakes, God made me —?! Well, we all make mistakes.
life is torture in its purest form

21. The 'Misfit' portrait from 1993, by a fourteen-year-old Caroline Reid.

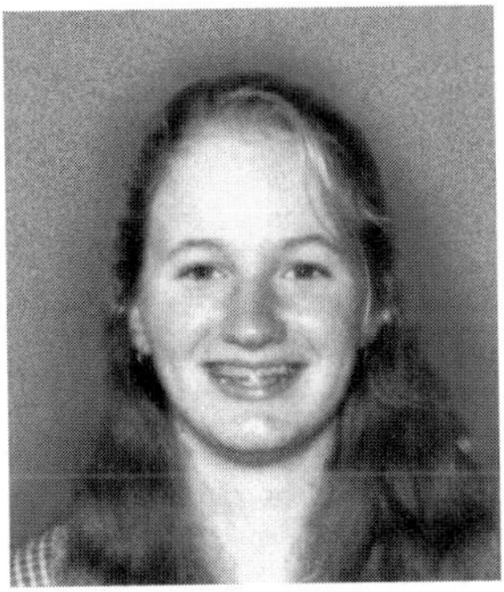

22. Caroline Reid in 1993, the same year she wrote many of her disturbing letters.

23&24. Victoria Police videotaped interview between Caroline Reed Robertson and homicide detectives. Robertson is questioned about strange documents found in her flat; the hospital dressing from the previous night is still on her hand.

25. Caroline Reed Robertson - a photograph released in 2000 by Victoria Police after sentencing.

26. Artwork featuring Rachel from Susan Southall's exhibition at the Centre for Contemporary Photography, March 1999. Rachel had gone missing at the time of the exhibition.

For wisdom is more moving than any motion;

she passeth and goeth through all things by reason of her pureness.

EVENING

Jealousy that drove a woman to murder

POLICE NEED YOUR HELP

KILLER: Artist's sketch.   MISSING: Notice that alerted public to the killer's disappearance.   LINKED TO HER DEATH: Rachel Barber, 15, who was lured by her babysitter.

Babysitter killed teen beauty in a fit of obsessive rage

Family friend plotted to kill teen, court told

Diaries reveal loner's bizarre obsession

Killer wanted to be Rachel

20 years for killing to steal beauty

Obsessive murderer jailed for 20 years

27. Headlines reverberate across the nation: press coverage of the murder was widespread and intense.

In his opening address Justice Vincent told the packed court that while a great deal was known about the circumstances surrounding the crime, material relating to other important matters 'remained silent'. But the broader sequence of events was clear and essential features on which sentence would be determined had been set out in the narrative provided by the Crown.

The judge, summarising the case against Robertson, said it was clear that the defendant had developed 'some level of fascination' with Rachel as far back as 1997. Her writings suggested that this became an 'abnormal, almost obsessional' interest. And Justice Vincent said the prisoner's reference to the proposed disfigurement of her victim's body in the murder plan was indicative of the degree of jealousy she felt towards Rachel and her family.

The reconstructed notes indicated to him that it *had* been the prisoner's intention to assume a false identity after murdering her victim. But he thought this a 'curious' scheme, lacking the careful planning of the actual murder plot. Evidence suggested that little thought had gone into the activities which followed the young dancer's death, or into Caroline's own 'curious disappearance' which was to culminate in her developing a new identity. No financial arrangements had been made before the murder to help facilitate the identity-swap plan; no careful scheme had been formulated to help dispose of the victim's body – and, His Honour noted, Robertson must have been fearful of the risk of attracting attention when faced with the prospect of removing the body from her wardrobe to the country.

By contrast, the murder plan involved a number of steps, and considerable time to execute, he said. Robertson's every action had been aimed at keeping Rachel Barber under control, while carefully avoiding arousing suspicion. 'I find the deliberation and malevolence with which you acted extremely disturbing,' he said. Despite all the unknowns in this bizarre case, he was satisfied Robertson had encompassed the young dancer's death in her thoughts for a substantial period before finally moving against her. 'In any event, whatever period may have been involved, there can be no doubt that your actions were carried out after extensive deliberation, and to a great degree, in a calculated fashion.'

Justice Vincent considered that the 'device' the prisoner

employed to induce Rachel Barber to her home had also been given considerable thought. The victim would have been vulnerable to this approach by Robertson: 'Indeed, what normal person would have contemplated the terrible existence of such a chilling design or that she was the subject of such hatred?' he said. 'I have no doubt that you appreciated that the combination of a slightly adventurous but harmless secrecy, and the prospect of obtaining what she referred to as "a heap of money", that would enable her to purchase some shoes that took her fancy, would have been very attractive to a person of her age and apparent temperament.

'Your planning in this respect possessed subtlety and demonstrates the operation of a devious mind and your possession of considerable manipulative abilities.

'I suspect that the twin fires of a powerful obsession with the perceived attributes of Rachel Barber, and an intense hatred of her for possessing them, increasingly consumed your thoughts, driving out any serious consideration of the practical unreality of achieving your desire, and motivated you to act before you were fully prepared. This view is, I think, consistent with your general conduct at that time.

'What is apparent in the material before the court in relation to your planning is the total absence of any suggestion or impression that you ever gave thought to the individuality or humanity of your victim, or any sense of the significance of taking a life. You appear to have been totally self-absorbed, concerned only with your own life situation, feelings and desires.'

The judge said that this self-centredness had resulted in the death of a youngster who, in spite of Robertson's research, she clearly *did not* really know or understand. Justice Vincent, his voice occasionally breaking with emotion, said it was a simple reality, contrary to Robertson's distorted perception, that there were no perfect lives or perfect people. All individuals were unique *and* irreplaceable in a society where every life is inviolate and should not be unlawfully taken. 'That is both a profoundly important moral principle, and a proposition of law based, in part, on sheer necessity, if we are to live together in a decent and civilised community,' he said. 'You have broken that precept, bringing about the death of Rachel Barber, motivated by envy of

240

her for her family, her beauty, and her personality, and above all, I am satisfied, because you believed that she would be likely to have a happy and successful life of a kind that you anticipated that you would never experience.'

But, he said, it was also possible to feel sympathy and sadness for Robertson, whose level of self-esteem was so low and whose deep-seated, longstanding self-hatred and envy of others were so intense that she was prepared to kill in order to achieve her 'unrealisable and unreal dream'. But her crime had created more than one victim, he said, referring to the Barber family's Victim Impact Statements, which conveyed the pain of having a young life criminally and senselessly taken. This was a reminder, he said, of the impact of crime on those intimately affected by it. 'For most in the community, in time, what you have done will become a distant bizarre occurrence,' said the judge in a quavering voice. 'But for some, and I refer to the family and friends of your victim, the anguish will remain, sometimes intensifying as milestone events take place in their lives or the lives of those around them, but ever present and constantly evoked by everyday life occurrences.'

He said that psychological and psychiatric evidence had been of limited assistance to him because of Robertson's inability or unwillingness to provide further information about aspects of her background or of the crime itself. But what *had* emerged, said Justice Vincent, was that the prisoner suffered from a deeply entrenched personality disorder.

Directing the court to the evidence of Dr Barry-Walsh, Justice Vincent referred to Robertson's home life. He noted Robertson's account of poor relationships with her parents and the numerous mentions of her obesity, which had resulted in her being marginalised and bullied at school. Her writings supported the poor self-image she later developed. It was clear, he concluded, that Robertson's alienation as she grew older increased her sense of anger. But the lack of detail in relation to the crime, and the absence of necessary information on her background, had left everyone speculating.

Justice Vincent told Robertson, who sat in the dock weeping, her head still bowed, that in sentencing her he had taken into account her age; the nature of the offence; the time she had already served on remand; and her eventual change of plea, which indicated her remorse. But, given the impossibility of understanding the motivating factors underlying the murder, he harboured grave reservations about her future and still considered that she posed a serious threat to other members of the community.

Jailing Robertson for twenty years, with a non-parole period of fourteen years and six months – but deducting from her final term the 627 days she had already spent in pre-sentence detention – the judge said he was still not confident that she showed any real insight into the significance of her crime, and suspected that her reactions were based on self-pity.

'Perhaps,' he said, 'the situation will change with the passage of time and with increasing maturity, you will find yourself able to make a full disclosure.'

PART THREE

Appeal

I have my own suspicions but they are no more than that . . . I still don't think any of us have a particularly wonderful understanding of Caroline, or the murder itself . . . I am left with that sense of not being one hundred per cent certain about anything at all.

DR JUSTIN BARRY-WALSH, FORENSIC
PSYCHIATRIST FOR THE DEFENCE

31

LETTERS TO RACHEL – EXTRACTS
FROM THE SECOND YEAR

The days leading up to the first anniversary of Rachel's death . . .

Tuesday, 8 February 2000

Dear Rachel,

Yesterday was torrid. I took your daddy to the doctors as suggested by Michael Clarebrough and he totally collapsed while he was there. He hyperventilated, got the shakes, was crying, lost his mobility, got pins and needles in his hands, and numb lips, on top of the continued pressure in his chest. It was very distressing.

Kathy, our doctor, ordered ECG and blood tests but she thinks the symptoms are related to a post-traumatic panic attack. He's had about four of these now, always slightly different. He admitted to Kathy that he falls into depressions, sometimes three or four times a day, and admitted to periods of depression before your murder as well. She's told him to see Michael Clarebrough once a fortnight and she is going to prescribe him anti-depressants which will also relieve his panic attacks. He couldn't even hold a paper bag to his mouth to breathe in carbon dioxide. When he left he was walking like Frankenstein or like someone recovering from a stroke. He eventually got back to the car but couldn't even hold a pen to sign his name properly. Afterwards he laughed about it but said he was scared at the time . . .

This time last year you had approximately twenty-one days to live. I have a book on how to have thin thighs in twenty-one days. Sometimes twenty-one days seems like a long time but then so does the last hour of school on a hot day. Twenty-one days more.

I wonder if Caroline Bloody Reed Robertson has any regrets. I wonder if she wished she could turn the clock back. Only twenty-one days, Rachel, a number of years that will elude you. You will never be twenty-one years old, or eighteen years or sixteen. Darling, I'll have to leave now, I'm getting tired.

Loving you for ever,
Mum.

15 February 2000

I went back to work today for the first time since the committal hearing. My boss Deb let me have some more time off. It wasn't too bad today, but I don't know, by the end of the day I was so miserable. I can't ever get over this, Rachel. I so desperately need you. Come on, walk or burst, as you so often did, through the front door, laughing and shouting for fun.

Caroline must be made accountable for what she has done.

17 February 2000

Dear Rachel,

It's 11.35 p.m. and Dad is tinkering on the guitar in the living room. The television was turned off at 7 p.m. and we had a musical evening . . .

When Dad came back with Ashleigh-Rose she must have played her new flute for about two hours, sipping water and playing Celtic pieces. She's going to play in a flute quintet at her secondary school fete.

Heather played her violin and was very excited – she could sight read a new piece her teacher was going to show her. We are at long last getting past the scratchy bits and she knows four open notes and four string notes and is very proud of herself. She also played the clarinet for us and can play 'Mary had a Little Lamb' and 'Hot Cross Buns', and also played a long G note for sixteen seconds. She wants to play at school assembly next week.

So from 7.45 until 9.45 we adoring parents sat and listened. I said, 'Once it was dancing,' and that was nearly every night. Ashleigh-Rose and Heather are now developing their own individuality – their own space. Rachel, the guts were knocked out of this household. It became a very silent house without you – without their choreographer and director. There was no dancing, no theatre productions. But now they are re-forming the family entertainment soirées. Music – yes, but no dancing. Just then I thought of Garry Disher's *The Bamboo Flute* because in this story, after the father had returned from war, there was no longer any place for music. And I suppose that's a bit how I felt – for a long time. Once I could never have imagined a time without music.

I could see Daddy smiling again. He saw Michael Clarebrough today and I believe it went very well. He wants your dad to keep a journal so I'll buy him one, even though your daddy doesn't think it will work.

29 February 2000

Well, dear Rachel,

Today is a leap year. If you had been living it would only have been your fourth leap year, and yet of course you are not. And for the leap year reason I feel as if this date represents your death. But your death date will also appear to go on for three days. Like your disappearance, discovery and funeral. Everything in slow motion.

On Sunday morning I went to church by myself. I sat there thinking that, regardless of the outcome of the trial, Caroline would still be accountable before God. As I was listening to the readings I felt as if God had spoken to my heart and asked me directly, 'Do you believe in capital punishment?'

'You know I don't,' was my response in thought.

Rachel, the answer that came back was so immediate it was as if God had said directly, 'So then, why should I?' I understood this to mean that if I don't believe in capital punishment on earth why should I then expect God to believe the equivalent after death.

Rachel, it made a lot of sense. Caroline will only need to ask for forgiveness. God would know if her heart was sincere. But then, why would Caroline care for what God thought?

I came home after church thinking we'd go to the Bayswater Family Pet Care Day, like last year, but Ashleigh-Rose didn't want to and was watching *Those Magnificent Men in Their Flying Machines*. After a while I went to bed to sleep.

Later I decided to go to the Pet Care Day by myself, but Heather said she would like to go with me. I just thought it had been such a lovely day last year why not go and remember the day . . .

No letters were written from 1 March until 6 March 2000, the week of the first anniversary of Rachel's death.

6 March 2000

Dear Rachel,

See how long it has been? Our lives have been so full of grief this past week, it would be folly for me to try and remember it all.

The last week began with the thought that this particular date should not be remembered as 'one year dead', 'two years dead' et cetera, but rather, 'one year with God', 'two years with God'. Yet on 12 September, your birth date, I know at the same time every year, I will be thinking . . . sixteen, seventeen, eighteen years . . .

Your father and I relived your death date for three days. Monday, 28 February 2000 representing Monday 1 March last year. Then Tuesday, 29 February representing the day of your death, because if not for the leap year it would have been 1 March. And then Wednesday, 1 March as the day formally recognising your date of disappearance and death.

248

On Wednesday at about four o'clock we all went to the cemetery. Manni and his mum and dad had already been in the morning and many of your school and dance friends left flowers.

I placed notices in the *Age* and the *Herald Sun* in the In Memoriam section. I had problems with the *Herald Sun* because they did not want me to use the word 'murdered'. They said it would upset their readers. I said, 'I am a reader, I am the mother, and you are upsetting me.'

I had written:

Barber, Rachel, born 12th September 1983
Disappeared 1/3/99.
In loving memory of our beautiful daughter and sister,
Senselessly and cruelly murdered.
A tragedy that cannot be undone.
But we remember her soul can never be destroyed.
For Rachel is with God.
Remembered and loved by many.

I said to them, what about all the murder and mayhem in your paper every day? They said I could use the word 'taken'. 'What about "killed"?' I said. 'No,' came the reply, apparently from the supervisor. So I said, 'Forget it.'

I spoke to my boss Deb and she went on about the justice system again and I said it had already been *agreed* that you had been murdered. She said, they probably didn't want to distress little old ladies, like her friend, who read the Death and In Memoriam columns daily. But half an hour later this elderly friend was in the bookstore looking for a crime novel with a good murder plot!

Anyway, I rang up Rob Read to check the legalities. He said, fax the notice to him and he would ring the Media Liaison Unit. Later on the same day the *Herald Sun* rang me back, apologising, and placed the ad for me.

Rachel, I know you wouldn't want us to continue to be sad but how can we not be? It's like your dad saying he'll see something funny on television and then laugh but think, 'How can I laugh when Rachel's not here?' I know what he means because I feel the same.

Susan gave us a photo album of graveside photographs that you may or may not approve of, but I find them really interesting and I am pleased she has done it.

My thoughts are all over the place. Sorry. I took your dad to see Dr Wallace for his check-up. I think the tablets are easing him. He seems as if he's floating. I'm the one who is very tense and irritable.

Last year was so hard. I mean the fortnight when no one knew what had happened to you. And we are reliving it all now – *every* day – *this* day. It was on 6 March last year that I called the policewoman behind the front desk a fuckhead. I still find it hard to believe. But I was so *frustrated*.

I've been lying here in bed remembering times we shared together. Do you remember the time Manni rang you from a public phone box in Moonee Ponds, at night, and told you how he had to hang up quickly because he was scared of some hoodlums in the street? You were sitting alongside me in bed and collapsed in tears. You wouldn't rest until you received a phone call from him at home. 'What will I do if they kill him?' you cried. 'I couldn't live without him.' And now of course Manni has to learn to live without you.

You were a funny girl sometimes, Rachel. I remembered the time you and Manni broke up, for I think thirty to forty minutes, and then how pleased you were when you made up. I remember watching you kissing and hugging Manni in the carpark behind the dance school while Rosa and I waited in our cars.

Tomorrow is my birthday. I'll be forty-one, and next year I'll be forty-two. So many years ahead without you . . .

8 April 2000

Dear Rachel,

March was an *awful* month – always will be. I have not kept in touch through these letters, and I am sorry, not only for you but also for your sisters and myself. My memory isn't very good and I've realised that so much of our lives is forgotten. Writing things down restores that part of our lives. I contemplated stopping addressing these letters to you. Thought I should just date them like a diary entry. But it is comforting speaking to you in the first person. And does it really matter what other people think?

I think I stopped writing because I was so desperately sad, but I need this sadness, Rachel, to 'recover', although that is not the right word.

So many things have happened.

We remembered so many significant days in March.

I saw Michael Clarebrough.

I went to the Victorian Missing Persons Meeting and met an assistant commissioner of the Victoria Police who asked me if I was the mother who had the problem with the police. I realise now that there was nothing they could have done to save you. I told him how Michael Clarebrough felt I should speak to the police but I was nervous of this. He felt it was a good idea and the outcome of this is that Michael spoke to the assistant commissioner and a meeting with him is being organised.

I've handed in my notice at work. That's it. I've made the decision, finally, with your dad's help, when we went to Indented Head for a weekend by ourselves.

Indented Head – so good – long drives along the Great Ocean Road to Lorne. Erskine Falls – so many steps. Dinners at pubs and walks through Queenscliff. Walks along the beach and mudflats. Afternoon tea at the Soho Gallery and Tea Rooms – an exciting place. We collected 'Henry Moore' rocks from the beach (rocks with interesting holes). Anyway, this time away by ourselves helped me with the decision to resign. I realised I had been expecting too much of myself.

Manni is doing well. He's got a place with a regular dance group on television in a new program called 'Stardust'.

We're taking a one hour walk each day . . .

I haven't seen much of my friend Chris lately. In fact I haven't seen much of anybody. We, too, now have a silent number . . .

I am pleased I am taking the rest of the year off. I will veg out. I will walk daily, garden and write. I will be creative. I will live the dream I once held for myself because your dreams were cut short.

I will write *for* you, and I will write for *myself*, and I will write for our family. I need to believe in my dreams, as you once taught your friends to believe in theirs.

Rachel, be with me for ever. Be with your dad and sisters, and give your darling Manni strength and hope for the future. Help him when the time is right to one day find a loving partner. He is only seventeen . . .

Love, Mum.

Later in the day . . .

Dear Rachel,

I'm scared. Help me, please, my darling Rachel, I'm scared for Ashleigh-Rose and Heather. How are we going to get through the next few years? I honestly don't know.

Ashleigh-Rose is now in Year 7. I remember your Year 7 and you grew up so much in that year. She wants to be grown-up, Rachel. She has a Year 8 friend over tonight. I can hear them giggling and being silly. I thought that because of all the tragedy last year Ashleigh-Rose would concentrate on school and tread easily, but I think she'll want to move on into independence more quickly than I am prepared to grant it.

I'm scared for their future. I'm scared because of the trial, and I'm scared because of all the media attention. There is apprehension in me, a bubbling, simmering confusion of despair. I want to cry. I want to raise your sisters to be happy and successful – whatever that means – but sometimes I wish that this had already happened. I'd like to wish my life away just to know I've done it. Raising children is a big task – and I failed you. I know your death wasn't my *fault* but I still feel I failed as a mother because I didn't get you through your teenage years safely. Some bastard killed you, and there was nothing I could do to protect you, and I still feel helpless for it . . .

15 April 2000

I'm truly sorry if the agony in my heart distresses you. How much do you love me? Hold me tight – close to your soul. Let me feel your love near. Let me dream of you. I feel jealous when Rosa tells me Manni has dreamt of you. I ask myself, perhaps selfishly, what about *our* family?

Do you think we betrayed you by not seeing your body? You do understand the police didn't want us to. I'm sorry if I'm saying things I shouldn't but I grieve so much and constantly go over in my mind whether the events of 1 March could have been altered. But then who is to say that Caroline would not have killed you on another day? It is so EVIL. And HATEFUL.

I'll tell you how I feel – I don't want to make new friends. My old friends don't contact me. I feel like a social leper. But then I don't make it easy for them. I cannot fail to talk about you. Even if I try not to, I still do. I feel as if we have been marked. Dulcie said she didn't think it was good for Manni to talk about you to the press because of his career, but it wasn't you or Manni who had done anything wrong. It is cruel. I don't want any part of it. Yet, I can still place the Reids' names on prayer lists and even pray for Caroline.

I so desperately want you back. I am scared of the coming trial and I am scared Caroline will get off. Is it true that money can buy freedom?

I am scared of struggling.

I feel everybody else wants to forget – to move on. But *I* can't move on. Your death is always in the present tense to me, yet when people talk of you they talk of you in the past tense – 'hads' and 'beens' and 'was' and 'used to's'. But for myself, Rachel, you are always present. I think of your quirky butterfly kisses – a thousand butterfly kisses, memories . . .

1 May 2000

Dear Rachel,

Today was the date of the arraignment. We thought we were going to attend this with your sisters but Paul Ross rang on

Friday to say Caroline would not be present and that an arraignment was really only the bit where Caroline is brought before the court and the charge of murder is read out to her. We thought this procedure would not have been too harrowing for the girls, who really want to attend court. Anyway, I have spoken to Paul twice today. There is a tentative date of 25 September for the trial. There is to be another committal mention on 15 May to confirm the number of witnesses.

Paul said that he wished Caroline would have the 'common decency' to tell us what happened. But Rachel, we know Caroline can be deceitful, so how could we ever believe her anyway? Paul Ross still uses the word bizarre to describe the murder, and the more I hear, the more it sounds exactly right . . .

I do want to go inside Caroline's unit but we can't go until after the trial. But I promise you we shall. It's symbolic to me. I want to take you out of there and bring you home.

I don't know how often I'll keep writing these journals. I'm surprised by the energy it takes from me.

Maundy Thursday

Dear Rachel,

I must apologise for yet another unfinished letter. I do try to keep my letter-writing time to you private, but one of your sisters came in and I am conscious that I must not favour writing letters to you over their company. I love you all equally.

I have been reading a great deal since my last day at work. This is good for me. I hadn't read properly in two months because my spirit felt bound up by the stresses of work. I've just finished reading *The Reader* by Bernard Schlink. One passage was about someone finding a grave where a funeral ceremony was being held. It described tall, bare trees between old gravestones, and a cemetery gardener or an old woman with a watering can and gardening shears. That is how I am, a woman with a watering can and gardening shears. I shall be for the rest of my life.

I have always felt that a cemetery has a subculture all of its own. One is thrown into another world. Surreal. Grieving parents and visitors become a new race. We exist with our memories, with our watering cans and gardening shears, we exist with our jam jars, vases and fresh flowers. Dead blooms remain at headstones alongside headstones freshened with new ones. No one would ever dream of removing another's dead flowers, because those dead flowers represent personal contact with their loved ones. But I will spray the roses near your grave with insecticide to prevent blackspot and mildew. I will water other people's roses for them on hot days and in my absence I hope they do the same for you.

And may God have forgiveness for my grieving heart in wishing accountability on Caroline.

It's a scary time ahead of us.

9 May 2000

My darling Rachel,

I was saying to your dad last night that time has stood still. You could just as easily walk through the door and it could be the same day you went missing. Your presence is still that real.

Ashleigh-Rose has been extremely distressed lately because she is scared of forgetting you. 'That's one reason why we have put more photographs of Rachel up in the house,' I said. It's not that easy, though. She says she has forgotten what you *sound* like.

One of the big magazines has contacted us and we have agreed that Megan Norris can write your story – our story. It's not the story of your death or the trial, rather it's about you, your place in the family and how the family is redefining itself without its magnet. She will also ask Ashleigh-Rose how she feels and include Heather as well. She will write a story over the next few weeks and it will be printed the week the trial finishes. Megan seems very sensitive.

I am walking every day, Rachel.

Love, Mum.

Midnight, 14 May 2000

My darling daughter Rachel,

It is ten minutes to Mothers' Day and I grieve for you as I did that first hour we were told of your death. No mother should experience the murder of a beloved child. You didn't die, you were *murdered*.

I was trying to explain to your sisters today how I can forgive the part of Caroline that is the baby she was born. I can have compassion and feel sadness for her as she was twenty-one years ago, but I shall always feel anger for the adult Caroline who murdered you. I can forgive the baby Caroline but I cannot forgive the woman Caroline. And I ask God to forgive the woman.

29 May 2000

Dear Rachel,

Your cousin Tom was fifteen yesterday. I remember the deep-thinking Tom said at your funeral, 'Well, Aunty Elizabeth, I thought I had an answer for everything. But I haven't got one for this.' I could not ring him up and wish him happy fifteenth birthday. Ben is sixteen. Lindsay must surely be fifteen – no, I think she's sixteen now. It's not fair, Rachel. Those three cousins, Ben, Tom and Lindsay were all younger than you. And now you have stood still and they have caught up.

Ashleigh-Rose will be thirteen soon, so she'll only be two years younger than you. But this is not fair because you were nearly four when she was born. And now I am thankful for those first four precious years shared alone with you. My darling baby, I miss you so very much.

31 May 2000

I rang a friend yesterday. It was good to have a chat but her conversation hovered around you and details of the coming trial. Not that I am in a position to tell her anything, only what had been in the papers.

The problem with friends who haven't seen or heard from us in a while is that they want to talk about you, and although I haven't got a problem with that, I can't help feeling that they go away and all they are thinking is, she can't stop talking about Rachel. Your dad said either way we can't win. If we talk about you all the time it's, 'Oh dear, look at them, you think they would move on . . . ' and if we don't talk about you it's, 'Isn't it terrible, they can't bear to talk about her.'

My friend was saying how dreadful it must be for us and how she couldn't even imagine what it must be like, but at the same time how dreadful this must be for the parents of the girl accused of your murder. I said to my friend, just imagine if it had been *her* little girl who had been murdered. The phone went silent for a moment. It is an unbearable, yet lived-with tragedy.

Your dad and I feel this continuing need to defend your character. It's like . . . Gee, Rachel was murdered. What had she done to make Caroline murder her? It makes me sick that people who don't know you are prepared to make generalisations about you. Your friends and colleagues and old friends know exactly what you were all about and knew there was absolutely nothing you had done to create this madness.

Caroline acted selfishly and out of pure evil. I heard tonight there had been a fire at Deer Park Women's Prison and that four prisoners had been injured. I thought, well, I hope it is not Caroline because I want her to stand trial and accept responsibility for what she did. I don't want anything to delay the trial.

3 June 2000

Even though I accept that you are dead, I cannot accept that you don't exist. Somewhere – somehow – you exist . . .

Perhaps if we had known you were only going to live for fifteen years we might not have driven you to all those ballet classes and dance concerts and ballets. And if we hadn't let your free spirit develop into the wonderful person you were at your death, you wouldn't have been *you*. The sad irony is, if you had grown up to be someone else, then Caroline may not have murdered you. Once again I am falling into the well of ifs – and how deep is that well?

So then, we cannot change our past but we can rewrite our future. We only ever have one chance of rewriting our future and that is in the present. Caroline could have chosen not to kill you – even at the final moment – she could have rewritten her future. The future can take many paths but the past is only ever the one path.

The future is a matter of choice.

10 June 2000

My beloved Rachel,

We did not clothe you for your burial. Your abandoned body lay there at Kilmore to be taken by police and dissected. We were not given the opportunity to embrace you. To gently dress you in lace knickers and lay your last concert dress across you.

Police advised us not to view your body. It had been decomposing in a shallow grave for nearly ten days. Neither could we view your body because of security for the trial. Rights become the rights of the convicted. The victim's family loses its rights in favour of the protection of the killer of their child. That is how it feels. Feelings cannot be denied.

Rachel, we were gutless. You were ours and we, above all others, should have had the courage to face your changed body. It was *you*.

My God, Rachel, forgive me, my darling. Forgive us . . .

1 July 2000

I have been reading *Heaven Eyes* by David Almond . . .

Rachel, you were brave. You taught your friends to dream. You flapped your wings and flew.

19 July 2000

Paul Ross rang today to say he had been thinking of us and to tell us that the prosecuting barrister will be Jeremy Rapke. Paul said if he was to have any preference for a barrister it would probably have been him. We won't hear for another month about witnesses.

Last night your father and I both had disturbing dreams. I dreamt I was sobbing uncontrollably about you – constantly – throughout the dream, without rest. This seemed to be mixed up with some science fiction drama. I was sobbing, in this fictitious setting, about your murder.

Your father dreamt he was collapsing with a panic attack. He couldn't move his legs and he eventually died. He said he did not remember you being a part of the dream.

However, about a week ago, maybe not even that, I dreamt I knew you were dead but I asked this weird photographer if he had any photographs of you – while you were living. He had been a snooping photographer and showed me photographs of myself, topless. He said he did have photos of you but showed me instead a video of you while you were younger – about eight years old. I then became part of the video. You were wearing the pastel-coloured mauve, pink and green striped sundress that I didn't particularly like but you loved, and you were always wearing it. Then you were running upstairs to meet me as I was running downstairs to meet you, and we hugged and hugged. It was like I was there with you and the hugging felt physical. The dream then jumped to you running across darkened roof tops, jumping from chimney top to chimney top until you were out of view . . .

I had morning tea with my boss today. Even though I'm not working any more I like to keep in touch. I was browsing in the shop afterwards when a customer of mine came and said how sorry she was for me when she heard. She had been overseas. This was happening at least once a day when I was working, and was one reason why I needed to leave work. I still have a problem with the fact that I went back to work so soon after your death. It *was* too soon and I still feel guilty about it. It seems disrespectful.

I have told Paul Ross that after the trial we feel we should see the forensic photographs of you. I said to him I know he isn't a social worker but would appreciate his support in this. I also discussed the need to go into the unit where you were murdered. It feels like we have not really had much involvement with what happened to you after your discovery, nor involvement with what the police know, because of the coming trial. We are sure there is still more we do not know about.

24 July 2000

I imagine your happy face near me. I can grab out to empty space and draw into my breast treasured memories. I remember you so strongly I find it despairing you cannot simply walk through the door and sit on the bed with me.

I still sleep with your little white cotton Bloch top. Can this ever end? You were so real. So alive. Now you are the invisible Rachel. Humankind writes tales about invisible men. Spirits are the living invisible, presences of those once living in flesh. To become invisible, must one die? The wind is invisible but it makes its presence felt. It's a force not to be disregarded. Neither then should we disregard people's departed souls.

I love you, Rach.

Love, Mum.

(Now, as I review these letters in February 2001, and I read 'Neither then should we disregard people's departed souls,' I should like to add a warning for Caroline: 'Beware, Caroline, beware of Rachel.' But such terror would be beyond Rachel's nature to even think of.

Caroline does not need Rachel to haunt her. Caroline's actions will haunt her themselves. So Caroline, if you feel haunted by Rachel, it is not Rachel who haunts you – but your own evil deeds.)

Friday, 28 July 2000

Dear Rachel,

We had an interesting night on Wednesday night.

Unfortunately Ashleigh-Rose had been ratty about home-work. She was just beginning to settle into it, and Heather was painting her salt-dough masterpieces, when someone came to the front door.

'I'm looking for a household full of people,' I heard a deep man's voice say. 'Does an Elizabeth Barber live here?'

A six-foot-plus-tall, two-foot-wide policeman stood there on our veranda.

Your dad invited him in and said, 'We've been subpoenaed as witnesses to the trial.'

'Who has?' I asked, looking at Ashleigh-Rose's ashen face.

'You, Ashleigh-Rose, and me,' said your dad.

Heather was sitting very quietly at the table, continuing to paint, ignoring the large policeman standing near by. She could see the very official-looking documents, with the stamp from the Prosecutor's Office on them, that the policeman had brought with him. And she could see the five dollars attached for travelling expenses.

I noticed the policeman's gun at his hip and looked at his shoulders and at his blue leather jacket – Victoria Police. He looked like a big cuddly bear, very friendly looking. And he was very kind, particularly when he realised how young Ashleigh-Rose was and how nervous your father was at the prospect of being a witness. His name was Senior Constable Neil Tilley.

He said that even though we had been subpoenaed it didn't necessarily mean we were going to be called. This would be confirmed two or three days before the trial. He went on to explain the process to Ashleigh-Rose, saying that at her tender age if she was called it would probably be possible for her to be questioned on a video link-up. He said to all of us that if we didn't understand any particular question we were asked at the trial then we should not answer it until the question had been repeated or clarified. He said it is sometimes a good idea to close your eyes. He said to Ashleigh-Rose that sometimes the defence counsel will try to convince you, for instance, that perhaps the colour of someone's clothing was purple and not red, but if you remember it being red, you must say red. He suggested we visit the Supreme Court before the trial, maybe call the court network people and sit in on another trial just for a little while to see how witnesses were questioned. Nobody can hurt you, he said to Ashleigh-Rose.

Later I commended the caring attitude of this senior constable to the assistant commissioner whom I met at a 'Missing Persons In Suspicious Circumstances' meeting.

After he left (and meanwhile Heather had disappeared into another part of the house) we went back to the living room. Ashleigh-Rose sat down and sobbed. She didn't just cry. She sobbed. And she trembled. 'I just wanted to *go* to the trial,' she said. 'I didn't want to be a *part* of it.'

'It's all getting very real,' I said. 'You don't have to go to the trial if you don't want to, apart from being called as a witness and then we'll look into that video link-up possibility.'

Rachel, Ashleigh-Rose was adamant. 'I want to go to the trial. I want to hear everything. I just didn't want to be a witness.' Ashleigh-Rose was eleven when you were murdered. Now she's thirteen.

She was upset like this for about twenty minutes, when we heard Heather's serious little voice say, 'I didn't get five dollars.' We stopped and laughed . . .

29 July 2000

Your grave looked so lovely today, Rachel. The grass was mown and the white pansies in the terracotta pots were in full bloom against the grey granite of your headstone. I thought of you, nine feet down. So far from reach – so sad.

There is no fear in the aftermath of death. I mean your decomposed body – your bones. I don't feel apprehension on seeing the forensic photographs of your body. In fact I would like to see them before the trial.

I said to your dad yesterday that all of this – the trial, being subpoenaed, the magazine article – all this seems removed from you. Official and important, but not a part of you. You died – no, correction – you were murdered, nearly one and a half years ago and yet this still goes on. Until the trial has finished your burial has not been completed.

3 August 2000

Your cousin Tamzin rang tonight from Coffs Harbour. She spoke to all of us for about two and a half hours. She said that during the committal hearing it seemed to her as though

Caroline was writing down addresses of witnesses. I had forgotten addresses of witnesses were given out in court. There is absolutely no way I will allow that.

We will be going to the court network at the Supreme Court on 17 August and I have begun to think about a Victim Impact Statement.

12 August 2000

Caroline has been so wicked, so wicked. She needs to stay in prison for a very long time. I don't want to face the reality that one day she will be wandering around free . . .

15 August 2000

Rachel, I've just realised that apart from our friend David, who calls in once a fortnight, and the man I reported, who still seems to call in about every eight weeks – apart from them, my friends seem to have abandoned me. Even some members of my own family find coming to the house too difficult. Memories. This is why I see myself as a social leper. Your dad reckons that's the wrong expression but I cannot think of another one to adequately describe how I feel.

Through all of this I have been thankful for your Granny Susan who is there for me. I can talk to her about you, Rachel. Nanny Joy is also there for me but I cannot speak freely with her because she becomes too distressed, and then this distresses me. For instance, last night when I looked at a video of you dancing I really needed to speak to Mum. I rang her up but I couldn't tell her I had been crying. I thought of ringing Grandad Ivan, but like Mum, I feel the need to be careful when I speak to him as well. I don't want to upset them further. I thought of ringing Robbie but at 5.30 in the afternoon she would have been busy with her children. I do feel isolated, Rachel, and some people may say I am drowning in self-pity. But, Rachel, I miss you so much.

Ashleigh-Rose has a friend whose sister turned seventeen on the weekend. She went to her party. In four weeks time you would have turned seventeen. I would have a very excited seventeen-year-old, and what's more I wouldn't be fearful for my new teenager . . .

2 a.m., 26 September 2000

Dear Rachel,

Last week Paul Ross, the Homicide detective, called in to deliver our statements in preparation for the trial. He also had some interesting news. The defence have informed the Office of Public Prosecutions that there may be a change in the plea. This is only a slight possibility, but nevertheless a possibility. Yes, Rachel, she may plead guilty. Events may take a completely different course.

But 10 October will still be the date of action in the Supreme Court. Paul Ross also said that from the time of the verdict to the date of sentencing there could well be two weeks because of the nature of your murder. It is a uniquely bizarre murder. Caroline has committed, or allegedly committed, a murder that might be the first of its kind in European history in Australia. Maybe the judge will be setting a precedent in his sentencing.

It was during Paul Ross's visit that I said I would like to work as a chaplain, possibly in the police force. He said, doesn't that take about eight years training? To be honest I'm not sure how long it would take. But first I would have to do a Bachelor of Theology and follow this by training as a chaplain. And Rachel, since Friday I believe God, crazy as it may seem, has guided me towards this. Working as a chaplain with victims of crime seems to be the absolute right direction. It's this decision that has made me feel so positive and good and I can't believe this has happened two weeks before the trial. I feel as if a weight has been lifted off my back – yet I feel guilty for feeling so good when last week, before this decision, I was feeling so wretched. Nothing is going to bring you back, Rachel, and I did make a public statement that some good was going to come out of all the tragedy. And, thank God, your dad is working with me on this.

I discussed it with your dad and he said, 'Go for it.'

I am making good out of evil.

6.30 a.m., 3 October 2000

The Olympic Games closing ceremony was great, but unfortunately I was very agitated. There were so many parts of it that reminded me of you. The dancing! Kylie Minogue singing 'Dancing Queen' (the song your friends from Canterbury Girls wanted played at your funeral but the words were not appropriate). Jimmy Barnes was singing, and remember, you have danced with Jimmy Barnes on stage. Everybody was so alive and so happy and I cried.

It's gone beyond saying it's not fair.

5.30 a.m., 10 October 2000

Events changed yesterday afternoon, just as Paul Ross had suggested.

I must admit I felt, or at least acted, in an extremely ungrateful way. I woke this morning realising that I should have been saying thank you to God and thank you to Paul and thank you to the Office of Public Prosecutions for doing their job so well.

I walked into the house about 3.45 yesterday afternoon with Heather. Your dad had driven Ashleigh-Rose to her pottery class. Susan rang me about five minutes after I walked through the door. Poor Susan, she must have wondered at my reaction. The OPP rang her because they could not contact me: the defence had contacted them yesterday afternoon – Caroline would be pleading guilty.

I should have been pleased – relieved. Even Heather knew it was good news. She said, 'Mummy, doesn't that mean she gets to stay in jail?' But instead I thought, 'She's getting off easy.' One side of me wanted her to stand in a courtroom for two weeks and be confronted by what she did to you. I wanted her name to be printed in the papers. And suddenly I realised that this had been the revenge I had wanted. I had wanted the public to know you had had no part in asking for your own death. All too often the public fall into the trap of saying that if someone has been murdered, then the victim must have contributed somehow, particularly where the accused knows the victim. This is what is so appalling in this wicked and selfish crime.

I rang the OPP after Susan had spoken to me, and the following advantages were pointed out: Caroline is unlikely to appeal on the guilty verdict since it is her own plea; a jury cannot be conned by a clever defence barrister, and there will be no trial, so witnesses do not have to be called.

I realise now this is the absolute best result. The OPP have done their job – Paul Ross has done his job.

And then I thought, in an outrageous way, that I too held deep inside a hope that Caroline had *not* killed you, only because for me it seemed more reasonable to accept that a total stranger had killed you than anyone who even remotely knew you. Anyone who knew you would not have wanted to kill you.

30 October 2000

My darling Rachel,

Caroline *did* plead guilty and 25 October was set for the plea hearing, which we were told would be heavily swayed towards the defence. And yes, my darling, there were lots of your family and friends there for support.

I think of the words your Nanny Joy wrote to me this week, after the plea: 'I think of all the past years enjoying Rachel, all those lovely family occasions, birthdays, christenings, Easter holidays, Christmases . . . all the while we looked forward to the next time, Caroline could well have been plotting how to bring our dear Rachel's life to its end.'

Caroline came out and I was thinking, you *silly* girl. I sat down after the judge left the courtroom. There was no way I was going to stand for Caroline.

She was a very sad and depressed woman, but Rachel, she was not insane. She cold-bloodedly plotted and killed you. It is cruel, wicked, evil – all of that – yet I pity her.

But the judge must not soften, because her act was evil. Let's not forget what she did to you. You are the victim. You were her perfect victim.

No more letters were written for the remainder of the year.

Developments ...

32

PROFILING A KILLER

A completely transformed Caroline Reed Robertson was escorted back to the Metropolitan Women's Correctional Centre at Deer Park to begin her twenty-year jail sentence.

Through Rachel's death, Robertson had finally attained her magical goal of becoming someone completely new, said Dr Barry-Walsh outside the Supreme Court. 'In destroying her, she recreates herself. That's exactly what's happened.'

Robertson, her golden-brown shoulder-length curly hair tied neatly off her face, looked far removed from the miserable girl who had been arrested twenty months earlier. Slim and attractive, her slight frame revealed the outline of ribs through her clinging white top. She certainly resembled someone very close to the Jem Southall of her imagination.

So perhaps her fantasy, in some respects, offered an acceptable ending – even if it meant spending a significant amount of her adult life behind bars; even if it meant an existence far from Jem's planned retreat in Bondi or Byron Bay.

'She's playing out a whole new fantasy role now,' observed the Melbourne-based criminal profiler Claude Minisini after studying voluminous reports on the killer and her crime. 'She's back to playing the victim again, a role her writings tell us she is familiar with.

And this time she appears to be playing it to perfection. "Look at *me*, I'm being punished *again* . . . *I'm* the victim."'

Minisini is the director of a consultancy firm called Forensic Behavioural Investigative Services. This highly regarded authority on criminal behaviour and killer psychology has studied the Rachel Barber murder very closely and remains intrigued both by the motivation for the killing and by Robertson herself. A former member of the Victoria Police Rape Squad, Minisini honed his craft at the FBI's internationally recognised profiling unit, Quantico, in Virginia. The lessons he learnt during fourteen months of intensive study during the early 1990s, which included interviewing and studying some of America's most notorious serial sex killers, has given him a valuable insight into the make-up of the criminal psyche, into the predatory nature of murder, the motivating factors underlying such killings, and the varying ways in which murderers kill.

Studying victimology, grisly crime scenes, known serial killers, repeat sex offenders, and those suspected of multiple murders, Minisini has devoted his career in latter years to the study of serial rape and murder. His success in profiling has resulted in much collaboration with Australian police departments, including his work on the Frankston serial killings, which cost three Melbourne women their lives.

The art of profiling, while originally viewed with some scepticism by police and psychologists on its introduction in the United States in the late 1970s, was the FBI's response to the escalation in the numbers of serial killings. With many crimes unsolved, experts developed and refined the technique, which involves matching the psychological make-up of a likely suspect with the crime scene left behind and the type of victim chosen by the killer. Profilers are consulted around the world.

'Profiling,' Minisini explains, 'is based on the premise that behaviour reflects personality. And there is so much about this crime – from the predatory way in which Robertson chose and targeted her victim, to the manner in which she executed the killing, and, of course, her behaviour after the event – which reveals volumes about her complex personality.'

Minisini says that in any violent crime certain behaviours are clearly exhibited, from the way the victim dies to the manner in which the killer disposes of the body. These things, and others, give the profiler a graphic picture of the interaction which has taken place between killer and victim. Every little detail tells its own story.

'Robertson exhibited many behaviours during the time leading up to Rachel Barber's murder, during the crime, and afterwards which tell us a lot about her,' says Minisini. 'They allow us, in effect, to walk in her shoes, as do her writings – all of which give us a keen sense of what occurred before the killing, why she chose Rachel as her victim, and what took place during that final fatal interaction.

'In profiling, we start with the victim. We look at factors like when and where the victim was approached, where the death took place, the method by which she was murdered, what effort was made to hide, or dispose of the body, the type of injuries inflicted, either before or after death. All of these things offer an insight into the killer's personality, helping me, in essence, to build up a behavioural ID.'

The most striking thing about Robertson's identifying behaviour to an observer like Minisini is that it placed her well outside the stereotype of a female homicide offender. International data shows that it is exceedingly rare for women to kill. A study of homicide published by the Australian Institute of Criminology in Canberra reveals that only one in ten murders in Australia between 1989 and 1999 were committed by women. When women kill, it says, their victims are generally intimates: lovers, partners or children. Most crimes are committed in the context of a longstanding abusive relationship, and the typical female killer is aged around twenty-nine.

But Robertson was much younger than this when she killed Rachel Barber – and unlike the stereotypical woman offender, who is unemployed, she had a stable job. She was also single, whereas the typical perpetrator would be married or in a de facto relationship. Finally, Robertson had a comfortable middleclass background, while the typical female killer would be from a lower socio-economic background.

Robertson's choice of victim and her motive set her aside too, since not only did she kill someone outside her family but she chose to target another female – which is extremely rare. Few women kill other women, and even fewer kill distant friends, or commit murder out of jealousy. The only factor she shares with the more typical female killer is that she chose to carry out the murder in her own home.

To Minisini, the unusual motive and nature of the Rachel Barber case set it apart from many of the other murders he has studied. Moreover, he says, it is very unusual to compile the personality and criminal profile of a killer who has already been caught. In some respects this means working backwards. In most cases Minisini would study the crime scene and the nature of the death, and examine the victim. All of the information gleaned would give him an understanding of the type of offender most likely to have committed the crime, and offer some insight into the motive.

In this case, the killer's identity being known, there were many other significant factors that told him not only why Robertson chose Rachel Barber as her victim but *why* she killed her in the way she did. They also explain her behaviour in the lead-up to the crime, and in the days following the murder.

Robertson's writings reveal, as does her behaviour, the startling story of a girl who, rightly or wrongly, perceived herself to be a victim. They convey the clear picture of a girl who had a vision of where she wanted to go in life, and what she wanted to be. But lacking the means to achieve these things, she retreated into fantasy.

'From the piles of letters and writings (which certainly seem to span at least a seven-year period as best we can gather) we can see her anger slowly building up. I see her as an inadequate individual and her letters take us through a journey of extremely low self-esteem and low confidence, which would understandably have made her an isolationist, leaving her void of the skills she'd need to successfully interact with others.'

Given her poor interpersonal skills and inability to interact with girls her own age, it was little wonder that her writings illustrated deep paranoia and a belief that she was being gossiped or laughed about. These hurts, real or imagined, says Minisini, would have triggered her subsequent retreat into the safety of her imagination, where she could dream of a more acceptable life.

Fantasising, he explains, offered her the chance to be someone

272

else, someone successful and attractive who mingled in showbiz circles; someone who could amaze friends on Oprah's 'If You Could See Me Now Reunion', leaving them incredulous that she had finally left behind the 'little deadbeat scum bag' she perceived herself to be.

Minisini remains in no doubt that Robertson role-played being someone else, until Rachel Barber became the object of her fantasy. When the fantasy lost its buzz, it would have taken a sinister turn, evolving into a dream of death.

'A fantasy is a daydream in which everything ends perfectly,' says Minisini. 'We all have them and they all involve role-playing some part in which everything turns out the way we want. It's the usual pleasant harmless stuff and goes nowhere.

'But this woman, like many killers I have seen, appeared to live most of her life in fantasy. She would have "acted out" the role of being someone like Rachel Barber over and over again, until it lost its appeal. Then, in her developing new fantasy, she would have role-played killing the victim who symbolised everything she wanted – acting it out in her mind until it was perfect in every little detail, before finally crossing the line into a dangerous new realm and actually killing her.'

Minisini says it is known from studies of murderers that each has a perfect victim in mind. 'Some murders, especially serial killings, are the products of that fantasy. They are almost invariably committed by highly organised and intelligent killers who plan to act out in real life the fantasies they have had for years. These killers often look for someone who is an ideal or perfect victim in their fantasy. It could be that a victim fitting that ideal just happens to come along and finds themselves in the wrong place at the right time – a victim of opportunity. But more often than not, the victim is someone a predator actively targets. Robertson's 'perfect victim' was young, pretty and talented and a performer too – exactly the type of victim Robertson needed to fulfil her fantasy.

There were other reasons, though, why Rachel was ideal. And Minisini agrees with Justice Vincent's view that Robertson targeted the girl partly because she was known to her and was someone she could build some sort of trust with, so that she could lure her victim away and isolate her from help. 'She was accessible and vulnerable, and would probably not offer resistance which might result in a loss of control for Robertson, who would have wanted to have avoided attracting attention.

'This was anything but a crime of opportunity. There are no signs here of primitive behaviour or spontaneous, explosive rage. The level of planning and organisation is indicative of an extremely intelligent person.' He said that the careful way Robertson had prepared the double-knotted noose suggested she'd done this well in advance. It wouldn't have been possible for her to have rustled this up while attempting to overpower her victim.

Minisini read court reports stating that Robertson had 'some intelligence', and found this an understatement given the scholarship she had won to Camberwell Girls Grammar, and the cunning nature of her plan. 'I suspect, given the evidence about her plan and writings, she is much more intelligent than has been recognised.' He noted from reports that Robertson's IQ was 114. And he was cautious about any medical assessment based on observations gleaned in just two hours with a manipulative killer capable of convincing anyone of anything. Minisini says the strong element of 'preparedness', and the length of time the crime had been taking shape in Robertson's thoughts, showed that she intended to execute a perfect crime and get away with it.

Minisini believes that Robertson's ruse of the psychological study she invited Rachel to take part in must have been very convincing. She had the foresight to consider where and how she would kill the young girl, ensuring that the secret meeting remained confidential to increase her chances of escaping undetected.

The drugging referred to in Robertson's plan, while strenuously denied by the killer, would have been central to keeping Rachel under her control, he claims. He doubts very much whether a killer acting out a detailed fantasy would have suddenly chosen to diverge from that plan. Alcohol could also have formed part of the plot to subdue the victim, in combination with drugs to minimise noise and resistance. In spite of Robertson's denials that either was administered, the autopsy did not rule out the possibility that both were used, he points out.

Minisini feels the same way about Robertson's proposed disfigurement of the victim, referring to Justice Vincent's observations in court that it indicated Robertson's 'wish to smash and destroy that other person': a crime of rage and hate. Again, this disfigurement clearly formed part of her fantasy, so why abandon it? Given the advanced state of decomposition of the victim's body, it is again very difficult to discount the fact that Robertson might well have vented her anger on the victim in this way. It is also in keeping with a highly organised personality executing a very deliberate plan, since disfigurement would hinder identification of Rachel Barber's body.

Ligature strangulation as a means of killing is very significant too, says Minisini. Relatively quiet, it would be a clean and easy method of murdering a victim less than half the size of the assailant. In her orderly way Robertson would no doubt have considered this her best option since she would not want evidence scattered around the scene. Minisini notes that Robertson had written of her intention to hire a carpet-cleaning firm to remove traces of evidence. She had clearly given this aspect of the crime some thought.

But Claude Minisini believes Robertson would also have selected strangulation because of the up-close, personal nature of this method. 'We know that killers with a desire to retain control have a need to fulfil their ultimate fantasy by watching a victim's life ebb away – knowing that the victim's fate is entirely in their hands. It is the ultimate in power and control. Everything about this crime is calculating, cold and cruel.

'Would she have been anxious though?' Minisini asks. 'Yes, of course she would . . . and particularly on the day of the planned murder . . . so it is understandable she would have taken the day off . . . She also took a huge risk afterwards, transporting the body to the country by van, and I imagine that too would have caused her great anxiety. But this would have been more related to getting caught than feeling anxious or upset about what she had done to Rachel.'

The evidence, he says, leaves him fairly sure that Robertson was not in shock or experiencing dissociation after the killing. He disputes the evidence of medical professionals who seemed convinced that her professed amnesia about the crime was genuine.

'That is absolutely not what her actions tell us. They tell us she was comfortable enough to spend time around her flat, with a dead body in her wardrobe – not the behaviour of someone ill at ease with what she has done. It says a lot about her as an individual, no doubt getting a secret buzz just being there with the body of someone she had killed. The fact that she could continue going to work, visit the Grand Prix with her co-workers, all suggests she wasn't at all uncomfortable or remorseful – rather that she has no conscience. Keeping the girl's body in her home for a few days would have allowed her the chance to relive the fantasy of the killing for a while, but being practical, she knew it would be appropriate to remove it to avoid detection.'

Choosing to dispose of Rachel Barber's body at Kilmore, says Minisini, was not a random decision either. Kilmore was selected because it was remote. Robertson would have known that neighbours were unlikely to spot her, or disturb her, allowing her sufficient time to dig a grave for Rachel Barber's body.

Minisini says it is interesting that Robertson, like other killers he has studied, attempted to infiltrate herself into the subsequent murder investigation, ringing the Barbers' home professing to be helpful, but in truth attempting to determine the status of the investigation. This behaviour is not unusual: some killers will offer to help in police searches while some have been known to hang around bars where detectives drink, generating discussions about a killing they've committed.

Neither is it unusual for killers to take 'souvenirs' from their victims, fuelling emotions of power generated by the actual conquest. They relive the murder each time they see the trophy – generally items of clothing, photographs from wallets or jewellery. Some male killers have been known to take jewellery from their victims and give it to their female partners, enjoying a secret thrill from watching it being worn. 'It's an extension of the dress-up notion central to role-playing,' Minisini explains. 'He notes that Rachel's two necklaces, her diamond earrings, and the topaz ring she'd been wearing when she disappeared have never been found. And neither have her dancing shoes, Humphrey Bear soft toy or dance bag. Robertson claimed to have no memory of the missing items. But, Minisini wonders, given Robertson's written admission that she stole from her family, branding herself 'a stealing baby', why wouldn't she have taken the possessions of a girl whose life she stole?

Minisini remains 'extremely cynical' about the suggestion of amnesia, stating that any recall of the finer details of her crime would interfere with Robertson's performance as 'victim'. 'I would say it is very much in her interests to remain amnesic about the killing because if people knew what had really gone on at her flat, no one would feel sorry for her at all. And being a victim, sympathy is central to her role-playing.' He agrees strongly with Justice Vincent's sentencing remarks that the signs of remorse she exhibited in court were most likely to be manifestations of self-pity. But he is not convinced that the passage of time might encourage the killer to make a full disclosure. Again, it simply would not be in her interests if she wished to continue to be seen as the victim.

Consultant forensic psychiatrist Dr Michele Pathe, formerly from the Victorian Institute of Forensic Mental Health in Melbourne, also remains cautious about the amnesia, although, given Robertson's ability to detach herself, she says it cannot be discounted. Even Dr Justin Barry-Walsh, who assessed Robertson for the defence, remains open-minded about the claims of amnesia. 'You would always have to be suspicious about the amnesia since so many serious offenders claim to have no memory of the actual events of a crime and that can be seen to serve a very clear-cut and obvious purpose,' he said. 'Most serious offenders will say they are amnesic, though I have to say that this case seemed to go further than that.'

But he admitted that since he had only seen Robertson briefly, he would have needed to have spent more than 'a couple of hours with her to be sure about anything.' And no, he could not rule out the possibility that her amnesia might not be genuine.

'I have my own suspicions,' he said, 'but they are no more than that. Even at this point, I still don't think any of us have a particularly wonderful understanding of Caroline, or the murder itself. Perhaps in the fullness of time, she may find herself able to talk about what happened a bit more clearly. You never know. Still, I am left with that sense of not being one hundred per cent certain about anything at all.'

One thing Pathe, like Minisini, is in no doubt about, however, is that Robertson's perception is that she is the victim in this case, her pity more directed towards her own plight than the fate of her victim.

A prominent Australian specialist on stalking and obsessive behaviours and now head of the world's first stalking and threat management centre, based in Melbourne, Dr Pathe describes the murder as a depressive homicide committed by a narcissistic killer. Narcissistic killers, she explains, are self-centred individuals incapable of empathising with their victims. Unlike some depressed people, who turn to suicide as a means of escaping intense emotional pain, depressed narcissistic people strike outwardly, killing others in response to perceived past hurts and humiliations.

'Homicidal depression can be considered narcissistic because it involves reactions to shame, and loss of pride,' explains Dr Pathe. 'These cases of homicidal depression where the losses are internalised are quite different from the psychological state of killers in 'anaclitic' homicides, which are reactions to external losses – like the loss of a relationship, a person, or an object. Since narcissistic people tend to be egocentric and focused only on their own feelings, they have difficulty forming relationships with others and are incapable of empathising with anyone else's feelings. Narcissistic people are able to establish attachments, but demonstrate reactions of anxiety and despair when those attachments later break down – striking out in response.

'What I see clearly in the Robertson case,' Dr Pathe says, 'are the feelings of shame and humiliation which result from narcissistic "injuries" and lead to serious loss of self-esteem and resulting depressive mood. They produce intense aggressive impulses and result in a general lashing out at others. When a narcissistic individual eventually unleashes their aggression, they are incapable of feelings towards their victim or family. They are thinking only of themselves and feeling sorry only for themselves who they see as the *true* victim of their actions. And this is what we have in Robertson's case.

'Robertson's writings are typical of those of a narcissistic envy killer,' states Dr Pathe. 'She sees *herself* victimised by the world. This warped victim scenario is commonly observed in studies on stalkers and obsessive personalities.'

Dr Pathe says closer examination of Robertson's writings reveals that her developing fixation with Rachel Barber led to close monitoring, or stalking, of her victim. 'While no evidence exists of an obsession in the

278

true psychiatric meaning of the word, there are certainly obsessional qualities about the lists she prepared on her victim. The ongoing surveillance became consuming over time.'

Making the distinction between 'obsession' and 'fixation', Dr Pathe explains that *obsessive thinking* involves unpleasant and intrusive thoughts that cause distress to the individual. But there was no hint of distress in Robertson's mind as she meticulously compiled lists about her victim's personality, her life, her family and her physical appearance. Her continued monitoring, which included photographing Rachel, applying for her birth certificate, and written observations on her dance school, boyfriend and family, all highlight the deepening fixation.

'The perpetrator also made other observations about the victim, such as Rachel dyeing her hair several different colours, and it is clear that by the time Robertson was arrested she had dyed her hair green and had been planning cosmetic surgery to transform her facial features, perhaps into those of her victim. All evidence of wanting to emulate her.'

Dr Pathe says intense interest like this often leads to stalkers experiencing a 'fusion' process with their victim as they over-identify with the object of their fascination. It might begin with emulating clothing, hairstyles, make-up – and grow until, in the stalker's mind, he or she is the victim of the situation. As reality blurs, this perception is heightened. While Rachel Barber was the real victim in this case, in Robertson's eyes Robertson herself was the victim, and Rachel was the cause of *her* pain and misery. 'We know of cases where stalkers, in their irrational frame of mind, blame their victim for stalking *them*,' says Dr Pathe. 'The reality is actually very different but that is how *they* perceive it.'

She agrees with Claude Minisini's observations that Robertson saw herself to be the victim in a hostile world that had mistreated and humiliated her. Like Justice Vincent, she believes that the killer was a self-absorbed young woman focused solely on her own feelings and desires. She is highly immature, Dr Pathe says – a self-centred individual with a 'very manipulative nature' who had begun to dissociate herself from reality and escape into fantasy. 'And it's likely Robertson had been quietly boiling with rage for some time before the murder.'

Though the courts had heard explanations from Robertson's assessing specialists that Rachel had been murdered by someone who wanted to possess her qualities, Dr Pathe believes the final act of killing the young dancer was much more of a 'lashing out' at the world for all the injustices the killer had ever suffered. 'Robertson's target was not somebody who had personally wronged her. Instead, Rachel exemplified the type of person who had previously oppressed and humiliated her. Robertson was striking back against the more powerful forces oppressing her. Her resentment against an unfeeling world, real or imagined, likely preceded her interest in Rachel, but then Rachel became the focus, the proxy, against whom she channelled all her resentment.'

She says that Robertson's typically self-referential and over-sensitive behaviour reflects someone inclined to project their anger and persecution onto others, having grown up to perceive the world as a rejecting, persecuting place. And why Rachel in particular? Pathe supports Claude Minisini's view that Robertson chose Rachel rather than any other fifteen-year-old as the object of her rage simply because she was easy to kill. 'Rachel Barber, unfortunately, became the accessible representative of all those people who had previously made her life a misery, by being successful and pretty and talented. Robertson knew she could get to her.'

Neither Dr Pathe nor Claude Minisini was surprised to learn that Robertson had built up a collection of magazine photographs of actresses, all fresh-faced, pretty and talented, like Katie Holmes and Claire Danes and, indeed, like Rachel. All symbols of what she wanted to be. This was, according to Dr Pathe, part of the fixation she developed in conjunction with her fantasy ideal, part of the fusion taking place between fantasy and reality, between herself and the person she wanted to be.

'It is a disturbing feature of the case,' Dr Pathe says, 'that the murder was premeditated by such a young woman over such a long period, with Robertson recording information on her victim, setting out her plan to lure and later dump her. All of this is consistent with the methodical, structured and highly organised personality she appears to be. But perhaps, at some level she never really believed she would do it. Yet the tragic reality is that she did.' Dr Pathe says it was clear that reality had already begun to dissolve from Robertson's life years before she murdered Rachel. Her writings certainly illustrate intense periods of despondency characterised by hopelessness, resentment and anger.

'I think the observations of her work associates illustrate a person living out some sort of fantasy most of the time,' says Dr Pathe. 'It's interesting that she makes constant mention of theatre friends that never existed and fantasises about becoming an actor, sometimes even talking as if she already was an actor. It shows she was using fantasy as an escape, either from the awfulness of her daily life or to protect herself from extreme emotional pain. Escaping to fantasy had the inevitable result of leaving her friendless . . . Allowing anyone to get too close would simply have exposed her fantasy life for the elaborate lie it had become.'

This ability to dissociate herself from the world, Dr Pathe says, while a feature in some sexual abuse victims, can also be used by others as an emotional safety device. For this reason Dr Pathe feels that it is dangerous to give too much credence to her so-called sexual abuse story, because it could well be false. Perhaps, Dr Pathe hypothesises, this is why Robertson didn't want the matter explored further in court, because it might not stand up to closer scrutiny.

Minisini also remains sceptical about any sexual abuse claims. He sees them as another manifestation of the notion of Robertson as a woman who lies and manipulates. He views the issue of sexual abuse as a careful strategy aimed at generating the sympathy required by a person still needing to be perceived as a victim.

Melbourne-based criminologist Judy Wright also agrees, saying that while Robertson's defence claimed there was no advantage to be gained in raising the issue of sexual abuse unless it were true, she believes the defendant had in fact a great deal to gain. 'Especially if the claim is false, because it not only feeds into the notion that she is a victim, but it is an ideal diversion and an effective means of creating at least a little doubt in everyone's minds. The defence asked why it should be raised at all, only for Robertson to refuse to allow it to be used as part of the defence plea. But I would say the primary advantage lies in making the suggestion itself. Just by hinting at the possibility of some past sexual trauma, even if it isn't true, leaves everyone wondering. She doesn't need to take it any further which means it cannot be fully explored by the Crown, or disputed. So either way it works for her.'

Wright, who once worked with serial sex offenders during her years with the Office of Corrections and now teaches criminology at a number of tertiary institutes in Melbourne, cautiously raises another point: prison libraries, she says, are filled with books on coping with sexual and physical abuse, and overcoming dependencies. This provides an opportunity for clever offenders to familiarise themselves with helpful information while on remand. This information might help an offender successfully portray herself as a victim at a pending hearing, but not enough to stand the test of close scrutiny if it were questioned. However, Wright asks, given insufficient detail, even if sexual abuse were true, would it be an excuse for murder?

'It's always fascinated me that when we have male offenders we rarely look at their victimisation, yet with women, there is certainly a tendency to pathologise their crimes – even medicalise them,' says Wright. 'With men, while we might well accept they have had a hard life, it never excuses what they have done.' Yet, she argues, medicalising the behaviour of female offenders is now almost routinely employed in the defence of women, particularly those on serious charges. But with men, their crimes are often simply put down to anger and violence. 'You don't hear many men saying they were depressed at the time they committed an offence because their hormones were fluctuating or that their testosterone levels were too high, making them aggressive and angry. We almost accept that it is part of male make-up for them to be outwardly angry, so they don't need an excuse. Yet with women, we instantly assume there *must* have been some underlying medical reason to have caused them to behave in such an anti-social way.'

She poses the question: what if Rachel Barber had been abducted and murdered by a twenty-year-old son of a family friend, instead of a twenty-year-old daughter? Would the same background reasoning of deep depression, self-loathing and perhaps sexual abuse, have explained such a crime? 'I doubt it,' says Wright. 'It would instantly raise suspicions about a sexually motivated crime: a pretty young dancer becoming the subject of unwanted interest and a strange infatuation, all the more understandable if the perpetrator is male. We'd say the victim was abducted and lured to the perpetrator's home and the crime would be bound to be seen to have sexual connotations. No doubt the young girl rejected his advances and he would, most likely we assume, have sexually assaulted her before killing her in the heat of the moment. It would make more sense.

'Would we care that he'd been bullied at school, had feelings of despair over his parents' marriage break-up, or his general depression? Would we listen to his bizarre writings being read out in court and feel sorry that his cries for help didn't receive an appropriate level of response? How would being a *male* misfit excuse murder? Even if he hadn't gone to the extraordinary lengths of planning the killing in fine detail like Robertson did, would any of these same arguments raise any sympathy? Do the crime, do the time. No sympathy.'

So Wright is certain that a medical explanation for a male's criminal behaviour would raise little public sympathy. 'Research amongst offenders shows that just as many males as females have been sexually abused as children, probably more. Yet experts assessing females are much more likely to raise these issues in pre-court assessment reports, sometimes perhaps suggesting to offenders during interviews that there might be such a background. I note from Robertson's case that in cross-examination one of the assessing doctors admitted he had asked her if there was a past of sexual abuse. Robertson had not volunteered this information, but had raised it only after being questioned by a doctor.

'The defence use the argument that if it *had* been a lie, she would have raised it earlier in the proceedings, especially if she was making it up for sympathy,' says Wright. 'But *earlier* in the proceedings she was maintaining her innocence and going for trial. The issue of sexual abuse was raised pretty quickly once she changed her plea and was about to front court, where she'd be facing a heavy jail sentence.'

One thing that Wright finds intriguing is what she sees as a general community discomfiture at seeing women as wilful, violent aggressors, just as capable of venting unresolved rage on victims as men. 'Why do we find this notion so hard to grasp?' she asks.

'Women can be just as angry, just as violent, and kill for all the same reasons as men. They too might want something so badly that they would be prepared to kill for it. Men do. Yet it is not socially acceptable to see a woman being outwardly destructive and angry. We prefer to think she must be mad rather than bad, and look for a medical reason to explain the behaviour away. It is so much easier to see the woman as a victim, one that couldn't have really wanted to *deliberately* cause harm. So if she says she was abused, coerced or just unbalanced, it is simpler to believe her.'

Robertson, observes Wright, relied on all three of these rationales in her defence. First, in her original story, she claimed that she'd been coerced by others. When that didn't look like working, stories of her depression and disturbed mind were raised. And finally, when she was staring at a lengthy jail term, the abuse story reared its head.

'And let's not forget the amnesia,' adds Wright. 'She wouldn't be the first offender to raise that. It is not unusual for perpetrators charged with serious crimes to have memory lapses about the most crucial parts of their crime: "I don't remember exactly what happened, but one minute I was standing there and the next minute he was dead on the floor and I had a knife in my hand."' Wright wonders if this 'blacking out' is just a convenient way of avoiding recall on the part of a criminal who cannot face consciously acknowledging the rage they are capable of effecting during a homicide. Loss of memory allows them to reconstruct a different version of events, one they can live with, one that makes the aftermath of a murder more bearable. Or, as she suspects in Robertson's case, one that allows her to continue masquerading as the real victim. 'It's interesting that she remembers some things quite clearly about her crime: she's certain she hired a van and that no one helped her dump the body; she remembers for sure that she didn't drug the pizza – then forgets other important information.'

Though Dr Pathe describes Robertson as a despairing young woman whose writings were filled with desolation, Wright focuses on the hate lists where the killer writes, 'I hate not getting what I want.' This, she says, offers a vital insight into the mind of a determined young woman who is focused entirely on her own wants and needs. A woman who would later be prepared to smash the object she hated for having everything she lacked.

But Dr Pathe says she believes it was the ultimate blending of fantasy and reality that led to Robertson's unrealistic switched-identity scheme. 'It is almost magical thinking, childlike in many ways. Yet this warped perception of reality convinced her that, given a new nose and cosmetic surgery, she would be a new perfect person with a perfect, happy life. In reality, of course, it could never happen.'

Pathe, Minisini and Wright all agree that, ironically, Robertson no longer has the need to escape an intolerable reality. In prison she now has a structured, secure environment suited to her organised nature – and one where she possibly has more purpose and more sympathy than she ever had before.

And all three experts agree with Dr Barry-Walsh that Robertson *has* gained considerably from her victim's death. She has finally achieved her dream of creating a newer, happier, more contented version of herself and is settled in an environment where there is no pressure on her to perform or compete. 'That's the tragedy of it all, isn't it?' says Dr Pathe. 'Through this awful crime she *has* transformed herself, achieving her dream of becoming slim and attractive and much closer to the image of her victim. She is much more at ease now, having succeeded in removing herself from the 'nobody' she perceived herself to be. The court case and surrounding publicity has, no doubt, given her considerable fame. By killing a pretty young girl with so much promise, she is liable to have gained a degree of respect in prison and would have earned a bit of a name for herself. She's hardly going to be surrounded by a bunch of particularly glamorous girls, so there won't be too much competition for her in jail. And being a murderer would certainly place her on the top echelon inside, so she is much more likely to be one of the celebrated ones.'

Furthermore, Dr Pathe suggests that Robertson may well have *fused* with her victim in the way that stalker-killer Mark Chapman did with his victim, John Lennon. In jail, he began to resemble Lennon, even marrying a Japanese Hawaiian woman who in turn closely resembled Lennon's widow. In killing Lennon, Chapman became more like the musician he fantasised about being than he ever was before. This type of situation is typically true of someone like Robertson as well, says the doctor. 'In a strange, twisted kind of way Robertson has finally achieved what she set out to do . . . she has acclaim, notoriety and what she dreamed of most – recognition. She *is* somebody now.'

Judy Wright agrees, though she believes Robertson's newfound contentment in prison might be more to do with the fact that Robertson finally achieved her goal of *destroying* her victim. 'Robertson dreamed about it, wrote about it, thought about it – and finally she did it. Why wouldn't she be happy now? She got what she wanted. Her victim's death. And I don't believe for a moment she's sorry – just sorry she got caught.'

Wright joins Claude Minisini and Michele Pathe in supporting Justice Vincent's view that, for the time being at least, Robertson presents a 'real danger' to the community at large. As Minisini concludes, 'Justice Vincent refers to the danger of someone else becoming the unfortunate subject of her fixation and took this into account as a significant factor in his sentencing of Robertson. I couldn't agree more. I believe we are dealing with someone really dangerous here – someone who is still role-playing her new fantasy – even now, in jail. Playing the victim suggests to me that she would continue retreating into fantasy, continue role-playing, and is therefore capable of transferring her fixation onto someone else.

'I note from her doctors that they say she is remorseful for her crime. But I find that hard to believe given her personality. It's superficial to accept her explanation that she changed her plea out of remorse. I think she's incapable of it. In my opinion, while waiting for her trial, she's regrouped, reassessed her situation and thought to herself, "No, this isn't going to work." On the premise that she'd get a lighter sentence by pleading guilty – she's admitted to her crime.

'I see her as a calculating, clever, though superficial, individual,' says Minisini, 'with a reckless disregard for anyone but herself – and no conscience. And that's why she's not telling anyone what really went on. The only thing we are sure of is that this crime was the first time she actually acted out a fantasy . . . and she got caught. What we don't know is exactly how long she had been role-playing it. And it leaves me wondering, given that she's finally removed the object of her fixation – whether, in her fantasies, she might find someone else in the future.'

33

INSTANT RECALL

In the Deer Park Women's Prison another transformation was already under way. Caroline Reed Robertson was reinventing herself into yet another persona – that of a model prisoner.

This new identity shared none of the characteristics of the enraged young woman who had formulated a plan for murder. Slender and fragile-looking, this new person was co-operative and pleasant; sociable with staff and fellow inmates; helpful to the less capable women prisoners; compliant in her own rehabilitation. Comfortable and at home. This dramatic change was noted by assessing psychiatrist, Dr Justin Barry-Walsh, who found her rapid adjustment to the regimentation of prison life very 'disconcerting'.

'The woman before the court was certainly not the young woman I interviewed in prison,' he observed some months after her incarceration. 'And she is absolutely not the same shy, over-weight girl who killed Rachel Barber. She is so well adjusted there and so "at home" that you can't help but feel prison has filled her emptiness. In a sense I think this is because prison provides structure and constraints. For someone like Caroline, it undoubtedly offers a sense of purpose and identity.'

Still, he admitted that her very rapid transformation made him uneasy. 'Her ability to settle *so* comfortably and to establish an entirely new lifestyle *so* quickly, has, perhaps, been the most troubling aspect of this bizarre case,' he said. 'She has adapted, perhaps, too well; there's something certainly very creepy about that.'

Despite a tumultuous introduction to prison life, there was no doubt that Robertson had finally found a safe environment where she could rebuild her life. Far from being lonely and unhappy, she appeared more at ease psychologically and had even made new friends. Thanks to the protection of a group of women inmates, she was no longer the target of beatings or threats. She was no longer intent on injuring herself, or feeling suicidal. And even her epileptic seizures had ceased, supporting medical opinion that they had probably been anxiety related.

In the two years since Robertson's arrest for the murder of Rachel Barber, no one had ever witnessed any signs of violence or aggression from the prisoner towards any of her fellow inmates. Even Sneddon, who was supporting her in jail, found this quite remarkable, saying that violence within the system is commonplace and provocation is part of everyday life. He recalled that during Robertson's early days at Deer Park, when she was noticeably depressed, she didn't even have the strength, let alone the desire, to fight stronger, more violent offenders who would have targeted her for the prescription medication issued to her by prison doctors. He considered it unlikely that she ever gained any benefit from the anti-depressants, sleeping tablets, or even her epilepsy medication. They would have been seized without any resistance from her.

While Robertson had apparently never had a drug problem, nevertheless in prison she completed a drug education program. She also assisted staff in helping some less able prisoners with their educational programs. Her new self-confidence could perhaps have been attributed to her involvement in a number of self-improvement and study courses. She was pursuing new interests, from creative writing to woodwork, and had embarked on a Bachelor of Arts degree. And finally she was fulfilling her true goal – studying film and drama. Robertson's work with Sneddon brought other rewards too: she had completed courses in spiritual development. Caroline Reed Robertson had come full circle.

Yet Robertson's treating psychologist, Michael Crewdson, detected a certain irony in the prisoner's new life. 'She is very dependent on prison life. Her unit is her home and her current close fellow prisoners are her family,' he wrote. 'There is a sad desperation in the way she has adapted. In many ways she has no choice.' He found it tragic, he said, that after many tearful sessions with her during those early months of incarceration, she would end their sessions saying: 'I have to go home now.' Others assessing Robertson expressed concerns that the prisoner's youth and her lengthy period of incarceration undoubtedly placed her at risk of becoming severely institutionalised. This would have important implications for her long-term future management in prison.

Robertson's defence lawyer Colin Lovitt told her plea hearing she was happier in prison than she'd ever been in the outside world. And while she'd rejected authority and regimentation at home, inside it suited her. But the stark contrast between Robertson's new life and the circumstances of her victim had not been lost on the Crown. Even Justice Vincent noted the tragic disparity in his sentencing, saying that finding an appropriate penalty had been 'extremely difficult' in a situation where everyone had lost. 'But none as much as Rachel Barber from whom you took everything.'

The prisoner, he noted, might pose an ongoing threat to the community – to anyone who might become the unfortunate object of her fixation in the future. Her potential for re-offending had been a significant consideration for him in determining her twenty-year jail term. It was one which reflected the gravity of her crime and illustrated the concept of retributive justice. A term substantial enough to protect the public and serve as a general deterrent to other like-minded individuals. And more importantly, one which upheld the 'unequivocal denunciation of our community in such fatally destructive behaviour'.

His optimism that time might allow a full recollection of events on Robertson's part seemed forlorn at the time. But just five weeks later, a new development would change everything.

By mid-December 2000, Robertson was back in discussions with her lawyers. Vital gaps in the evidence looked set to be filled, shedding new light on the circumstances of Rachel Barber's murder. News of these new revelations emerged at a preliminary hearing before the Court of Appeal on 27 April 2001, when Robertson asked for leave to have her twenty-year jail sentence reviewed.

Formal notice of Robertson's appeal was first lodged with the Supreme Court on 12 December 2000, as the Barbers braced themselves for a second painful and empty Christmas without their eldest daughter. They were unaware of this new development until the end of January, when news of the pending appeal filtered through to the Office of Public Prosecutions. Robertson's lawyers indicated that they intended to argue for a reduction in her sentence on the basis that it was too excessive given her age, her plea, and the lack of prior convictions.

For the police, however, an appeal was not unexpected. Criminals facing lengthy jail sentences have little to lose, and often contest their sentences on the basis that they are too severe.

To prevent many baseless appeals clogging up the judicial system, there is a filtering process in place. In a preliminary hearing at the Court of Appeal the presiding judge, or president, reviews all cases in which offenders are appealing against the length of their sentence. In some cases, prisoners appeal against both their sentence *and* their conviction. In these cases the appellant, maintaining innocence, asks for their case to be re-opened by the Court of Appeal in the interests of justice. They claim to have been wrongly convicted and want the conviction and subsequent sentence overturned. But the majority of offenders, like Robertson, simply contest the severity of the sentence itself.

After hearing legal argument from counsel representing the Crown and defence, the president determines whether or not an offender has reasonable grounds on which to pursue an appeal. If he believes grounds exist, he will allow the appeal to go before a tribunal of three judges. If he feels there are insufficient grounds, he will dismiss the request.

Five separate preliminary appeals were listed before the Court of Appeal president, John Winneke, on the morning of Friday, 27 April 2001, each involving offenders taking issue with the length of their sentences. In each, Winneke took extreme care to point out that his function was a supervisory one, and it was not his job to say whether a final appeal might eventually win or lose.

Two requests from convicted criminals seeking to appeal sentences had already been knocked back that morning by the time Caroline Reed Robertson was brought into the Green Room of the Court of Appeal. She arrived in a security van from Deer Park more than an hour earlier and had been lodged in the cells underneath the building waiting for her case to be called. She walked across the plush green carpet and past the lines of olive-coloured leather seats from which the courtroom takes its name. She appeared to be a vastly different prisoner from the pale, downcast and nervous young woman who had stood before Justice Vincent in November the previous year.

She was dressed in a white skivvy top and navy fitted pants, her golden shoulder-length wavy hair scraped back into a ponytail. Her close resemblance to the Jem Southall identity she had sketched in her stylised drawings was eerie. Her further weight loss, which attracted hushed comments from court staff, saw her looking more like her new persona than she could ever have dreamed possible. In her drawings she'd fantasised about a new slim figure, golden-blonde locks, a natural complexion, smart tailored pants. Now she was the living image of her sketch.

There was also a confident new step in Robertson's stride as she walked briskly up the side of the court towards the dock, separated from the public gallery by a reinforced glass partition. A few feet behind the glass sat the victim's mother, Elizabeth. It had been Elizabeth Barber with whom Robertson had shared her aspirations of being an actor. And Elizabeth who had encouraged her to join a local children's theatre group. Now she sat pale and nervous as she waited for another glimpse of the young woman who'd admitted to killing her daughter; the same young woman who'd babysat their children, chatted to Michael Barber as he'd mowed the lawns of the little house across the road from the Reids, and who'd sometimes used the Barbers' family computer. Indeed, just weeks after the preliminary appeal hearing, the Barbers had accidentally discovered, when cleaning out the hard drive on their home computer, a draft of an essay written by Caroline in which the central character, named Rachel, ends up being locked in a mental asylum. A copy of this essay was subsequently passed to the Office of Public Prosecutions.

Now, carefully avoiding eye contact with her victim's mother, Robertson adjusted her fine-framed metal spectacles. She acknowledged, with a smile, a young woman sitting at the back of the court. She appeared to be a new friend, about Robertson's age; a face not previously seen during Robertson's plea or sentencing hearings.

Elizabeth Barber had only heard about the preliminary appeal hearing a few days earlier, and had been informed that Robertson was unlikely to make a personal appearance. The hearing, she'd been warned, was likely to be a non-event; a paper shuffle among lawyers, over in a few minutes. Robertson's request to appeal was likely to be instantly rejected. If it *were* successful, the process could take months. And even if it were unsuccessful, the prisoner could re-appeal again within fourteen days. There would be no result today. So she was told it would not be worth her while attending. Elizabeth Barber thought otherwise.

Mike Barber refused to join her, claiming there was little point to the exercise. Nothing would bring Rachel back, he said. Secretly, though, Elizabeth suspected he was daunted at the prospect of revisiting the imposing court complex, of reliving the process all over again; of having no closure when the family had already been struggling to come to terms with last year's jail sentence. And she wondered if he might be even more afraid of the anxiety he'd experienced during Roberton's earlier appearances; frightened of another panic attack.

But Elizabeth vowed she would be there to remind people who the real victim in the case was. She didn't *want* Caroline Reed Robertson assuming the role of victim. Yet by her notice of appeal, Robertson was claiming she was being victimised by the system; being punished too severely. As Robertson's lawyer later put it, this was a sentence Robertson considered to be manifestly excessive. Elizabeth Barber determined that her presence was a necessary reminder of the family's loss; of Rachel's loss; of the price an innocent fifteen-year-old had paid for another's jealousy. Rachel, in the legal process, had already become the *deceased*; another type of victim. Perhaps by now Rachel might not even warrant a mention. The appeal process, said Elizabeth, would be entirely about Caroline; about *her* unfair harsh treatment. The victim's mother wanted to look Rachel's killer straight in the eye and be sure Caroline knew Rachel still had a voice in the proceedings.

In court, Caroline Reed Robertson's comfortable, relaxed demeanour was in direct contrast to the highly agitated state of the victim's mother as she sat with her hands tightly clasped together, waiting.

The president invited Robertson to move from the dock to a seat directly in front of the bench where he could address her. Winneke confirmed he'd read all the evidence; the witness statements and doctors' reports; the judge's sentencing remarks. He explained his own role in the proceedings, telling Robertson that if her appeal had any reasonable prospects of success he would order it to go on to the full Court of Appeal. But this didn't mean her appeal would eventually succeed, simply that it had reasonable prospects. The Court of Appeal had a very different role to that of the sentencing judge whose task had been to hear all the evidence in her case. The Court of Appeal, said Winneke, intervenes only in cases where a judge's discretion in sentencing might be considered erroneous. Or where the sentence was too harsh for the crime.

Robertson's lawyer, Colin Lovitt QC, was not present in court that morning, though the prisoner told the hearing that she had expected him to represent her. Several attempts had been made to contact him, but when a brief adjournment failed to trace either the prisoner's lawyer or his report, another barrister, Nick Papas, agreed to represent Robertson. He spoke briefly with the prisoner in the cells during the adjournment. He knew of her case since he had reviewed it in another role for Legal Aid.

Robertson sat silently as the court was told about her crime; a cold-blooded murder, executed by a very young woman with no prior criminal history, in 'extraordinary circumstances'. Winneke agreed. Robertson's case had been based on facts which the criminal courts rarely saw. But all this had been taken into consideration by Justice Vincent, *the* most experienced trial judge, who had included his observations in 'very detailed and considered sentencing remarks', Winneke said.

Winneke also noted that there were 'exhaustive efforts' made by both sides to reveal more about the circumstances leading up to Robertson's crime. But each of the persons who sought to achieve some insight into Robertson's mind was frustrated because of what was said to be real, or unreal, amnesia.

Mr Papas responded by saying that although the plea had involved 'most experienced counsel' and a very experienced judge, Robertson's QC, Mr Lovitt, had struggled 'to come to grips with what this case was about in terms of instructions and explanations'.

Then Mr Papas told the court something quite extraordinary. Robertson, he explained, had told him she was experiencing 'detailed improvement in her recollection'. She was now able to provide the court with fresh information which could explain, 'in an aggravating or mitigating way', her conduct at the time of the crime. Mr Papas added that this new material meant the prisoner could offer details to explain her role, 'her participation', in the murder of Rachel Barber. And because of her impaired memory at her plea and sentencing, this crucial material had been unavailable to Justice Vincent.

But, argued Mr Papas, if Justice Vincent *had* been aware of these details, it might have influenced his subsequent sentencing and perhaps resulted in a different outcome for Robertson. He further contended that her appeal was being made on the basis that her twenty-year jail sentence had been at the upper end of, if not outside, the range of sentencing options available to Justice Vincent. Even the prisoner's parole period of fourteen years and six months, he contended, was considered manifestly excessive for such a young offender with no prior convictions. For all these reasons, he urged the court to consider granting Robertson a full appeal hearing.

But Winneke said he was prepared to neither allow nor deny the request. Justice Vincent 'was a very experienced trial judge who had engaged in very careful consideration in this case, and very careful sentencing,' he said. And even with a lack of information in the lower courts, this didn't mean there had been any sentencing error. Justice Vincent had sentenced Robertson with *all* the available evidence before him. However, if this new material *had* been presented to him, it might possibly have explained the facts of the case in a 'more understandable way,' Winneke said.

Winneke called for time to explore the new information and adjourned Robertson's application to a date to be fixed. This, he said, would allow Mr Papas more time to speak with the prisoner, and to collect further details for the court.

Retiring from the bench to his chambers, Winneke was unaware of a drama about to unfold behind him. As barristers collected their piles of documents and chatted amongst themselves, the victim's mother took a few paces forward, blocking the entrance to the dock where her daughter's killer was standing. Elizabeth Barber had sat silently throughout the hearing, trembling with nerves. Her anger had been building as she listened to arguments on Robertson's behalf, claiming the sentence was excessive – too harsh for such a young offender. Overcome with rage and frustration, Elizabeth Barber confronted Robertson, standing directly in her path as prison guards unbolted the door to allow the prisoner to pass. She stared intently into the killer's face. Robertson tried to look away.

But two years of pent-up grief and distress spilled from Elizabeth, erupting into the silence of a stunned court. She was oblivious to the warnings of the officers guarding the prisoner. 'Stand back, madam! Stand back!' commanded the burly male guard.

'You think *you* are being treated too harshly, do you? *Too harshly*!' Elizabeth shouted. 'You think your sentence is unfair? You were not fair to my daughter . . . you were not fair. You gave my daughter death . . . *You* were *unfair* to my daughter. You are a killer . . . a killer . . . '

Obviously concerned by these developments, the guards closed in on the prisoner and the tense silence continued as the despairing mother refused to move. 'Stand back, *please*!' urged a female guard, pushing Robertson past. But Elizabeth, her voice loaded with emotion, screamed at the back of Rachel's killer as she hurried down the aisle towards the staircase and was ushered into the sanctuary of the cells below. Barristers stopped in their tracks, lifting their grey-wigged heads to observe the commotion. Journalists leaving the press bench in front of the dock stood in silence, too astonished by the unexpected outburst even to take notes. A routine court appearance had just been transformed into another news break.

Stunned by her own actions, Elizabeth Barber rushed from the court, sobbing. 'She *is* a killer. She is *not* the victim here. Rachel was the victim. Rachel. Yet *she* feels hard done by and unfairly treated. How can that be?' Lawyers waited for things to clear before creeping past in an uncomfortable silence, avoiding the tears of a grieving mother; avoiding the tangible, unmistakable grief every person in the waiting area could feel.

Outside in the street, a TV journalist ran briskly up the footpath towards Elizabeth, asking for an interview. While the journalist went to organise her camera crew, others crowded around, keen to hear a mother's thoughts on the morning's proceedings.

'How much sympathy did *she* have for Rachel?' Elizabeth continued. 'She says she suffered from amnesia. Yet now that it suits her, it appears her memory is coming back. She had no memory at the Supreme Court, though she remembered my daughter begging for her life, pleading with her, "Please, please don't."

'She should do the time that was allotted to her, but she thinks the courts have been unfair to her, too harsh. How much sympathy did she have for Rachel when she was squeezing the life out of her? And how much more can she remember?

'I wanted her to see my eyes. They are Rachel's eyes. I wanted her to look at me and see Rachel.'

Throughout the afternoon and evening the story made news on TV and radio broadcasts. *Distraught mother confronts her daughter's killer.* By the following morning it was news around the State as the newspapers picked up the story. *Envy killer lodges appeal – teen's murderer remembers more* stated the weekend's *Herald Sun*, reporting the latest twist in one of Australia's most bizarre murders.

Caroline Reed Robertson was making headlines all over again.

But not for long.

Because of the backlog of appeal applications waiting to find their way into the Court of Appeal, a lengthy waiting game followed Caroline Reed Robertson's preliminary appeal hearing.

It would be eight long months before her name surfaced on the court's lists.

Her case, still on the grounds that her punishment had been 'manifestly excessive', was finally listed to be heard on 16 February, 2002.

But on 5 February, just days before she was due to make her

final appearance in court, Robertson changed her mind again; this time formally withdrawing the appeal.

Robertson offered no explanation for the sudden turnaround. Speculation was rife that she'd been given 'sound legal advice', no doubt warning her that she might not only lose her appeal, but receive a stiffer sentence.

Either way, she simply signed off on the official court documentation, indicating that she wished to abandon her appeal against the length of her sentence. There was no going back.

So, finally, by February 2002, almost three years after stalking and strangling Rachel Barber, the wait was over for the Barber family. A lawyer from the Office of Public Prosecutions contacted the Barbers with the news.

The Barbers had harboured hopes that any information from an appeal hearing might at least fill in some of the gaps in their knowledge of Rachel's final hours. But their hopes of adding a date to Rachel's headstone recording the exact day of her death, and the time she died, would be locked away with many other disturbing unknowns.

PART FOUR

Rachel

Our beautiful daughter. Is our journey now complete?
Have we finally departed your grave?

ELIZABETH SOUTHALL

34

THE IMPORTANCE OF
PHOTOGRAPHS

I wrote in a letter to Rachel not long after her death concerning the importance of photographs. I remember my cousin Michele telling us how lucky we were to have so many photographs of Rachel, and recent ones too.

Yet the most recent ones were described to us as horrific. 'Prepare yourselves,' we were told, and we were asked to sign indemnity forms.

Photographs. We have photographs of our memories. We have now seen photographs from all of Rachel's life, her birth – and death.

What a struggle this has been. We were unable to view her body for reasons I have already given, but we experienced guilt for abandoning our daughter to the laws of the land. And how ridiculous this sounds. We had searched, we had struggled with police to find our beautiful daughter and yet, when she was found, we did not even ask the detectives who announced her death if we could go to Rachel's side. We never asked. And then when we were strongly advised not to see her body because this would jeopardise the trial we never argued. Did we accept this all too easily?

Somehow at the time it wasn't important. It was the

conclusion of our mammoth quest that was important. We might as well have been fighting Arthurian black knights and dragons, so hard had our struggle been.

But with time we felt we had abandoned Rachel. How could we not have insisted on being near Rachel? Could we not even have shared a silent moment in the same room? Could we not have sat beside Rachel with a sheet over her body, protecting our eyes from whatever it was we could not see because of the trial? Could we not have sat there and held her hand?

Paul Ross wanted to protect us. He had always been our gallant knight. He told us how he would look at the loveliness of Rachel's photographs adorning our walls. He told us there was no resemblance between these and the forensic photographs. Over a period of two years the subject would be broached. He wanted to spare us from a lasting memory of Rachel's decomposed self.

'Remember her as she was,' cried my distraught mother. 'Rachel was so beautiful. Don't do this to her, please,' she begged. 'Think what Rachel would want. Don't leave Michael with ugly memories of his beautiful daughter.'

At first I did not want to see the photos. I was scared. But seeing the photographs would not replace our memories of a physical contact with Rachel. Caroline not only murdered Rachel and stole her life from us, she stole from us the parental right to be with our daughter's body after her death. By wrapping her, and burying her in a shallow grave at the conclusion of a hot, hot summer, she also denied Rachel the right of having her mother and father say goodbye and embrace her body. A right denied for the protection of memories. A right denied so justice could be done.

Did Mike broach the subject first? Was it Mike who said, 'Rachel's not in a position to tell us we can't see her death photographs.'

We were advised to cremate Rachel, so horrific were her decomposed remains. But we knew Rachel had always said, 'If ever I die young I don't want to be cremated.' So we thought, we all die, we all decompose – often at different rates, but decomposition always has the same result – bones. Rachel knew this, and from her knowledge that her bones were to be left within the confines of our planet earth, we imagined her saying, 'Hey world, I existed here once.' So we did not cremate Rachel.

But we were denied access to our daughter's body before its burial. And now we were being denied access to our daughter's photographs. What was the hidden reason for this? Perhaps Rachel's body was not at rest, nine feet down, clothed in rosewood. Maybe she had been cremated against our will. I know this was not the case. But there was always the hint of these disquieting mind games.

We spoke to Michael Clarebrough, our psychologist, who said this was a decision we would have to make for ourselves. Not what the police thought, or what my mother thought, or even what *he* thought. What mattered was what we thought. I asked him if he had viewed the body of his brother who had been murdered in his twenties, and if he had, was his lasting memory this image, or rather the memories of his brother's life? Michael said he had seen his brother's body and that his memories have always been of his living brother. It is to these memories that Michael continues to wear his brother's motorbike jacket.

From the time we decided we should see Rachel's photographs there were always the gentle put-offs, or not so gentle put-offs. 'You are Supreme Court witnesses. You must wait until after the trial,' or 'Counselling must be sought on this matter.'

Caught up in the photograph dilemma was my realisation that we had forgotten to arrange for prayers to be said over Rachel's body. Some months earlier I had been watching a movie about a passenger jet crash in the United States. Those killed were to remain on the tarmac overnight covered in blankets until the investigators arrived the next day.

One senior fire officer had said, 'I don't know, this doesn't seem right. Shouldn't they at least have a few words said over them, you know, like a prayer.'

The other officer said, 'Yes, I've just arranged for a priest to say prayers over each body.'

Until then it hadn't occurred to me that Rachel had not had a prayer said over her body until her funeral. Even though we had said prayers for Rachel's departing soul thirteen days after her murder, it was still twenty-four days before prayers were said close to her body. It seemed that this was one more right her killer had robbed her of. And it was our mistake, and only ours, for not thinking of it while we were immersed in shock.

In discussions with the State Coroner's office, I asked that, if it was not advisable for families to view a body because of forth-coming court procedures, could it be possible for Homicide detectives to advise families further in this area? To tell them that if they wished, a police chaplain could be asked by the State Coroner's office to say a prayer over their loved one? Provision should also be made for religions other than Christianity.

The Principal Registrar wrote in reply:

> Arrangements can be made at any time for prayers to be said whilst a person is retained at this office. A number of religions require that whilst a person is retained, their 'holy man' spends the night at this office.
>
> In your case I note that it was necessary for Rachel to be retained for ten days. In most cases this period is two days and issues such as religious observances are dealt with by the funeral directors.
>
> We attempt to be responsive to the needs of people who come into contact with this office. In the circumstances outlined by you, arrangements could have been made for prayers to have been said for Rachel. In future, if contacted by family members with a similar request to that as outlined by you, we will make every effort to comply . . .

I was pleased that this service was possible. But the main issue for me was that in our shock we had *forgotten* to contact the office. We didn't stop and think, 'Oh yes, we must arrange this today.' How comforted we would have been if this service had been made known to us. The Registrar did say that I could contact him further if I had other queries relating to this matter. But, at the time, it appeared to me that he had missed the point, so I did not reply. I have since discovered that the Coroner's office have an information booklet for family and friends about the Coroner's process. Perhaps this could be where such information could be put, possibly in the 'Practical Issues' section, under funeral arrangements.

After Caroline had been sentenced we again tackled the subject of photographs. The Homicide department really did want to protect us from images they considered would be too distressing. 'We don't need to be protected any more,' we argued. 'It is your protection of us that is making us distraught.'

Paul Ross said he would inquire further. Rob Read from the Victims Advisory Unit also said he would pursue the matter for us. Rob explained that there were other factors for Homicide to consider before allowing us to view the photographs. But after a lengthy discussion he had said, 'What right have we to play God?'

On 14 December 2000, having signed an indemnity form, and in the presence of Rob Read and our psychologist Michael Clarebrough, we sat before a very thick but ordinary-looking photograph album.

Rob Read told us he had taken the liberty of looking at the photographs first and had marked with sticky tabs the spot where the photographs of Rachel's body began. He explained that a lot of the photographs were of Caroline's flat and her father's Kilmore property.

'Are you ready?' I asked Mike.

'Ye-es,' he said, in a 'come on – get on with it' tone.

Rob Read warned us again that the photographs were horrific. We opened the album, flipping through the pictures of Caroline's flat with some curiosity.

The next page was marked with a tab.

Immediate relief. It was Rachel. Our daughter was dead.

I have likened the story of the photographs to an archaeological dig. There were photographs of each layer of the gravesite as it was meticulously investigated. It was obvious why parents could not be present. Our first response would have been to have lifted our beautiful parcel in our arms. It would have felt just like the image I've mentioned of the little girl who found her puppy, dead, in her Christmas parcel. We would not have noticed the exposed flesh and the raw bone. We would have recognised, as we did, our Rachel.

What I don't think we would have been prepared for was the smell. Mike said he felt this would have stayed with him for ever. He wondered how the investigation team dealt with the smell. How difficult this must have been for detectives. For the forensic pathologist.

I had prepared myself for this. Susan had shown me a book she had of black-and-white photographs showing body remains from Sarajevo. My first thought was, oh how grotesque – not the photographs themselves, but rather that some photographer had been inclined to photograph such grief, such misery. However, looking at the photographs, if I imagined these remains as modern sculpture, I could see the work of Henry Moore. Ugliness is often only how we perceive an image.

Paul Ross had warned us that the photographs did not resemble Rachel. Rob Read repeated that the photographs were horrific. The Homicide Department had struggled to protect us from ourselves. And looking at the photographs of what was once our daughter, we could understand their reservations. But these images were not grotesque to us. That is how it was. We saw the Rachel within.

My first words were, 'I can remember massaging those shoulders.' Shoulders? Her beautiful neck could now have been a beautiful spring cut from the finest gems.

I could not see her toes. Where were her toes? Had the detectives left them in the soil, buried beneath the bark floor? She was a dancer. All her life she had needed her toes. We needed to see her toes now.

We turned the page and the photograph we now viewed was of Rachel on the forensic table.

'There,' said Mike. 'There are her toes . . . She looks as if she is asleep,' said Mike. 'Remember her asleep in bed?'

'Yes,' I answered, gazing at the photographs everyone else thought were so awful. There was our daughter, resting, as if asleep.

'Her hands,' I said. 'Look at her hands.'

Her hands did not appear decomposed. Her beautiful hands. The image I shall remember for ever. They glistened. Perhaps she had been frozen.

And I remembered Caroline's hands in the Supreme Court. It's the image I shall have imprinted on my mind, from the day of sentencing, for ever. I sat looking at the profile of a murderess, looking at her hands. The hands that squeezed the life out of our daughter.

Hands. I think of this image. Hands are creators. Hands are caressers. Hands hold newborn babes. Hands speak of love and hands mould hate. Hands beat. Hands withhold. Hands kill. Hands had once nailed feet and hands to a cross, and in this image is depicted both hate and love.

Our beautiful daughter. Is our journey now complete? Have we finally departed your grave?

I wonder, is it possible to massage a soul?

35

UNCONDITIONAL LOVE

Did Rachel's killer really appreciate the magnitude of her evil act? It was a crime of self-obsession, a self-obsession that took over the reality of the present. Let's say that if she could not appreciate the magnitude of it – then how much of her act *is* she guilty of? How much of her crime are others guilty of? The unhappiness of the teenager? The obsession? The killing?

In making excuses for murder it is not enough for one to say that one has had an unhappy childhood. There are many people for whom childhood has not been the idyllic fairytale. Although my own childhood had been happy, it was not without its difficulties. I was bullied at school in Years 7 and 8 at an Anglican Girls Grammar because I had a Down's syndrome sister two years younger than me. I can remember the taunts. 'You're mental like your sister.' I can remember being pushed backwards into a locker and locked in. I can remember the repulsion of a girl walking towards me in the corridor and spitting in my soup. And my parents' marriage ended when I was sixteen – as did Caroline's parents'. But I did not choose to murder someone, and I say 'choose' because in premeditation one is choosing to kill. Caroline is guilty of Rachel's murder.

I remember saying to the press on the steps of the Supreme

Court after Caroline had been sentenced to twenty years with a non-parole period of fourteen years and six months, that I wished Caroline had been given counselling earlier, before she had destroyed a beautiful life. I remember thinking over the ensuing months after Rachel's murder how we had said to the press that we wanted the family of the woman charged with the murder of Rachel to know that we felt nothing but compassion for them. I told family and friends that Gail and David need not share any sense of responsibility.

But these feelings perplexed me after the sentencing – after hearing the angst in Caroline's letters and her written pleas for help as a lost teenager. These thoughts troubled me because for once I was wishing we had not made these statements. Caroline's parents, I thought, must share the responsibility. More importantly, I thought, they shared in the demise of their own daughter.

I emphasised to the media how important it was for children to receive unconditional love. I stressed that children need to know they are loved – for who they are – regardless of their shortcomings.

These ungracious feelings towards her parents really bothered me. Not only for the raw anger I now felt towards these two parents but because of the lack of compassion beginning to encroach on me. And I sobbed – I was angry with myself. Gail and David were not on trial, and never had been.

There are many adults who have suffered a miserable childhood, suffered abuse – physical or mental. There are also those who have walked through their journey and become outstanding people in spite of it. Recently I was speaking to the mother of one of my children's friends who was fostering a baby boy. I discovered that in the last three years she and her husband had fostered close to thirty babies and children. They had both experienced difficult childhoods and it was out of this background that these parents, with two children of their own, had decided to help other children facing difficulties, to help parents needing assistance in the care of their children.

From Gail's comments in the days when we were neighbours, we were aware that Caroline was an unhappy teenager. 'She won't let me near her,' were the cries of helplessness from Gail. Gail couldn't *reach* her. She told us that Caroline had called her an unfit mother.

I had suggested counselling for Caroline, and for herself. I told her that Rachel was seeing a counsellor to help her with difficulties in relation to a dance teacher. But Caroline didn't want to see a counsellor.

I remember saying to Gail, if she won't let you near her just hold onto her, wrap your arms around her, in your heart. I tried to explain to Gail that I thought Caroline could have blamed her for sending her father away because at sixteen I blamed my mother for sending my father away. Why couldn't my mother make my father happy? My relationship with my mother broke down during these years. We became alienated.

I told Gail it wasn't until I was in my twenties and married that I realised it wasn't my mother who had sent my father away. I had come to see that the relationship between two people *can* irretrievably break down for one reason or another. It wasn't always just one party sending away another party. I told Gail that one day Caroline would come to her again, but for now just to keep on loving her. (Caroline, your mother does love you. I think perhaps she has been trying for years to help you, but in her despair she didn't know how. Let her in. Caroline, none of us are perfect, least of all parents.)

A separation, and often the stressful years leading up to a divorce, can put unfathomable strain on a family. Parents can forget the inner needs of their children. The Reids were financially comfortable. Materialistically, the children lacked for nothing. Their children had the opportunity of a good education. Caroline's family had neighbourhood status. Caroline was always pleasant to us, and obviously she was to others too, because she babysat for several families in the district, not just us.

Some people have said to us, 'Where did all your prayers get you? Where is your God? Your Rachel is dead.' But God is not responsible for Rachel's death. Caroline's parents are not responsible for Rachel's death. It was her killer, Caroline, who chose and plotted over many months to kill Rachel. As far as our God is concerned, our God chose to save Rachel's soul. Our prayers were answered. Rachel was found and brought home.

Rachel's sisters cannot understand why, as Rachel's mother, I have a certain amount of compassion for her killer, even now. Sometimes, like living through the month of March with its many dates of anguish, the compassion I feel for her leaves me despairing and angry. Though it is not the act I pity for the killer, for having seen a photograph of the telephone cable that was used to kill Rachel, a photograph I saw *after* Caroline's sentencing, I realised it was a cable with a knot that could have been released by a simple slackening of tension. Our daughter's life could have been spared. It was never an accident. Our daughter was slain in a way that could not have been more personal. Caroline's full strength would have been needed, until Rachel's last breath expired.

In my wildest hopes I thought her killer, having been intent on killing Rachel – and after placing the death cable around Rachel's neck – had changed her mind on hearing Rachel's plea, 'Please, please don't.' I had thought perhaps this was what her killer meant by 'accident' because then, when she had pity for our daughter and changed her mind, she had discovered to her horror that the ligature could not be slackened. I thought that the crying tantrum the witness had heard could have been Caroline, appalled.

But the death cable *could* have been slackened. Simply by letting go.

It is for the person, the soul within the killer, I have pity for. The person who did not experience a feeling of self worth for who she was, even with all her mistakes; the person who did not perceive an unconditional love, before she despaired to kill. Instead *I* am left despairing. Despairing at my compassion. I am not saying she did not receive this love but rather that it was her perception that she did not. One day I hope Caroline can feel the warmth of love. If I were her parent I would want to hold her in my arms, to say, one day everything will be all right. I have been abhorred by the sensation to want to do this myself. But how can I? I still fear for Ashleigh-Rose and Heather. And it is my *mother* love for these two breathing children that holds me back. On her release, will Caroline be any less dangerous? A scary thought. Someone love her, before it is too late.

I need to repeat that it is important for children to feel unconditional love from their parents. Even for those who kill. Perhaps for some, nothing could be more healing than the embrace of their parents' innate love. Killers were once born, were once babes with parents. Some killers have parents who can see beyond their child's abhorrent crime and love their *baby*. The child within the killer, their child who is now an adult, is still their *child*, whom they once cradled with hope.

Some say Caroline was experiencing remorse when she changed her plea. Some say she was sorry she was caught and, realising her chances of a 'not guilty' verdict were slim, decided to plead guilty so that she would receive a lesser sentence. Whichever way one looks at it, Rachel did not receive a lesser sentence. Whichever way one looks at it, we have not received a lesser sentence.

Throughout the eighteen months or so leading up to Caroline's sentencing, because we were possible witnesses, all the way through we were excluded from the details of Rachel's murder for the sake of the impending trial. We couldn't visit the unit where Rachel was murdered. The police, knowing we had never been in Caroline's unit, didn't want us to. The less we knew the better. We couldn't visit her first gravesite at Kilmore before the impending trial. We were advised against seeing her body because of the impending trial. We couldn't even see photographs of her body before the impending trial. We couldn't speak to the forensic pathologist. We couldn't attend the committal hearing. We couldn't tell Rachel's grandparents how she was murdered until the committal hearing, nearly a year later. We only told Rachel's sisters how she was murdered during the December 1999 school holidays. We were not allowed to tell Rachel's beloved Manni how she was murdered. Rachel's friends went to the committal hearing and were confronted, for the first time, with the story of how her life was squeezed out of her. And so many other little things.

If Caroline were truly remorseful, wouldn't it have been

kinder to plead guilty earlier? But I realise that none of the above would have even occurred to her. And quite fairly, I say, why should it? How many people would realise that because of the security of the coming trial we could be made privy to none of this? Or – think about it – to you, if ever you found yourself in the same ghastly situation.

Is it any wonder that, when told the day before the trial that Caroline was to change her plea, I greeted this news with anger?

I remember the anxiety I felt in the weeks leading up to the day of sentencing. I found myself on a new passionate quest. I got it into my head that I wanted our Victim Impact Statement to be read out in court.

But I remember the social worker from the Office of Public Prosecutions was quite concerned for our welfare. It seemed our request would not be possible.

'Why would we want to do this?'

'Because,' I said, 'I want to personalise the victim. I want the killer to feel the impact she has had on our family.' I considered that if Rachel's family and friends had listened to pleas on Caroline's behalf at the plea and mitigation, then surely at the time of sentencing, the killer and her family could listen to the impact Caroline's actions had had on our family. After all, the document was called a Victim Impact Statement.

For several reasons it was not possible for the statement to be read in court. If ever our idea could have had a chance, it should have occurred when the Victim Impact Statements were tabled in court at the plea hearing.

Then we were told that Victim Impact Statements were simply not read out in court. Essentially the statements were for the judge or magistrate to read, and for the defence lawyer or defendant. It would technically be a misuse of their purpose for them to be read out in court and perhaps it would be regarded as an interruption by a judge to 'normal' court proceedings. My answer to this was that the case was already bizarre, so why not be more bizarre?

I was so headstrong on this. As far as I was concerned all the way through those two years we had been prevented from being involved. Our daughter, in a sense, had become the property of the State. She was now the deceased – the body. Although at the Supreme Court I did find comfort in the fact that both the judge and the prosecuting QC had referred to Rachel by name. And there was a degree of acknowledgement of our grief from the defence barrister through his use of the word 'child'.

The reading of the Victim Impact Statement became an issue for me. I quickly began to see it as one more right we were denied. I didn't want to listen to reason. I rang the Office of Public Prosecutions constantly prior to the day of sentencing. At one point it was suggested by a friend that I should perhaps ring the Judge's Associate. The prosecutor Jeremy Rapke, QC, was unfortunately away at another case. I wrote a letter to him so he would find it on his return. It was a letter my stepmother happened to see on my computer screen before I posted it. She was so distressed because I had said 'our Victim Impact Statements' and had included hers and Rachel's other grandparents' statements as well. She then rang the Office of Public Prosecutions, saying she didn't want their Victim Impact Statements to be read out because they had not written them for the general public. At first I was annoyed by her intrusion but realised how wrong my assumption had been, caught up in my zeal. I had liked Susan's comments in her Victim Impact Statement regarding Dante's *Inferno*: 'Caroline betrayed the bonds of friendship and the oldest responsibility known to man: the relationship between guest and host.' She told me Dante placed such people in the lowest circle of hell. In the Inferno, the lowest of the nine circles of hell contains the traitors and rather than be tortured by fire they are frozen in ice.

I contacted the Office of Public Prosecutions saying that even if only our own Victim Impact Statements could be read I would be happy.

It felt as though I was fighting a new battle now, a battle against our own team. But it was pointed out to us by an American friend of my father and stepmother, who was a forensic psychologist, that if my reason for wanting the VIS to be read out in court was for Caroline to hear and digest its contents, then it simply would not happen. She would tune out or even disrupt the proceedings in the court, and the judge probably would not consider this favourably. I could not believe we were changing our minds. Again – for the security of the trial.

Prosecutor Jeremy Rapke, QC, offered to see us in his rooms on the day of sentencing before the procedure began. He told us that having the VIS read out was not usual and strongly, but caringly, advised against it. He was a lovely man. However, if we insisted, he said he could make the request to the judge and had also taken the liberty of informing the defence counsel it was a possibility. But we found ourselves agreeing it would not be in the best interests of sentencing proceedings.

I recall the defence QC referring to our Victim Impact Statement as a remarkable document and, looking back over this document, there are a number of issues I wish to share now.

Mike and I never believed in capital punishment and still don't. No amount of tears (and there will continue to be many) or revenge can ever bring our beautiful girl back. She has proudly left her mark on those who knew her. She will always be remembered with love.

Capital punishment is too easy. If someone has committed such a heinous crime as this they need to be made accountable for it in *this* life. Caroline not only broke the law of God, she broke the law of the State.

As a result of this tragedy our family was shattered beyond belief, and even though we try so hard to repair ourselves there is always some memory tearing at a repaired seam. My fear is, what will happen when we have stitched so many times that the seam can no longer be repaired?

We were once a very ordinary family and now our family has ceased to trust. We taught our children trustfulness and respect, and to be understanding of others. Yet sadly we now feel this willingness to have faith in people cost our daughter her life. No parents can protect their children from so evil a crime.

Rachel must have suffered both mentally and physically, and will never be in a position to share this abominable horror. Someone has had to be her scribe. Someone has had to try to tell her story, and our story. Megan and I have endeavoured to do this. After Rachel's murder nothing was going to bring her back, but Rachel had always wanted to make a positive impact on the world. She wanted to be a dancer. She wanted to be a star. As Rachel's mother, I hope the writing of this story will, in some way, do for Rachel what Caroline robbed her of. I hope her short life can have a positive impact on others – somehow.

Up to the time of sentencing we had not been made privy to the full evidence, as I have said, and were still greatly troubled by the many unanswered questions, some of which remain. On which day did our daughter die? At what time did our daughter die? What happened to our daughter's jewellery, her shoes and her Humphrey Bear? And . . . *why*?

Our inability to understand the trauma Rachel suffered haunts us still. Was she taunted with the prospect of her death? What did her killer mean when she suggested meditation to Rachel, to help with 'unpleasant things'? Did Rachel know, then, that she could not escape? All questions that unceasingly rock our being.

We understand that the defendant killed Rachel possibly because she was consumed with envy of her happy life. It is tragic that Caroline had never seen the Rachel who had not been happy. The Rachel who struggled academically at school, the Rachel who gave up dance at thirteen due to ill health and an over-disciplinary dance teacher. The Rachel who at fourteen told her father something we had known since she had left her dancing school: 'I know why I am so *miserable*, it is because I am not dancing.' And finally, the Rachel who decided to return to dance, but to musicals and contemporary dance because she was now afraid of her first love, classical ballet.

Although sometimes frustrating, as teenagers can be, Rachel was an exciting and fun girl. We allowed her to leave school at fifteen so that she could follow her dream and because we wanted her to be happy. Everyone talked of how beautiful she was but she had an inner beauty, an inner joy too. An ability to bring joy to others – though her sisters are the first to remind me that they did argue at times as well.

It is this that makes the crime so unbearable, even more evil and cruel from Rachel's point of view because she had so much hope and promise for her future. She had struggled through school and with herself, but had always persisted. Rachel's school friends remember how she was always going on about this. One friend in particular told us that Rachel would say, 'It's important to believe in yourself and follow your dreams.'

In taking Rachel's life so cruelly Caroline stole Rachel's dreams and hopes, and ours for our daughter. The most shocking aspect of this crime is that it was so carefully planned and carried out, with no conscience or consideration for the suffering it would cause our family, or her own.

Rachel was vibrant. We torture ourselves daily with the thought that someone so physically alive and spirited could have been wiped out so suddenly, so unexpectedly. Our deepest sorrow is for Rachel – not for ourselves – at the moment when she must have realised that she had been baited and caught.

We have been helpless in our grief because we were unable to say goodbye. And every time we visit her grave we are faced with the reminder of so many unknowns. In March 2002 we still wonder what date to put on her headstone. Police are confident she died on the night of the 1st, but should we put 1 March or 2 March 1999? If we were to ask her killer, could we believe her? I think we will take the advice of Rachel's sister, Ashleigh-Rose, now fourteen, who feels we should put 1 March 1999 as it represents the day Rachel was lost to us.

We went through a period of isolation too, because even friends were afraid, and we found ourselves taking on their grief, their awkwardness, their attempts at saying the right thing.

One friend said after Rachel's funeral, 'Elizabeth, my mother said, let this be a warning never to let even teenagers out of your sight.' I replied, 'She was coming home from school, in daylight. How many children travel on buses, trams and trains daily, to and from school? We were not being irresponsible.'

Another friend said before the committal hearing, 'Elizabeth, don't blame yourself. All teenagers go through rebellious periods.' I replied, 'Only trouble is, Rachel was not going through a rebellious period.'

Both of our breathing beautiful children kept us focused as we struggled to support them through the traumatic time no child should ever have to experience. We are tempted to continue to teach them at home, as we did for the last school term of 2000, but we feel that this is not in their best interests. I know Heather would love it – but would she thank us for it later? If we fail to respond to the needs of Ashleigh-Rose and Heather, if we crumble, what good will we be as parents?

As I indicated earlier, Ashleigh-Rose and Heather did not know how their sister was murdered until December 1999, when we told them at the kitchen table, sitting with their counsellor. Ashleigh-Rose says of her counsellor, 'Catherine is a great help. She is helping to show me how to release my anger by screaming into pillows, and screaming in the pool.'

Ashleigh-Rose is always angry about her sister's death and is quite unforgiving. She wrote in her journal when she was twelve: 'I miss you so much, Rachel. All I want to do is scream at every one I know. Inside I'm screaming for help but I just don't know how to tell everyone how to give me that help, because I don't know what type of help I need. I mean, I have counselling, and that is one type of help, but I feel closed in. Sometimes I don't know *what* to do, like whether to just go to my room and listen to music or just think of all the good times we used to have, Rachel. And I'm grateful for the times we had together but Rachel, I only had you for eleven years, and I can only remember about six of them with you. I was too young to remember earlier. Mum and Dad had you for fifteen. Right this very moment I feel like crying but it won't come so I hold it in. I know it's bad to hold it in but sometimes you have to. I don't like knowing that you are gone, Rachel, and knowing that the murderer of you is still alive . . . '

And after the sentencing, Ashleigh-Rose said at the Supreme Court: 'She took my sister's life. I hate her for that and will hate her for ever. I used to be the middle sister, now I am the oldest daughter in our family. I wasn't supposed to be and it is all her fault. Our lives will never be the same now.'

Heather found it difficult to discuss Rachel with anyone, relating to her counsellor more as a friend with whom she can chat about school and other friends. We have encouraged this relationship, so she will know that her counsellor will be there for her when she needs her. Ashleigh-Rose noted that when anyone mentioned Rachel's name, Heather would quietly remove herself from the room. So it surprised me how open Heather became to the press, and that she had spoken freely to one journalist: 'After the sentence Heather Barber, ten, who bears a striking resemblance to Rachel, said she was still worried about Robertson but was glad she would serve at least another thirteen years in jail. "I was very worried, especially when I heard about it the first time," said Heather, who plans to take up dance studies next year. "People say I've got the same actions as Rachel. I keep thinking about it [the killing]."'

Heather, then aged ten, said in her Victim Impact Statement: 'I feel very, very angry for what Caroline has done. I knew she was weird the first time I saw her. I loved Rachel because she was my sister. But I hate Caroline because she killed my loving sister Rachel. And I hate her for what she did. And I mean that. I think she is a, excuse my language, but a *bitch*, more than that which I won't say. I really do hate Caroline, really I do.'

As their mother I was concerned with the degree of hate expressed by Rachel's sisters, but having spoken to my counsellor and theirs, I realised it was important for them to express their grief as *they* experienced it.

The police believe that the girl who reported seeing Rachel on the tram, Alison Guberek, would still have been alerted to her disappearance by the media attention that was created on the Tuesday of the second week. But if we had given up and gone home on that first Thursday and not continued with our poster campaign, what then? If Alison had not come forward on the Monday night, would the press release still have gone out on the Tuesday? Would there still have been a gut feeling that urged the Missing Persons detectives on?

We felt compelled to continue our search for Rachel, whatever the cost. Michele said to me much later in regard to our Church Street escapade, 'You remember our fear. We weren't being irrational. No one else was helping. Our feelings were right.'

It is chilling to think that Caroline chose a perfect victim but it is even more chilling to think that this was also very nearly the perfect murder. I wonder how many children sleep on the streets at night because parents are advised to go home and seek special counselling, as we were by the local police. And I wonder how many of those children have been murdered, but were presumed to be runaways because the teenager just happened to fall into a high-risk group. Even if there was just one, like our Rachel, it leaves parents and police in a very difficult situation because there are no answers.

Rachel was dead that first night. Even if the local police attitude had been different in the first week, the outcome would still have remained. At the same time though, if sales staff in the retail industry treated customers the way we perceived ourselves to have been treated, many customers would be lost. Perhaps what I am referring to is courtesy.

But maybe the issue of understaffing and stress-related issues in the police force should not be ignored. Detective Chief Inspector Rod Collins said on the radio some months after Rachel's murder (after having spent many police hours searching for another girl they believed had been abducted, only to discover she *had* indeed run off), 'We're damned if we do and we're damned if we don't.' I think that sums up the impossible situation police in general find themselves in with regard to missing teenagers.

In telling our story I must emphasise that I have never been out for blood. It is Caroline Reed Robertson, formerly known as Caroline Reid, who killed Rachel. Nothing the police could have done would have ever altered that. The only thing that a swifter police reaction could have achieved would have been a lessening of our suffering in that period when Rachel was missing. The waiting game would not have been so appalling.

I discovered some long months after the murder of Rachel that a part of our trauma was misplaced anger. To be fair to the police, the highly unusual circumstances surrounding Rachel's disappearance must have placed the local police in a no-win situation. But we found their apparent lack of concern hard to accept. Although with time and with counselling and further meetings with the local police in the presence of our psychologist, we came to approach the situation with some understanding.

So we acknowledge the burden for police, regarding missing persons, as an extremely onerous one, particularly with missing teenagers because they are the most likely to return. Is it any wonder some local police would prefer to delegate missing persons to a separate police department, with a staff of twenty? The catch cry: in an ideal world. Even in our non-ideal world, I personally feel the Missing Persons Unit should remain a separate department. During 1999, the Missing Persons Unit, with a staff of ten, was amalgamated with Homicide. If one rings the Missing Persons number one is greeted with the response, 'Homicide Department'. Yet police still adamantly say Missing Persons is separate, but under the umbrella of the Homicide Department. Couldn't it at least have its own telephone number?

It is now over three years since Rachel was murdered, and our remaining daughters have a problem that is unsolved. They still have an older sister but their relationship to each other has altered. Ashleigh-Rose is obviously reluctant to adjust to an older sister role, while Heather can't come to terms with the change at all. 'I was always the youngest sister,' she says, 'and now I hear people call me the *younger* sister. I will always be the youngest.' Yet one day Rachel will become the youngest *older* sister. Will the girls feel the need to adjust again?

And I, even now, feel awkward and dislike the question people often ask, 'And how many children do you have?' It is surprising how often this question comes up. I have experimented with answers. 'I have three.' (Hoping they don't ask me their ages.) 'I have had three but now I only have two.' 'I have three, but my eldest was murdered.' On the odd occasion, to save hassle I have answered, 'I have – two' (as if I need time to think about it). But then I have been riddled with guilt at the denial of Rachel's fifteen years. Fifteen years cannot be discounted. And why should I have to worry about other people's awkwardness? As far as I am concerned Mike and I *still* have three children. I just can't use that answer because inevitably the next question is, 'Oh, and how old are they?'

When I was working I found myself telling a customer I had

a sixteen-year-old daughter. And again, on meeting new people, for instance when Ashleigh-Rose started at secondary school, I would come across parents or teachers who would hint, 'Just wait until they get into their mid-teens . . . ' I *know*. But how can I *say*? How?

The mother of one of Rachel's friends told us her daughter had said, a couple of weeks before Rachel was murdered, 'Mum, Rachel is so blissfully happy.' And I ask, was she so happy that she was unable to be aware of danger?

My husband Mike says, 'Tomorrow, everyone will forget our beautiful Rachel.' This is a fear shared by our girls. Ashleigh-Rose already says she has forgotten her sister's voice and is terrified of forgetting her altogether. She withdrew from a friend who told her to forget Rachel and 'get over it and get a life'. This distressed her greatly. But what Ashleigh-Rose has failed to understand is that this twelve-year-old friend was only trying to help. And if my adult friends find Rachel's death uncomfortable to deal with, how can we expect children to deal with it?

In our society death is taboo, particularly the death of a child. (So what does that make murder?) And it shouldn't be taboo. Maybe it is time for open coffins to be returned to the parlours, the living rooms, and for death to be brought back into the home, so that as new generations of children grow, so will their acceptance of death. The dead are not to be feared. Rather, it is sometimes what kills them that should be feared.

EPILOGUE

31 March 2002

Dear Rachel,

So long has passed since I wrote to you last. The writing of your story has enveloped my complete consciousness. It makes every March without you more real.

Before writing this book about you I had been comfortable living in denial. I knew you were dead, but it was still easier to speak to you through these letters and pretend you were not dead. These letters made me feel comfortable. Rachel, I didn't want to lose touch with the essence of you. You will always be real for me – but now – in spirit only. What did I say at the conclusion of the chapter about the forensic photographs? 'Our beautiful daughter. Is our journey now complete? Have we finally departed your grave?' I cannot speak for your dad but, I think I *have* finally departed your grave. But only through acceptance. It is a tragedy we learn to live *with* – not move on *from*. Your murder will be a continuing presence for our remaining years.

Rachel, your Manni completed his two-year Diploma of Dance. You, too, would have completed yours. We are still close to the Carellas. Your sisters look upon the boys as five big brothers. Rosa says, 'We will always have a place for each other,' and she is right.

I told very few people that Megan and I were writing this book because those I did tell said, 'Well, if you think it will help *you* work things through.' But they missed the point. It wasn't written for me. The letters I have written to you, many of which are not here in this book, have been for me – *and* you – when it was easier for others in their awkwardness not to see me, or not to bring the subject up. And in a sense neither was the book for you. It was written for the police, for psychologists, for grief counsellors, for clergy and pastoral care workers. It was written for other parents, and for those who experience death. Some grief can never be resolved.

'Let me be *me*!' Heather demanded one morning last year. Rachel, I wasn't listening to your youngest sister. I hadn't been listening for two years. Those two years of Heather and Ashleigh-Rose's lives are memories I will read about in your letters. Two years of childhood gone. Ashleigh-Rose has grown up so much. Eleven to fourteen is a big enough leap in one's life, even without the added grief that Ashleigh-Rose has had to encounter.

Maybe Heather spoke so forwardly to one of the journalists because she thought it was a chance for her voice to be heard. I cringed when I read that Heather planned to take up dance. She knew I had quite clearly said, 'I'm not going down that track any more.' I was adamant. Your sisters knew this. But it was because of this quite public affirmation by Heather that I allowed both your sisters to join in a local jazz school. But this wasn't enough for Heather. 'I want to learn jazz and *ballet*,' she'd said.

One morning I drove Heather to a ballet school open day but left an hour later saying, 'I can't do it, Heather. I can't.' Rachel, your whole being had been dance. The experience was so distressing, and Rachel, so sad. A tug of feelings. Finally in desperation Heather declared, 'Let me be *me*!' And I realised, Rachel, that if you had still been alive you would have been there with Heather sorting through the ten years of ballet uniforms buried deep in the laundry cupboard, sorting through at least fifteen pairs of ballet shoes, jazz shoes and character shoes. How could I not let Heather be Heather? I let you be Rachel.

So we drove on to another ballet school. I walked in and breathed in the familiar smells, saw the wooden floors, the ballet buns, heard the sounds of classical ballet class, and saw expectant joy in your sister's face. So I said – yes. She may decide at the end of a year it's not what she wants but at least I have given her a chance to be herself.

I felt quite ill that afternoon. Heather had been rummaging through the bags of ballet uniforms, spilling memories across the couch and onto the floor. She found the whole caboodle. Leotard, tights, skirt and ballet shoes. The furniture was pushed back, her hair went up in a bun and out came the old Royal Academy of Dance video.

Justice Vincent said at the sentencing, 'The anguish will remain, sometimes intensifying as milestone events take place . . . ever present and constantly evoked by everyday life occurrences.' Rachel, this will always be true, even when your sisters are defending their rights to be who they are; and even when quite insignificant tasks occur. I remember something your dad told me: that just mowing the lawn is difficult for him, because he is reminded of the times he mowed the lawn at Mont Albert. Caroline would stop him on the way home from college and chat to him, while he rested his arms on the handlebar.

But Heather didn't look like a clone of you. She looked like Heather being allowed to be Heather. I saw a joy in Heather I hadn't seen for quite some time. It's the smile, you know. One can tell real joy in a person by their smile.

And I smiled.

Rachel, you left an imprint in this world. Your short life gave so much energy to your dad and the loss of you has left a festering wound in him, so much so that he cannot find the words to express his loss. You were the Rachel he knew before you were even born. And maybe in response to his words, 'Tomorrow, everyone will forget our beautiful Rachel', he too will recognise your short life did have meaning. I don't mean that your murder had a reason. There is no acceptable reason for the act of your murder. The act will always be evil. And it could diminish one's faith in God and humanity.

So wouldn't it be better, Rachel, if something grew from this destructiveness? The day after we were told of your murder, absurd as it seemed then, I said that some good would come from it. To make good out of evil. To change the destructive nature of your murder and help people understand that there is a resurrection from death, not only for those who have died, but also for those left with the grief, the seemingly unconsolable 'whys'. That even in our physical existence, our souls are nurtured.

And for me, as a Christian, there is also an Easter story in your death. Always will be. Throughout the desolation and torment of March, throughout the 'anniversaries' of your murder, relived every day; throughout the tears, *every* year, I will always emerge at Easter. A time your sisters look forward to, a time for Easter eggs and hot cross buns. But Easter is so much more than that. Easter is Christ's suffering remembered, and a journey through death made victorious in the resurrection.

Rachel, during the writing of this book I could not continue to write letters to you. I had simply used too many stores of emotional energy. I said to your Grandad Ivan, with regret, 'I can't do both.' His answer . . . 'But this book is the definitive letter – this says it all.'

Love to you, my darling Rachel.

ACKNOWLEDGEMENTS

It was Elizabeth's father, Ivan Southall, who instigated the writing of this book. As a writer, he always recognised the importance of this story, but said it was one he couldn't write himself. So he urged Elizabeth to tell it, and we thank him for that.

However, Elizabeth felt that she could not tell this story on her own either, because she wanted to give both Rachel's family's account, *and* the account of the crime that cost their daughter her life. So Elizabeth approached Megan, who had written a story on Elizabeth's family. We had become friends, and would tell the story together.

We have written what we hope is a balanced and accurate story of Rachel's murder. But we could not have done this without the tremendous support of our editor at Penguin Books, Suzanne Wilson, whose patience and sensitivity helped us through the enormous task of turning a pile of paperwork into a readable story. This material included Elizabeth's exercise books filled with notes taken down during Rachel's disappearance, and her journals and diary entries, letters (many written in the middle of the night), Megan's pages of shorthand notes from the court case, piles of transcript and evidence. Together we spent many late nights at Suzanne's house, collating our material and combining our stories into what we hope is a revealing insight into a murder and a loss that should never have happened. We must also thank Suzanne's ever-patient husband Stuart for the many cups of coffee which accompanied those late-night editorial sessions. He will be glad to have his family home back.

We would also like to thank our own husbands, Mike and Steve, for their support in making this book possible, and our children Ashleigh-Rose and Heather, Alex and Peter, who have also encouraged us in this project.

There are many others who have willingly given their time or contributed information to this book, to ensure the story we tell is both fair and accurate. So we wish to thank the following for all their help in this task:

Elizabeth's mum Joy, and dad Ivan Southall; her stepmother, Susan Southall; her parents-in-law, Rose and Arthur Barber; her brother Drew, and sisters Robbie and Melissa whose comforting cuddles meant so much; cousins Michele, Ian, Jan and Jamie; aunts Betty and Babe; niece Tamzin; nephew Shaun Connors and Renée; the Carella family for their ongoing support and love – Emmanuel, his parents Rosa and Tony, his brothers Robert, Domenic, Frank and Michael.

We wish to thank Ted and Betty Blacker; Assunta Pellicano; students and their parents from the Dance Factory, Richmond, along with the staff, especially Vicky and Mark, and Dulcie Lee; David Vo for the use of the poster on the back cover and his help during the search for Rachel; Cathy and Alec Djoneff who paid for the petrol during the long days and nights Elizabeth and her family drove around the city – and for a weekend away in the months after Rachel's death; also their daughter, Ellen Djoneff who was one of Rachel's closest friends; John, Chris, Alex Griffiths and his mates; Carlo, Tate and Richard; Sandra and Russell Simos and their daughter Laura (Rachel's close friend), as well as her sisters and brother.

We gratefully acknowledge the co-operation and assistance of the Victoria Police, especially David dePyle, Neil Paterson, Steve Waddell and their fellow officers at the Missing Persons Unit;

Detective Sergeant Paul Ross and other detectives from the Homicide Squad; Senior Constable Neil Tilley; we thank Amber at the Victoria Police Freedom of Information office for her assistance in obtaining relevant information and photographs; Dougall from Victoria Police Media Liaison for his help in obtaining statistics and checking factual information; Rob Read from the Victims Advisory Unit; Jenny Mouzos from the Institute of Criminology in Canberra for her co-operation in providing information on women who kill; Hermann Metz and the team of scientists at the Police Forensic Science Centre in South Melbourne; Prue Innes from the Supreme Court Media Office; Bronwyn Hammond at the Office of Public Prosecutions for her patience in fielding Megan's numerous telephone calls in her quest to check information, and Bronwyn's colleague Matthew Bastinion; Annie Davies for her support during the court process; the Court Network System; Alison Guberek and her family; the Suzan Johnston Modelling School; St Hilary's Anglican Church and Mont Albert Primary School for the many casseroles provided during the two weeks of Rachel's disappearance, and Heathmont East Primary School for their support, especially with Ashleigh-Rose and Heather.

Thanks, too, to Rachel's Grade Four teacher, Miss Ellen; Lindsay Frost of the Salvation Army and fellow captains; Management and Staff of the escort agency we mention in our story; counsellors Michael Clarebrough and Catherine Bauld; Dr Kathryn Wallace; Dr Pam Brewster for constant de-briefings; Dr Michele Pathe, Dr Justin Barry-Walsh, Claude Minisini and Judy Wright for their invaluable insight into the psychological aspect of criminal behaviour; prosecution barristers Robert Barry and Jeremy Rapke QC; John Spooner from the *Age* who kindly donated his fee for the use of his artwork to victims of crime; front cover photographer Andrew Raszevski and Icon Media, who kindly donated the photograph of Rachel for us to use; Cathy Larsen our designer for her fabulous book design and Julie Watts and Robert Sessions from Penguin Books for their support and belief that ours was a story that needed to be told; Denis Pye for her many hours of photocopying, sandwiches and cups of coffee during our major editing sessions. Deborah

Holland and Chris Harrington of Books In Print – thank you for your support; Tony Stanton; the inner-city support organisation who sent the Barbers a cheque for $1000 to help cover expenses after Rachel disappeared; and to Patrice Fidgeon for her help sourcing news clips and support throughout the project. And finally, to the many others who handed out posters, helped in the search, or contributed their time to the publication of this book.

Elizabeth Southall and Megan Norris, 2002

PHOTOGRAPHIC CREDITS

Every effort has been made to trace copyright holders of photographs. The publishers would appreciate hearing from any copyright holder not here acknowledged.

FRONT COVER AND SPINE: Photograph of Rachel Barber kindly donated by Icon Media.
BACK COVER: Missing person poster designed by David Vo.

PICTURE INSERTS
The numbers below correspond to numbers of captions.
1: courtesy of Alan Foon, Foon's Photographics, Wonthaggi.
2, 3, 5, 8, 11, and 12: courtesy of the Barber family.
4: photograph by Ashleigh-Rose Barber, courtesy of the Barber family.
6: courtesy of Susan Southall and the Barber family.
7: courtesy of Susan Southall and the Barber family. Photograph copyright © Susan Southall, 1995.
9, 10: courtesy of Dulcie Lee, Dance Factory.
13, 15, 17: courtesy of the Melbourne *Herald Sun*.
14, 18, 19, 20: courtesy of Freedom of Information Unit, Victoria Police.

16: courtesy of John Spooner, the *Age*.

21: courtesy of Freedom of Information Unit, Victoria Police.

23, 24: videotape stills courtesy of Freedom of Information Unit, Victoria Police.

25: courtesy of Freedom of Information Unit, Victoria Police.

26: courtesy of Susan Southall. Artwork copyright © Susan Southall, 1999.

27: Main article courtesy of the Sydney *Sun-Herald*. Headlines, from top to bottom, from the *Age* (1 February 2000), the Melbourne *Herald Sun* (26 October 2000), the *Australian* (30 November 2000) and the Melbourne *Herald Sun* (30 November 2000).

Caroline Reed Robertson's letters obtained courtesy of Freedom of Information Unit, Victoria Police.